Contemporary Art in Latin America

Painting

Graphic Art

Sculpture

Architecture

Fp THE FREE PRESS, *New York*
Collier-Macmillan Ltd., *London*

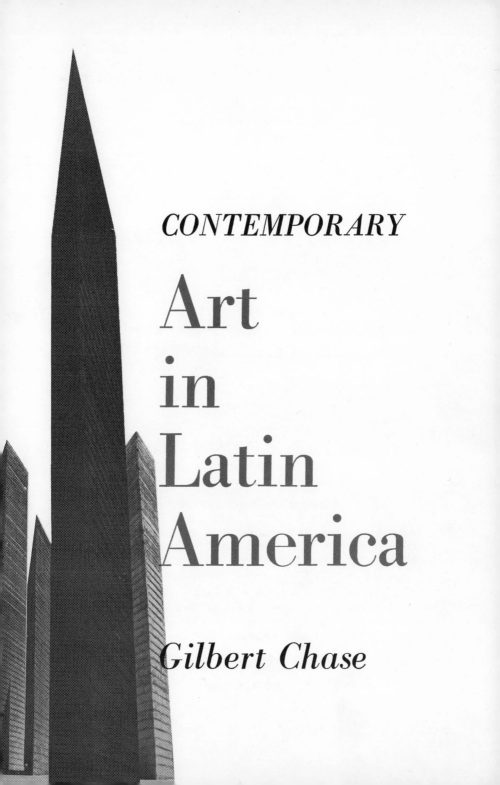

CONTEMPORARY

Art
in
Latin
America

Gilbert Chase

For
KATHLEEN

The Free Press, A Division of the Macmillan Company,
866 Third Avenue, New York, New York 10022

Collier-Macmillan Canada Ltd., Toronto, Ontario

Library of Congress Catalog Card Number 70-78890

Printing Number
1 2 3 4 5 6 7 8 9 10

Preface

To the best of my knowledge this is the first book in any language to attempt a general survey of contemporary plastic arts and architecture in Latin America. Though it may have the merit of a pioneer work, it doubtless reflects the difficulties inherent in dealing with four major arts in eighteen countries, in an area and a period (roughly 1920 to the present) as yet not systematically explored, documented, or evaluated in the critical-historical literature of modern art.

With the exception of architecture and the Mexican muralist movement that began around 1920, the recent art of Latin America has received scant attention in reference works and histories of modern art. To take an example at random, the Skira *Histoire de la Peinture Moderne: De Picasso au Surréalisme* (Geneva, 1950) mentions only three Latin American artists: Orozco, Rivera, and Siqueiros, the famous triumvirate of the post-Revolutionary muralist movement in Mexico. Each has three identical entries in the index, and the references in the text are brief and perfunctory. In a chronological table, under the date 1922, they are mentioned thus: "*Mexico*, Manifesto of the painters Siqueiros, Orozco, and Rivera." On page 130 they are cited as "significant" representatives of "social realism" (coupled with the art of Soviet Russia). None of their paintings is reproduced or discussed. For the European authors of this work, the whole of modern Latin American painting is reduced to three Mexicans with a manifesto.

In the *Dictionary of Modern Painting*, edited by Fernand Hazan, Orozco and Rivera are included along with one other Latin American painter: Joaquín Torres García of Uruguay. This at least is a change from exclusive focus on the Mexican muralists. Bernard Myers, in *Modern Art in the Making* (New York, 1950), has a chapter titled "America Today" that deals only with the

United States. However, in his concluding chapter, "The Modern Artist and Society," Myers discusses the "Mexican Renaissance" of the post-Revolutionary period. He has nothing to say about the art of any Latin American country except Mexico (he subsequently published another book, *Mexican Painting in Our Time* [New York, 1956]). Thus the bibliography continues to be preponderantly weighted toward Mexico.

It is true that all these books were published some years ago, and that since 1960 increased attention has been given to the contemporary arts of Latin America. The series of illustrated booklets *Art in Latin America Today*, issued by the Pan American Union in Washington, D.C. deserves particular mention. Thus far the series includes Argentina, Brazil, Chile, Colombia, Guatemala, Haiti, Peru, and Venezuela. In contrasting format (and price !) is the large and lavishly illustrated volume titled *The Emergent Decade*, with text by Thomas M. Messer and artists' "profiles" in text and pictures by Cornell Capa (Ithaca, 1966), dealing with Latin American painters and painting in the 1960's. The illustrations are splendid; letters exchanged between Messer and various Latin American art critics constitute much of the text. The impressively thick catalog of the exhibition *Art of Latin America since Independence* (New Haven, 1966) contains numerous black and white illustrations and useful biographical data.

When it comes to biographies and monographs, Mexico again gets the lion's share. Only in architecture do we find a fair number of monographs dealing with other countries, such as Paul Damaz's *Art in Latin American Architecture* (New York, 1963), Henry-Russell Hitchcock's *Latin American Architecture since 1945* (New York, 1955), Enrique Mindlin's *Modern Brazilian Architecture* (New York, 1956), Stamo Papadaki's *The Work of Oscar Niemeyer* (New York, 1960), Klaus Franck's *The Works of Affonso Eduardo Reidy* (New York, 1960), Sibyl Moholy-Nagy's *Carlos Raúl Villanueva and the Architecture of Modern Venezuela* (New York, 1964), and Willy Stäubli's *Brasília* (New York, 1965). In South American architecture, the main interest appears to be concentrated on Brazil, especially since the creation of the new capital, Brasília, with its official buildings designed by Niemeyer.

In preparing the present survey I have of course consulted the available literature in various languages, and the catalogs of individual and collective exhibitions—especially those of the biennials of São Paulo (Brazil) and Córdoba (Argentina). The *Bienal Americana de Arte* of Córdoba, held from 1962 to 1966, is especially significant for two reasons: it was devoted exclusively to contemporary art of the Americas, and was sponsored mainly by private industry, Industrias Kaiser Argentina (an automobile manufacturer). Such industrial sponsorship is recent and still unusual in Latin America, where governments have been the traditional patrons of art. Another example is the Instituto Torcuato Di Tella in Buenos Aires, which has a division of visual arts that during the 1960's became a leading international center for contemporary art in Latin America.

It has been gratifying to notice in recent years the rapid and effective increase of interest in Latin American art throughout the United States, as revealed not only by the large number of individual gallery shows but also by such important collective exhibitions as *South American Art Today* (Dallas Museum of Fine Arts, 1959), *New Departures: Latin America* (Boston Institute of Contemporary Art, 1960), *New Art of Brazil* and *New Art of Argentina* (Walker Art Center, Minneapolis, 1962 and 1964 respectively), *The Emergent Decade: Latin American Painters and Paintings in the 1960's* (Cornell University and The Solomon R. Guggenheim Museum, 1965–66), and *Art of Latin America Since Independence* (The Yale University Art Gallery and the University of Texas Art Museum, 1966). Some of these exhibits have circulated widely in the United States.

My own serious interest in the contemporary arts of Latin America began in 1945, when I travelled extensively in that area. This interest was nourished by years of residence in Peru and Argentina, and was further stimulated by subsequent travels that took me on various occasions to nearly all the countries of Latin America. There I was able to meet many of the artists, to see their work in studios, galleries, and museums, and to observe the new architecture *in situ*. In New York also, where so many Latin American artists have come to live and work, I was able to interview a number of them and to discuss their aims and methods.

I am indebted for information and documentation to many individuals and institutions, both in Latin America and the United
States, and to all of them I extend my thanks and gratitude.

I wish especially to thank my friend Dr. Vasco Mariz, of the
Brazilian diplomatic corps, at present Director of Culture in the
Ministry of Foreign Affairs, whose unfailing cooperation and
critical comments have greatly aided my study of the arts in
Brazil. It was under the direction of Dr. Mariz that the Ministry
of Foreign Affairs published in 1966 a valuable reference work,
Quem É Quem nas artes e nas letras do Brasil (*Who Is Who in
the Arts and Letters of Brazil*), which I have had frequent occasion
to use. The section on Plastic Arts was compiled by Clarival
Valladares, that on Contemporary Architecture by Vladimir Alves
de Souza. I wish also to express my appreciation to Dr. José Gómez
Sicre, Chief of the Visual Arts Division of the Pan American
Union; to the research staff of the Museum of Modern Art in New
York; and to the Galeriá Bonino of New York and Buenos Aires.
Many others in many countries have helped in many ways.
They are indeed too numerous to mention here individually;
but each will understand that what they have done to assist me
in this work is but a continuation of the long years of friendship,
hospitality, and cordial cooperation that my wife and I have
repeatedly and gratefully enjoyed in the countries of Latin
America.

Contents

PREFACE   *v*

1. MEXICO: REVOLUTION AND REACTION   *1*

2. THE CARIBBEAN AND CENTRAL
   AMERICA   *39*

3. NATIVISM AND MODERNISM ON THE
   WEST COAST   *96*

4. ARGENTINA AND URUGUAY:
   COSMOPOLITAN CURRENTS   *127*

5. MODERN ART IN THE TROPICS: BRAZIL   *181*

6. ARCHITECTURE AND INTEGRATION
   OF THE ARTS   *227*

SELECTED BIBLIOGRAPHY   *275*

INDEX   *281*

List of Illustrations

1. MATHIAS GOERITZ, The Towers.   *frontispiece*

                                    Following page 132
2. JOSÉ CLEMENTE OROZCO, "Modern Migration of the Spirit."

3. DIEGO RIVERA, *Temptations of Saint Anthony.*

4. ALBERTO DA VEIGA GUIGNARD, *Ouro Preto: St. John's Eve.*

5. JOSÉ CLEMENTE OROZCO, *Zapatistas.*

6. RUFINO TAMAYO, *Girl Attacked by a Strange Bird.*

7. WIFREDO LAM, *The Jungle.*

8. FERNANDO BOTERO, *Mrs. Rubens (No. 5).*

9. RÓMULO MACCIÓ, *Emplacement.*

10. OSCAR NIEMEYER, National Congress and Ministry of Foreign Affairs, Brasília.

11. FÉLIX CANDELA and MARIO PANI, Band shell.

12. CARLOS RAÚL VILLANUEVA, Olympic Stadium.

13. CARLOS RAÚL VILLANUEVA and ALEXANDER CALDER, Aula Magna.

14. ROBERTO GONZÁLEZ GOYRI, Concrete Reliefs.

15. GUILLERMO TRUJILLO, *End of the Feast*.

16. JOAQUÍN TORRES GARCÍA, Untitled work.

17. AMELIA PELÁEZ, *Fishes*.

18. CÂNDIDO PORTINARI, "The Mining of Gold."

19. ARMANDO MORALES, *Double Arch*.

20. GYULA KOSICE, detail from *Diyi All the Time*.

21. J. A. FERNÁNDEZ MURO, *Shot in the Back*.

22. MARCELO BONEVARDI, detail from *Sun Wheel*.

23. ALICIA PEÑALBA, *Small Winged Object*.

24. ROBERTO GONZÁLEZ GOYRI, *Dying Warrior*.

1

Mexico:
Revolution
and
Reaction

*T*HE Mexican Revolution began in 1910 as a revolt against the régime of the eighty-year-old Porfirio Díaz, who had been virtual dictator of the nation since 1876. But it was also a revolt against the old order in general: the feudalism of the large landowners; the wealth and influence of the Catholic Church; the oppression and exploitation of the peasants and workers; the degradation of the Indian population; and the economic imperialism of foreign powers. Behind all this was the heavy heritage of Spanish colonialism, which the achievement of political independence in the early nineteenth century had not entirely overcome. The Indians and mestizos (of mixed Indian and European blood), constituting most of the population, were an economically and politically submerged majority. Art was the adornment of the privileged classes and culture the expression of an educated minority. The Revolution aimed to reverse these values. In the words of one of its intellectual leaders, the ethnologist Manuel Gamio, in his influential book *Forjando Patria* (*Forging a Nation*), published in 1916, "Mexico does not produce legitimate works of art as yet, because to be legitimate it should first be its own, a national art that would mirror, intensified and beautified, the pleasures, sufferings, life and soul of the people."

Nationalism was to be the dominant theme of the Mexican Revolution and its cultural aftermath. Gamio, a life-long defender of the Indian and champion of indigenous culture, proclaimed the doctrine that because the great majority of Mexicans were of Indian blood (in whole or in part) the values of Indian culture were essential for the complete and authentic expression of the national character. This doctrine was accepted as basic to the cultural program of the Revolution. The nationalist movement consequently emphasized the indigenous heritage of Mexico, not only in the contemporary folkways (including popular arts and crafts) but also in its pre-Hispanic traditions and achievements. The history of ancient Mexico was regarded as more important than the history of Spain. Art and archaeology were harnessed to recover and depict the glories of Tenochtitlán—the Aztec capital in the central valley of Mexico—and eventually the National Museum of Anthropology became a kind of secular national shrine. The Spanish conquerors, on the other hand, were depicted as cruel and bigoted, destroyers of native culture and exploiters of the Indian. Diego Rivera depicted Hernán Cortés, the Conqueror of Mexico, not as a glorious hero, but as a deformed embodiment of depravity.

Gerardo Murillo—"Dr Atl"

The first Revolutionary artist of Mexico, who set the example for using art as political propaganda, chose to call himself Dr. Atl, from the word meaning water in the Náhuatl language of central Mexico (the language spoken by the Aztecs). His real name was Gerardo Murillo (1877–1964), but in the history of Mexican art he is always known as Dr. Atl. He it was who told the astonished students at the San Carlos Academy of Art that "The end of bourgeois civilization is at hand!" Dr. Atl was a Revolutionary artist and a militant organizer even before the outbreak of the Revolution. In 1910, while Díaz was still in power, the régime incongruously organized the Exposition of Contemporary Spanish Painting to mark the centenary of the Mexican struggle for independence. The Mexican artists, with Dr. Atl as their spokesman, protested. As a result, they obtained a small subsidy from the government to organize an exhibition of their own. According to Orozco, it was "an immense, an unexpected, success." This event resulted in the immediate formation of an association of artists called the Centro Artístico, under the leadership of Dr. Atl. The group requested and received permission from the Ministry of Education to decorate the walls of the amphitheater of the National Preparatory School. By November the scaffolding had been set in place and the painters were ready to start work on the murals. Then, on the 20th of November, 1910, the Revolution broke out. "There was a panic," wrote Orozco in his *Autobiography*, "and our projects were ruined or postponed." Yet two precedents had been established: the association of artists under a militant leadership, and the painting of murals in public buildings as a group enterprise under government sponsorship. Both were to have important consequences some eleven years later, after the termination of the military phase of the Revolution.

When Porfirio Díaz was overthrown in 1911, Dr. Atl was in Paris exhibiting his wax-crayon landscapes. Returning to Mexico in 1913, he joined the party of Carranza, one of several Revolutionary leaders contending for control of the country (two others were the "bandit" leader Pancho Villa, and Emiliano Zapata, champion of "Land and Liberty"). Dr. Atl persuaded a number of the young artists, among them Siqueiros and Orozco, to join the forces of Carranza, whose headquarters were in Orizaba. There they carried on a propaganda war in words and pictures, chiefly through the medium of a newspaper called *La Vanguardia*, to which Orozco contributed a series of political caricatures. But when Carranza came briefly into power, Orozco was dismayed by the looting and the licentious conduct of his followers. His powerful and realistic drawings of brutality, greed, and destruction—a Mexican version of Goya's *The Disasters of War*—caused him to be regarded with disfavor.

Meanwhile, Dr. Atl, as leader of the World-Wide Workers' Organization, was in the thick of the Revolution. In 1915, when revolutionary violence was at its height, he appeared as a leader of the mob in Mexico City, throwing open the doors of the Church of La Concepción to admit the rabble eager for loot and goaded by a spirit of sacriligious ribaldry. As though taking part in a carnival, men donned sacerdotal garments and enacted a grotesque parody of the Mass, while others mounted to the pulpit to utter blasphemies and others again entered the confessionals and jeeringly exhorted the looters to confess their sins. Women, too, adorned themselves with sacerdotal albs, with bright-colored tunics snatched from sacred images, and with altar cloths worn as aprons. One woman, with the image of a child taken from the arms of a statue, obscenely mimicked, with howls and grimaces, the virgin birth.[1]

Similar scenes were repeated throughout Mexico during this decade of violent strife, of hate for the established order of powers and privileges. Yet Dr. Atl himself, writing some years later on the popular arts of Mexico, was to deplore the strong grip that Catholic imagery and religious sentiment continued to exert on the Mexican people:

The revolutionist who fought the church and the clergy, by suggestion or because he did not know what he was fighting, remained deeply religious and deeply Catholic. After looting a church, he carried the little pictures to his barracks or his home, lighted a candle before them, offered a triduum, begged of them protection for his family.[2]

The Mexican Revolution was full of such inconsistencies and contradictions, embodying ineradicable traits of Mexican character. When one of the greatest painters of the Mexican Revolution, José Clemente Orozco, came to write his autobiography, he was bitingly sarcastic about the dogmatic manifestos, the pseudo-aesthetic propaganda, and the doctrinaire pronouncements made by some of his more militant colleagues, such as Rivera and Siqueiros. The two latter artists in turn, differed sharply on the aims and means of Revolutionary art, and engaged in public polemics on the subject. Perhaps it was just this lack of monolithic structurization, the constant undermining of dogmatic positions, and the frequent discrepancies between doctrine and action, that

[1] Paraphrased from F. Ramírez Plancarte, *La Ciudad de México durante la Revolución* (Mexico, 1941).
[2] As quoted in Charlot, *The Mexican Mural Renaissance*, p. 216.

preserved the artistic vitality of the Revolutionary movement and kept it from complete bureaucratic solidification.

In the beginning, the Revolutionary movement was a revolt against narrow academic standards. Students at the official art school, the San Carlos Academy of Art, spent their time copying the same models in the same unchanging poses and learning to paint in the outmoded manner of the second-rate Spanish academic painters. Dr. Atl opened new vistas for these students. Roaming among the night classes, he spoke to them about the marvels of Michelangelo's frescoes in the Sistine Chapel and showed them his drawings of muscular giants taken from those glorious models. Dr. Atl had been to Italy and to France; he exerted the fascination of one who had known "the audacities of the Parisian school." In the poetic phrase of Orozco, he came into the classrooms with "the rainbow of the Impressionists in his hands." He awakened in the students a sense of individual and national identity. The words of Orozco again: "As we listened to the fervent voice of that agitator, Dr. Atl, we began to suspect that the whole colonial situation was nothing but a swindle foisted upon us by the international traders. Now for the first time the painters took stock of the country they lived in."[3]

Dr. Atl himself set the example of seeking his techniques abroad, his subjects at home. At that time he probably knew more about the techniques of painting and print-making, both occidental and oriental, than anyone else in Mexico. Though he learned much abroad, he refused to follow current fashions. As a lover of naturalistic landscape, he rejected cubism and all other abstract tendencies. He went to live on the slopes of Popocatepetl and devoted himself to drawing and painting the volcanoes and the fertile valleys of Mexico. Technically, his main concern was with the application of color. Being partial to pastels, he wanted to give them the permanency that they lacked. This he did by inventing the so-called Atl-colors, consisting of wax, resins, and petroleum mixed into a hard paste. These colors were applied like ordinary pastels to any surface chosen by the artist. They could be superimposed indefinitely while always remaining pure,

[3] Orozco, *An Autobiography.* Translated by Robert C. Stephenson. University of Texas Press, 1962, p. 20.

unmixed. Paintings executed with the Atl-colors have the soft, luminous quality of ordinary pastels, but with greater variety and richness of tones. Further variations of texture could be obtained by diluting the colors with petroleum or by melting them. Dr. Atl also combined his wax colors with other techniques, such as aqua-resina (painting on a white base prepared with white of zinc and casein paste). He used them also with simple water-colors and oil paints. His landscapes have a remarkable topographical and geological fidelity combined with a mastery of perspective and a variety of tones, at once delicate and rich. His aesthetic philosophy was based on the belief that "the representation of Nature is one of the loftiest expressions of the human spirit."[4]

Mexican Muralism

The violent, quasi-anarchistic phase of the Mexican Revolution came to a halt in December, 1920, with the inauguration of General Obregón as Constitutional President. As his Minister of Education, Obregón chose a controversial but dynamic personality, the philosopher-politician José Vasconcelos, to whom he entrusted a vast program of cultural renovation aimed at all sectors of the population, but especially at those hitherto deprived of educational opportunities. The program was not limited to the fine arts, but also embraced the folk, primitive, and popular arts and crafts. The latter phase was entrusted to three artists who were friends of Vasconcelos: Dr. Atl, Adolfo Best-Maugard (1891–1964) and Roberto Montenegro (b. 1886). In 1921 these three men organized an exhibition for which Dr. Atl wrote an authoritative catalog, *Folk Arts of Mexico*. Jean Charlot describes this as "still the best source book on the subject, which made a wealth of untapped patterns and designs available to painters."

The following year Best-Maugard was appointed Federal Director of Art Education, and soon afterwards he published his influential book, *Tradition, Renaissance and Evolution in Mexican Art* (1923). In 1911, Best-Maugard had been commis-

[4] Dr. Atl, *El Paisaje: un ensayo* (Mexico, 1933).

sioned by the anthropologist Franz Boas to copy pottery designs from the Valley of Mexico, a task that enabled him to compile an index of indigenous motifs. When the famous ballerina Anna Pavlova visited Mexico in 1918, Best-Maugard designed the costumes, sets, and choreography for a Mexican Ballet that she produced with immense success not only in Mexico City but in other capitals of the world as well. In spite of his interest in the art of ancient Mexico, Best-Maugard was convinced that the folk and popular arts of modern Mexico must necessarily be heterogeneous, including not only Spanish but even Chinese elements (the latter brought to the Pacific coast during the trade with China that flourished in the colonial period). With the aid of 150 assistants, Best-Maugard undertook to teach Mexican children to express themselves creatively through decorative painting and drawing. He developed a system of pedagogy based on folk art.

Meanwhile, Vasconcelos was commissioning various painters to execute murals for public buildings. The first to receive a commission was his friend Roberto Montenegro, who had just returned from Europe, where he had been living since 1906. Working in tempera, Montenegro used the absidial wall of a former church converted to a workers' center for a mural titled *The Dance of the Hours*, a conventional allegory depicting twelve female figures grouped around a knight in armor leaning against the tree of life. Proud of his initial commission, Vasconcelos later wrote in his memoirs: "Montenegro started there the movement of Mexican Painting that later transcended national boundaries. . . ." But it was a tame beginning for a movement that was soon to erupt like a volcano, creating scandals, riots, and controversies and spreading its influence over all the Americas. The painters chiefly responsible for this eruption were Diego Rivera, José Clemente Orozco, and David Alfaro Siqueiros.

Diego Rivera

Diego María de la Concepción Juan Nepomuceno Estanislao de la Rivera y Barrientos Acosta y Rodríguez (1886–1957)—more commonly known as Diego Rivera—was born on December 8,

1886, in the town of Guanajuato, high in the mountains of Central Mexico. From childhood he hated the church and the clergy, and was proud of being an atheist. When he was seven, the family moved to Mexico City, and at the age of eleven he enrolled in the San Carlos Academy of Art, attending classes at night while going to elementary school in the daytime. He found this burdensome. "What sustained me," he later said, "was the discovery of the pre-Conquest art of Mexico, for which I conceived a passion that was to influence my entire artistic life."[5] Later, as a fulltime student, he worked hard, "determined to learn all that tradition could teach me." This principle he was to follow throughout his formative years, both in Mexico and Europe. After pre-Conquest art, the most important of his early influences came from the famous popular artist José Guadalupe Posada (1851–1913), with whom he studied privately. Posada had an engraving shop, in which he etched illustrations for songs, ballads, stories, and jokes that were peddled as broadsides throughout Mexico, "all printed on sheets of colored tissue paper and sold from door to door." In his autobiography Rivera states that Posada "knew as much about form and movement as any man I ever met. It was he who revealed to me the inherent beauty in the Mexican people, their struggle and aspirations." Rivera's mural for the Del Prado Hotel in Mexico City, *Dream of a Sunday Afternoon in the Central Alameda*, clearly reveals the strong influence of Posada. In fact, Posada was one of the seminal forces behind the Mexican muralist movement, providing for its painters a repertory of images and symbols that evoked an immediate response from the Mexican populace.

Rivera also came under the influence of Dr. Atl, who urged him to go to Europe. This he was able to do in 1907, with a small government stipend. He remained in Europe until 1921 (except for a brief return to Mexico in 1910), studying first in Madrid with Eduardo Chicharro (an academic painter) and later chiefly in Paris. A trip to Italy in 1920 was especially important, for it awakened his interest in fresco painting. When he returned

[5] Rivera, *My Art, My Life*, an autobiography with Gladys March. The Citadel Press, 1960, p. 39. Other quotations by Rivera are from the same source unless otherwise indicated.

to Mexico in 1921 as a self-declared "Revolutionary artist," his artistic baggage was a collection of many styles, from naturalism to cubism, from Cézanne to Picasso, from impressionism to realism. The works of this period (1908–19) reveal his technical ability and his capacity for assimilation. Having assimilated the lessons of Renoir, Cézanne, Seurat, and the Fauves, he went on to capture the qualities of cubism, particularly as represented in the work of Braque and Juan Gris. He is said to have done some eighty paintings in the cubist style. The most significant of these, in view of Rivera's later commitment of the cause of the Mexican Revolution, is a painting titled *El Zapatista*, dating from 1915. The title, of course, refers to a follower of the Revolutionary leader Emiliano Zapata. Here we find the familiar elements of Revolutionary painting—sombrero, poncho, rifle, cartridge belt, mountains and volcanic craters in the background; but they are "decomposed" in the manner of cubism (e.g., the crown and rim of the sombrero are treated as separate pictorial elements), and rearranged in the pictorial space as a semiabstract composition.

At this time Rivera was fascinated by cubism as "a revolutionary movement, questioning everything that had previously been said and done in art. . . . As the old world would soon blow itself apart, never to be the same again, so cubism broke down forms as they had been seen for centuries, and was creating out of the fragments new forms, new objects, new patterns and—ultimately—new worlds." But when Rivera plunged into the cultural and creative aftermath of the Mexican Revolution, he saw no way of reconciling "revolutionary" art with Revolutionary ideology. As he explains in his autobiography, "When it dawned on me that all this innovation had little to do with real life, I would surrender all the glory and acclaim cubism had brought me for a way in art truer to my inmost feelings." But the glory and acclaim he "surrendered" as a minor cubist were as nothing compared to the glory and acclaim he received as the most militant and most favored non-revolutionary painter of the Mexican Revolution.

Although Rivera himself referred to *El Zapatista* as "probably the most faithful expression of the Mexican mood that I have ever achieved," he came to feel, under the influence of Marxist doctrine, that he was on the wrong track as an artist. In his cubist paintings he was undoubtedly being faithful to what Ortega y Gasset called "the imperative of the work of one's own time," but when he turned to Communism he responded instead to the social-political imperative of the class stduggle and the emergence of a "classless society." As he later told it,

> I foresaw a new society in which the bourgeoisie would vanish and their taste, served by the subtleties of cubism, dadaism, constructivism, surrealism, and the like, would no longer monopolize the functions of art. The society of the future would be a mass society.... A new kind of art would therefore be needed, one which appealed not to the viewers' sense of form and color directly, but through exciting subject matter. The new art, also, would not be a museum or gallery art but an art the people would have access to in places they frequented in their daily life—post offices, schools, theaters, railroad stations, public buildings.

The subordination of form and color to "exciting subject matter" was the decisive turning-point in the history of modern Mexican painting—coupled with the shift from easel to mural painting. For Rivera, this shift meant learning the virtually lost art of fresco painting, and this meant a return to the Italian Renaissance. Rivera regarded the transition from modernism to muralism as a sort of purification rite: "I intensified my labors to rid myself of modernist residues in my work. By the end of 1919 I felt that I had cleansed myself sufficiently to take the next step and, by research and study, prepare myself for my new career as a mural painter." And so, having sold some fashionable portraits, he took the money and went off to Italy to study the frescoes of the old masters.

Rivera spent a year and half in Italy (1920–21), completing "more than three hundred sketches from the frescoes of the masters and from life." The moment seemed ripe for returning to Mexico: his homecoming, he tells us, "produced an esthetic exhilaration which it is impossible to describe.... In everything I saw a potential masterpiece—the crowds, the markets, the festivals, the marching battalions, the workingmen in the shops and fields..." Soon he was given a wall to cover at the National

Preparatory School in Mexico City. This was a group project shared by other artists, among them Fernando Leal, Jean Charlot, Ramón Alva de la Canal, Siqueiros, and Orozco. The Mexican muralist movement, as a grand national enterprise, came to life on these walls. There were many individual styles, but one overriding subject common to all—Mexico.

From this time on, Rivera devoted himself without stint to the study of Mexican culture, history, and archaeology, and to its living folklore, the land, and the people—their fiestas, rituals, dances, costumes, celebrations, occupations. He went from one mural to another: the Ministry of Education (1923–28), the National Agricultural School at Chapingo (1923–27), the Palace of Cortés in Cuernavaca (1929), and his *magnum opus*, the National Palace in Mexico City (1930–35), the subject of which was the history of Mexico from the pre-Hispanic era to the present.

Rivera had already undertaken this vast subject in his murals for the Palace of Cortés (commissioned by Dwight Morrow, the American Ambassador to Mexico), for which he had done intensive research in primary sources such as the Sahagún Codex, the most comprehensive pictorial record of pre-Cortesian Mexico. For the National Palace murals he utilized this knowledge and developed the theme of Mexico's history on a grander scale. The results of Rivera's documentary studies of ancient Mexican life are impressively demonstrated in his large panel depicting the City of Mexico under the Aztecs just prior to the Spanish Conquest (*La Gran Tenochtitlan*), with its wealth of detail. This includes a panoramic view of the city in the background, a reconstructed iconography, a pictorial catalog of·social types from ruler to prostitute, costumes, adornments, artifacts, products, flora, fauna, and the notoriously gruesome detail of the severed arm of a slain captive offered for sale as meat. This is descriptive and documentary painting carried to the utmost limits of crowded detail and illustrative functionalism, pictorially redeemed by a masterly sense of composition and a striking use of color.

But the indisputable masterpiece of the project is the immense mural that occupies the five bays of the main staicase, which divides to the right and left after the first landing. Here Rivera painted a panorama of the history of Mexico, including its legendary past, when the god Quetzalcoatl presided over a Golden Age; the Spanish conquest under Cortés; conversion and oppression of the Indians; tortures by the Inquisition and branding of slaves; the leaders of Mexican independence (among them Hidalgo and Morelos); the defense of Chapultepec in the war with the United States; the execution of the Emperor Maximilian and the expulsion of the French; the régime of Porfirio Díaz and his generals; the Revolution of 1910 and its leaders; foreign exploitation of Mexico's natural resources; and finally the triumph of the social revolution, the victory of the working class, presided over by Karl Marx.

The whole mural requires careful study to grasp all of its details—indeed, the identification of individuals requires a coded diagram. In the panel depicting the Revolution of 1910 there are thirty-nine portraits of political figures, including Conservatives, Liberals, and Revolutionaries. The concluding panel, representing the class struggle, was completed in 1935, after a lapse of five years during which Rivera visited the United States. It reintroduces elements of gross caricature and crass political propaganda that are apparent in some of the frescoes in the Ministry of Education (*Night of the Rich, The Billionaires*), and falls below the aesthetic quality of the rest of this impressive mural, in which an "exciting subject matter" is sustained by the masterly deployment of form and color.

Something should be said about Rivera's work in the United States. After executing two frescoes in San Francisco in 1930, he was given a one-man show the following year at the Museum of Modern Art in New York, which attracted a great deal of attention. Other commissions quickly followed: the Detroit Institute of Arts, the Independent Labor Institute, Rockefeller Center These proved to be highly controversial, especially the murals for Rockefeller Center, of which the general theme was "Man at the Crossroads." Rivera gave this theme a Marxist interpretation, capped by a portrait of Lenin leading a group of workers. As Schmeckebier points out, "Lenin's portrait was an insignificant detail compared to the huge expanse of the wall." But doubtless it triggered a latent antagonism between artist and patron, leading

to Rivera's abrupt dismissal, cancellation of his contract, and the
eventual effacement of the mural. Rivera reproduced the mural
in the Palace of Fine Arts of Mexico City, and got his revenge by
including an uncomplimentary portrait of John D. Rockefeller,
Jr., "his head but a short distance away from the venereal disease
germs pictured in the ellipse of the microscope" (Rivera).

Diego Rivera remained a controversial figure to the end of his
life in 1957, and the controversy about his place in modern
art continued after his death. It would be easy to compile a
catalog of his faults and limitations, and these would be magnified
by the enormous quantity of his work, said to cover some 4,000
square meters. His documentary detail, his illustrative tendency,
his repertory of stock images, his preoccupation with propaganda,
his decorative folklorism, his blatant exaggeration—all have
evoked critical disfavor. But few question the grandeur of his
achievement or his importance in the national culture of Mexico.
He is at his best in his mastery of the monumental style and the
technique of fresco painting, as revealed in his work for the
Chapel of Chapingo, where the quintessence of all that he learned
from the Italian masters of the Renaissance is concentrated and
transposed to a personal and Mexican mode in the splendid nude
figure of the main wall, "Earth Liberated."

José Clemente Orozco

"José Clemente Orozco is the greatest painter produced by
America." This categorical value judgment by the Spanish art
critic Luis Cardoza y Aragón reflects a growing body of critical
opinion that has steadily enhanced Orozco's posthumous reputation. Justifying his judgment, the same critic continues,

> The virtues of other Mexican painters are to be found assembled in
> him, governed by his sincerity and passion.... His nature is the richest
> of all, the most complex and complete, rigorously disciplined and
> served through the refined wisdom of artist and man. Nobody feels
> more profoundly what he says or says more profoundly what he
> feels.... His drawing with its lineal impetus and his use of light is

enough to give him preeminence.... His drawing is the richest, most diverse, most eloquent, inventive and passionate of Mexico.[6]

José Clemente Orozco (1883–1949) is equally fascinating as man and as artist. His *Autobiography*, originally published in 1945, reveals that he was never taken in by the catchwords of the Mexican Revolution, the slogans of political propaganda, the confusion of social and aesthetic values, the dogmatic ideology of the Left, or the confining doctrines of nationalism. Throughout the *Autobiography*, Orozco appears as a "loner": a man who knew his own mind and kept his own council; a man who went against the tide even while he appeared to be going along with it; a merciless exposer of shams and pretentious attitudes; a man who looked for the truth, however horrible or disturbing, and faced it unflinchingly. Overshadowed by Rivera during his lifetime, he is the only one among the muralists whom the newer generations in Mexico recognize as a seminal force and a spiritual ancestor.[7]

Orozco received all his artistic training and all his formative experiences in Mexico. He was, as we have seen, directly involved in the militant phase of the Revolution, and bore witness to its excesses in an extraordinary series of drawings. Along with the influence of Dr. Atl—both artistic and political—the young Orozco was profoundly influenced by his contact with José Guadalupe Posada. As a student he spent "a few enchanted minutes" each day watching Posada at work; and this "was the push that first set my imagination in motion. . ." Furthermore, "Posada's engravings were decorated by hand, and it was in watching this operation that I received my first lessons in the use of color."

Orozco was a dissenter within the Mexican muralist movement. He declared that the emphasis on non-aesthetic content "leads us down the road to purely illustrative, descriptive painting, and

---

[6] Luis Cardoza y Aragón, *Orozco* (Universidad Nacional Autónoma de México, 1959).

[7] This applies particularly to José Luis Cuevas and to the group known as *La Nueva Presencia*, formed in 1961 by Arnold Belkin, Francisco Corzas, Leonel Góngora, José Muñoz, Emilio Ortiz, and Artemio Sepúlveda.

all the way to the impersonal photographic document, indeed to literary painting, which neglects form in order to declaim or tell stories—to anecdotal painting, that is." He summed up his own artistic creed in these words: "A painting should not be a commentary but the fact itself, not a reflection but the source of light, not an interpretation but the very thing to be interpreted.... It should consist of absolutely nothing but the plastic fact in its particular, concrete, and rigorously precise statement...."

This may seem a contradictory statement for an artist who was so deeply involved in the political and moral issues of his time. But what he undoubtedly meant was that whatever the plastic artist had to say about life, about humanity and society, must be extrapolated from the essential "plastic fact" of the work of art as a thing-in-itself—"particular, concrete, and rigorously precise." If such paintings as *The Trench* and *The Trinity* (his frescoes in the National Preparatory School, 1922–23), stand out as masterpieces of Mexican Revolutionary muralism, it is precisely because their uncompromising portrayal of self-destructiveness and human suffering through war and violence is not a commentary on the miseries and disasters of war but the fact itself, embodied in the plastic form. And the same could be said of the three frescoes in the same project, *The Franciscan and the Indian;* here the subject is compassion, translated into a deep and enduring emotion through the plastic facts of form and color. Orozco's extremely effective use of a subdued color range in these frescoes must be noted. He never used color in the purely decorative or rhetorical manner of Rivera. This can be verified in such a masterly painting as *Zapatistas* (1931) [Plate 5], where a rather conventional Revolutionary subject is transformed by the expressionist use of vibrant color harmonies.

From 1927 to 1934, Orozco lived in the United States, where he executed murals for Pomona College in Claremont, California (*Prometheus*, 1930), the New School for Social Research in New York City (1931), and the Baker Library of Dartmouth College, Hanover, New Hampshire (1932–34). This last, presenting *An Epic of American Civilization*, is one of his most ambitious and significant projects. Part I, "The Coming of Quetzalcoatl," depicts the pre-Hispanic past of Mexico; Part II, "The Return of Quet-zalcoatl," covers the period from the Spanish conquest to modern times, culminating in "The Modern Migration of the Spirit" [Plate 2]. This last panel is an allegorical counterpart of the first, which depicts the migration of the Indian tribes in search of their Promised Land. Here in the modern spiritual migration,

"a militant Christ-figure is shown, axe in hand and his cross at his feet, symbolic of an aroused and aggressive spirituality. He stands against a great junk heap in which appear the destroyed symbols of antiquated creeds and the confining forms of all religions. The release from spiritual bondage here symbolized becomes even larger in meaning in view of the destroyed war materials in the junk heap, representing the violence and hatred among men which is too often invoked in the name of religion."[8]

The main epic is unfolded in fourteen panels, though there are several other complementary panels to fill the remaining wall space in the library, including the central panels on the south wall depicting "Modern Industrial Man." The epic includes "Anglo-America" as well as indigenous and Hispanic America, but the last three panels—"Gods of the Modern World," "Modern Human Sacrifice," and "Modern Migration of the Spirit"—indicate a universal message for mankind.

The significance of the Dartmouth murals was aptly summed up by a historian of Mexican painting : "For the first time in the history of American art Orozco attempted to depict the epic of American civilization, not with the pseudo-intellectual symbolism of the New World's cultural and social history in the broadest the prairie-schooner frontier . . . but with a symbolic interpretation of the New World's cultural and social history in the broadest sense."[9] Orozco himself formulated the aesthetic basis of the Dartmouth murals in a statement published in New York in 1929 : a new art for the New World.

The art of the New World cannot take root in the old traditions of

[8] As quoted in Albert I. Dickerson, ed., *The Orozco Frescoes at Dartmouth* (Hanover, N.H., 1934).
[9] Schmeckebier, *Modern Mexican Art*. University of Minnesota Press, 1939, p. 81.

the Old World nor in the aboriginal traditions represented by the remains of our ancient Indian peoples. Although the art of all races and of all times has a common value—human, universal—each new cycle must work for itself, must create, must yield its own production, its individual share to the common good. . . . If new races have appeared upon the land of the New World, such races have the unavoidable duty to produce a New Art in a new spiritual and physical medium. Any other road is plain cowardice.[10]

When asked by Dartmouth College to make a statement in 1933 for a pamphlet on the murals Orozco said, among other things,

The important point regarding the frescoes of the Baker Library is not only the quality of the idea that initiates and organizes the whole structure, it is also the fact that it is an AMERICAN idea developed into American forms, American feeling, and, as a consequence, into American style. . . . This is not imitation, this is our OWN effort, to the limit of our own strength and experience, in all sincerity and spontaneity.

While acknowledging the "American" character of the Baker Library frescoes, it is nevertheless important to note that they were begun shortly after Orozco made his first and only visit to Europe, in the summer of 1932. He visited London and Paris, and traveled in Spain and Italy. What apparently impressed him most were the frescoes of Giotto in Padua (which he had previously known only through reproductions), and above all Masaccio's frescoes in Santa Maria del Carmine, Florence. Discussing the last panel of the Dartmouth fresco, dominated by the terrible figure of Christ chopping down his own cross, Schmeckebier writes,

It would seem as though Orozco, through his study of Masaccio, had discovered the basic principle of form used by the Byzantine craftsman on the walls of Sant' Apollinare Nuovo in Ravenna. The tall impressive figures are not the only parallel. In his coloration, his juxtaposition of pure color patches for their glittering iridescent effect, Orozco with his modern fresco medium has been working with principles long in use by Byzantine mosaic designers and revived by the Parisian Neo-Impressionists. Orozco's achievement, however, is by no means a stylization of Impressionistic scene painting (Signac), nor the glittering narrative panorama that Rivera made out of it, but a

[10] As quoted in Cardoza y Aragón, p. 118.

*thoroughly new form whose ultimate possibilities of development are
unlimited.*[11]

Returning to Mexico in 1934, Orozco was commissioned to
paint a large wall in the lobby of the Palace of Fine Arts, for
which he chose the theme *Strife*, as exemplified in the destructive
violence of modern civilization. From then on he was kept busy
with one mural project after another, culminating in his final
and crowning achievement, the frescoes for the Chamber of
Deputies of Jalisco, in Guadalajara (1948–49), completed shortly
before his death. Especially notable are his frescoes for the
Hospicio Cabañas, the University, and the Government Palace
in Guadalajara (1935–39), in which he developed a strongly
personal style that was both expressionist and monumental and
that was equally effective in historical subjects and in social
themes (*False Science and the Problem of Humanity*). For the
dome of the University of Guadalajara, Orozco designed four
major figures, representing respectively the Worker, the Educator,
the Scientist, and the Rebel. The Guadalajara frescoes are to
Orozco's *oeuvre* as the Sistine Chapel frescoes are to that of
Michelangelo. No one who has not made the artistic pilgrimage
to Gaudalajara will have grasped the full depth and scope of
Orozco's genius.

Orozco's drawings for the frescoes are masterpieces in their
own right. When the Mexican government, in 1947, organized
an exhibit of Orozco's works at the National Palace of Fine Arts,
the artist said: "That to which I attribute the most importance
are the drawings for my murals because they demonstrate how
much I have labored in what I consider the best and most characteristic part of my work. They reveal the most interesting moments
of my production, my own particular manner of working." In
self-criticism, as in all else, Orozco's judgment was lucid, pene-
trating, and honest. Most critics will agree with the opinion of
Bernard Myers, that "Orozco emerges as the towering figure of
the Mexican school."

[11] Schmeckebier, p. 99–100.

Siqueiros: Militant Muralist

Of the "big three" in the Mexican muralist movement, David Alfaro Siqueiros (b. 1896) was the man of manifestos, of polemics, of class warfare, of militant Communism. Born in Chihuahua, he came to the capital at the age of thirteen and entered the National School of Fine Arts (formerly the Academia de San Carlos), participated in the students' strike in 1911, joined the army of Carranza, and for five years took an active part in the Revolution. Later he wrote: "Without that experience it would not have been possible to conceive and to animate ... the modern movement in Mexican painting ..." After the Revolution he went to Europe, traveled in Italy and Spain, and at Barcelona, in 1921, issued his "Manifesto to the Plastic Artists of America," calling for "a public art, a monumental and heroic art, a human art, drawing on the example, direct and vital, of our great and extraordinary pre-Hispanic cultures of America." Returning to Mexico in 1922, Siqueiros took the initiative in organizing the Syndicate of Technical Workers, Painters, Sculptors and Similar Guilds, which was intended to formalize the solidarity of the artists with the working classes. The Syndicate issued a manifesto that set forth the artistic ideology of the Mexican Revolution. The over-all aim was "to liquidate the decadence of modern art" (a basic Communist tenet). Art should be a collective expression, hence it was necessary "to socialize artistic expression, to destroy bourgeois individualism." Easel painting was condemned as "essentially aristocratic," and "the monumental expression of art in mural painting" was advocated "because such art is public property." Art, in short, must belong to the people.

Orozco, in his *Autobiography*, made a devastating critique of this manifesto. He pointed out, for instance, that none of the artists wanted to abandon easel painting: they simply gave it another name, calling it "movable painting." As such it became acceptable, and it is a fact, often overlooked, that the Mexican muralists also produced a large quantity of easel painting. But the Manifesto of 1922 did formulate the general aims and criteria of the official line in post-Revolutionary Mexican painting. The

Syndicate also published a periodical, El Machete, to which both Siqueiros and Orozco contributed.

Although Siqueiros participated briefly in the National Preparatory School project, he accomplished relatively little as a muralist during the 1920's. In 1932 he traveled to the United States, where he executed some unsuccessful murals in California. He was becoming interested in the use of industrial paints, such as Duco (pyroxilin), which he applied with a spray gun. He asserted that the artist "must turn to materials that correspond to industry, that is, to the society of which we are a part." He was also interested in the dynamic exploitation of spatial and visual effects, experimenting (as Bernard S. Myers observes) with "a space that results from the multiplication of parts and the cinematic superposition of images that may be viewed from different angles." He first experimented with these techniques in Argentina in 1933, in a project for a private residence in collaboration with Spilimbergo and Antonio Berni. In 1939 he was able to apply these new techniques and materials in his first completed large-scale mural, Portrait of the Bourgeoisie, executed for the Electrical Workers' Union in Mexico City. He achieved an even more ambitious project in 1941–42, at a school called Escuela México in Chile, Death to the Invador (a double allegory of Chile and Mexico), working with pyroxilin on masonite. After his return to Mexico, Siqueiros was commissioned to do a large mural for one of the gallery walls in the National Palace of Fine Arts (1944–45), which he titled The New Democracy. It is dominated by the huge torso of a nude female figure that appears to surge from the wall "as though from the crater of a volcano" (Justino Fernández).

As the sole survivor of the famous trio of Mexican muralists of the first generation, Siqueiros has continued to receive public and private commissions for murals in Mexico, including some three-dimensional ones for the University City of Mexico (see Chapter 6). He made his big bid for fame as a historical muralist with a work executed in 1957–60 for the National Museum of History in Chapultepec Park, titled The Revolution Against the Porfirian Dictatorship. Striving for the grand epic manner, it remains an impressive anachronism.

Imprisoned in 1960 for "social dissolution," Siqueiros was released four years later and immediately began to work on an immense project, said to be "the world's largest mural," on the theme *The March of Humanity* at his studio-home in Cuernavaca. The total area is about 49,000 square feet. It is painted on an asbestos compound, each section framed with iron, so that it can be transported (it is installed in the new Auditorium in Mexico City). According to John Canaday,

> the mural includes passages of almost pure abstraction along with others of the most strident figurative expressionism, some of the latter being virtual repetitions of earlier murals varied by a technique that Siqueiros calls sculpture-painting. Two-dimensional passages rise into relief, with faces or whole figures swelling outward, and the mural is studded, as well, with fully three-dimensional wrought metal sculptures that are in effect totally disengaged from the wall.... The theatrical exhibitionism and the insistent noisiness, which are exaggerations of the late manifestations of many schools, seem quite intentional.[12]

It is evident, as Canaday writes, that Siqueiros intends "to conclude a tradition with a bang rather than a graceful bow."

Extra-mural Trends

Modern Mexican painting was never as monolithic as the dominance of the muralists made it appear from the outside. Even in the heyday of the muralist movement, during the 1920's and 1930's, there were many other kinds of painting going on in Mexico, reflecting various contemporary artistic currents, such as surrealism, Dada, magic realism, and neoromanticism. Justino Fernández dates the beginning of surrealism in Mexico from 1924—two years after the first major project of the muralist movement. It cannot be said, however, that any of these were important national currents or that they stirred up more than a ripple internationally. The work of such painters as Francisco Goitia (b. 1885), Manuel Rodríguez Lozano (b. 1895), Abraham Angel (1905–1924), María Izquierdo (1906–1956), Julio Castel-

---

[12] *The New York Times*, Jan. 3, 1968, p. 48M.

lanos (1905–1947), Agustín Lazo (b. 1898), Carlos Orozco Romero (b. 1898), and Frida Kahlo (1910–1954), revealed individual variety and independence from the doctrinaire nationalism of the muralists. And even the latter, as we have noted, embraced many different tendencies and modes of expression in their easel painting and their graphic work. Rivera had his surrealist phase in such paintings as *The Temptations of St. Anthony* (1947) [Plate 3] with its sexual imagery derived from the combination of vegetable and quasi-anthropomorphic elements, and *The Painter's Studio* (1954), with its array of fantastic "props" drawn from the macabre repertory of Mexican folklore and ritual. Orozco developed his own brand of expressionism in his easel paintings—for example, in the extraordinary *Resurrection of Lazarus* (1942)—and his pen and ink drawings, of which the *Truth* series (1945) carries satire to a pinnacle of high art. And in the case of Siqueiros one would have to take into acount not only his numerous easel paintings, but also his recent lithographs, such as the series on Vietnam (1968), where the plastic expression, combining abstract and figurative elements, takes precedence over propagandistic intent.

There was, then, considerable diversity in the visual arts of Mexico. Purely abstract art was slow to emerge and has never been a dominant tendency, in spite of the official support given to it in the early 1960's.[13] What all these counter-currents needed was an artist of sufficient stature to successfully challenge the prestige of the muralists and the dominance of the nationalist-socialist-realist school. Two artists capable of filling this need appeared on the scene almost at the same time: Carlos Mérida and Rufino Tamayo. The former was a Guatemalan and his career will be dealt with in the section on Central America (see Chapter 2). Mérida was active in Mexico from 1919; he was briefly associated with the syndicate group; he executed some murals for the Ministry of Education. But he soon turned to easel painting, with emphasis on color and form, leading to abstract or semi-abstract

[13] Of the eight artists chosen by the National Institute of Fine Arts to represent Mexico at the VI Bienal of São Paulo (1961), all but one (Gironella) were abstractionists of one persuasion or another: Waldemar Sjölander, Vlady (son of the exiled Russian novelist Victor Serge), Luis Nishisahua, Lilia Carrillo, Manuel Felguérez, Vicente Rojo, and Enrique Echeverría.

compositions, particularly during the period from 1932–37. His architectural murals are discussed in Chapter 6. Mérida was influential in pointing the way toward semi-abstract figuration and the freely inventive use of indigenous motifs.

Rufino Tamayo

Rufino Tamayo, born in Oaxaca in 1899, was the first Mexican artist to emerge conspicuously from the shadow of the muralists. It is true that he went through a social-political phase, as shown in *Glorification of Zapata, The Call of the Revolution, Rhythm of the Workers* (all 1935), and that he painted several important murals, notably *Birth of Our Nationality* and *Mexico Today* (1952). He also painted Indian types, women carrying jars on their heads, fruit vendors, corrido singers, women of Tehuantepec—in short, the whole indigenous-folkloristic repertory. As a young man he was appointed head of the Department of Ethnographic Drawing in the National Museum of Anthropology and Archaeology, awakening a deep and enduring interest in the indigenous cultures of Mexico. He also taught in the primary school system, including the rural open-air schools established by Vasconcelos. He came to have an intimate knowledge of Mexico and its people, past and present, justifying his statement, "I have very strong roots." But he never felt that the quality of being Mexican was incompatible with participation in the main currents of contemporary art.

Tamayo formulated his conception of art in these terms: "A product whose value derives only from its plastic qualities. Qualities obtained by means of a process of depuration until the essence is reached. A plastic essence ordered by a poetic sense, within the precious limitation of the picture. That is what I call PAINTING." In a statement made in 1960, Tamayo said: "There is no place in art for political or ideological manifestations. Painting is painting ... and there is no need of mixing it with any other thing. That has been the error of Mexican painting." In the same article he stressed the importance of being truly contemporary: "All the old molds of art and science have been broken.

A new era has been opened with interplanetary space travel. And if everyone is now looking for a new language, the painter cannot remain behind."[14]

Rufino Tamayo was brought to Mexico City at the age of eight, when both his parents died, and lived with an aunt who kept a fuel and fruit shop in the central market. While working there as a boy, Tamayo studied surreptitiously at the Academy of Fine Arts. He had his first one-man shows in 1926, in Mexico City and New York. He remained in New York for two years, and frequently returned thereafter. His first important commission was for a mural in the National Conservatory of Music (1933), for which he painted a strikingly unclassical muse of Music—a dark-skinned, half-draped Indian woman playing a lute. But his path in Mexico was made difficult by his aloofness from the dominant official group. In 1938 he accepted a teaching position at the Dalton School of Art in New York, and it was in the United States that his international fame was established. He liked the free and stimulating artistic climate of New York, where in 1939 he was deeply impressed by the Picasso exhibit at the Museum of Modern Art.

The influence of Picasso, along with that of Braque, had already manifested itself in Tamayo's painting; *Troubadors* (1934), for example, recalls Picasso's *Three Musicians*. After 1939, this influence became more apparent in such works as *Carnival* (1941) and *Woman with a Bird Cage* (1941). It has been suggested that Tamayo's celebrated *Animals* (1941) depicting two savage Mexican dogs, owes something to "Picasso's exaggeration of individual parts of the organic structure of a body for purposes of emotional impact." However this may be, the fact is that Tamayo applied this procedure not only in his well-known animal figures, but also in many of his human figures, as in *Woman Calling* (1941), *White Nude* (1943), *Man Contemplating the Heavens* (1944), *The Bird-Charmer* (1945), *Mother Amusing her Child* (1947). None of this makes of Tamayo a neo-Picassian painter, for any compositional traits or devices have been completely assimilated into his own unmistakably personal style.

The same remarks apply to another compositional element that

[14] *Diario de las Américas* (Miami, Florida), April 5, 1960.

makes its appearance in some of Tamayo's paintings of the 1940's, a crucial period in his development. This has been described by Robert Goldwater as

> the violently foreshortened figure moving either backward into the picture space, as in Woman Reaching for the Moon, or forward and out of the plane of the composition with sudden and intense gesture, as in Woman Reaching for You. ... The widespread running figures in the latter are already found in paintings of the 'twenties and 'thirties; now with slightly greater stylization the gesture is made entirely consistent with the more excited rhythms and increased abstraction of these later paintings.[15]

The emotional effect of *Woman Reaching for the Moon* (1946) is intensely lyrical, an effect enhanced by the extremely delicate yet vibrant harmonies of color. The greatly foreshortened female figure in the background of the remarkable *Self Portrait* (1946) owes its dynamic effect not to any forward or backward movement, but rather to the position of the outstretched arms.

Tamayo's mature style is marked by an increasing abstraction of the human figure, imaginative use of the pictorial space, formal balance combined with poetic sensibility, and an extremely subtle range of colors. In many respects he is the painter of the modern "age of anxiety," for the menace of strange fears and catastrophes hovers over such works as *Girl Attacked by Strange Bird* (1947) [Plate 6], *Fire*, *Cataclysm*, and *Total Eclipse* (all 1946). The style is capable of absorbing many kinds of subjects, even such conventional ones as Mexican women carrying jars on their heads (*Women of Mexico* [1944]), or small boys eating watermelons (a recurrent theme)—and transforming them into a unique personal expression. The style is also flexible, ranging from the almost abstract to the almost naturalistic—as in the splendid *Portrait of his Wife* (1946). "Portraits must be like their subjects," says Tamayo. But he has also said, "Painting is an invention." His technical skill and creative intuition are directed toward achieving a dynamic balance between representation and invention.

15 Robert Goldwater, *Rufino Tamayo*, Quadrangle Press, 1947.

The Next Generation

Chronologically as well as creatively, Tamayo appears to bridge the gap between the "old masters" of the post-Revolutionary period and the new generation, born around 1920. The main question is: Do any artists of this generation, have the potential stature of a Tamayo—that is to say, can they assure the creative (certainly not the ideological) continuity of Mexican painting? The answer, I believe, is in the affirmative. Three artists, in particular, give support to this affirmation: Ricardo Martínez, Juan Soriano, and Pedro Coronel. They resemble one another only in talent and originality: their individual styles are completely different. Coronel and Soriano are sculptors as well as painters; they have more in common with each other than with Martínez, who remains closest to the figurative ideal.

Ricardo Martínez (b. 1918) is a self-taught painter whose artistic talent was awakened when he frequented the studio of his brother Oliverio, a sculptor. From the beginning he chose to paint in the figurative mode, and during his formative years (1942–58) he did still-lifes, landscapes, and human figures. A certain monumental quality in some of the latter—*The Astronomer* (1944), *The Roots of the Valley* (1946), *The Maguey Picker* (1946), *Group of Figures* (1950)—pointed toward the definitive monumental style that was to emerge around 1959. The emphasis on the nude human figure—that is to say, on the essential humanity of the subject—is the characteristic trait of this development. The three massive male figures in *The Roots of the Valley*, overlooking a nebulous landscape from a high elevation, underline the unity of man and nature that is Martínez' basic theme—a theme also apparent in *The Maguey Picker*. But in the later paintings nature is rather implied, especially through the recurrent symbol of water, and sometimes of fire, than depicted and the human figure comes to dominate the entire pictorial space. Though there is often ample space around the figure (or figures), it contains no objects, but is used to emphasize the human subject through the play of light.

After 1959 a number of completely characteristic paintings by Martínez exist in which his mature style is fully defined. The most famous of these is *The Lovers*, which immediately projects that monumental, primordial quality, at once archaic and timeless, poetic and substantive, that is to be found in all his later work. The use of light is also completely characteristic : it is concentrated on the lower portion of the woman's body, emphasizing the zone of fecundity. The themes of motherhood and mother and child are recurrent; at least one, *Mother and Child* (1961), appears to carry an allusion to Mary and the child Jesus. Another recurrent theme is that of water—not water itself, but a woman or a man drinking water, emphasizing the gesture of bringing the cup to the mouth, as in a sort of ritual (*Woman with Water*, [1962]), or simply carrying water in the hand (*Man Drinking* [1963]). *Woman with Fruit* (1965), a monumental nude holding a single fruit in one hand, again presents the theme of fecundity. Love, fecundity, maternity, man's dependence on nature—these are the elemental themes in the painting of Ricardo Martínez. These he continually reshapes with the varied play of light and color, using both—but especially light—as dynamic determinants of the composition.

In the words of the Mexican art critic Rubén Bonifacio Nuño:

Four themes form the nucleus of Martínez' pictorial system: the correspondence of the human and the cosmic, the purposeful defeat of death and fulfillment of love, and the community of mankind in its unique reality.... He has avoided the superficially dramatic, so easy to achieve.... By his plastic style—his system of ample and precise curves and of absolute luminosity, his disdain for merely scenic effects [and] his masterly use of color—he has reclaimed for Mexican painting the sense of dignity and grandeur.[16]

Martínez' painting would not be what it is had he not delved deeply into the ancient past of Meso-America. But whatever he learned of archaelogy and ethnography he set aside in favor of the primeval human quality, the austere monumentality, of these early cultures. His men and women have Mayan features : this is one way of asserting their reality in time and place. But the total absence of secondary pictorial and descriptive details also

[16] Rubén Bonifaz Nuño, *Ricardo Martínez* (Universidad Nacional Autónoma de México, 1965), p. 11.

affirms their essential humanity and cosmic identity outside of time and place.

Both Soriano and Coronel move within that pictorial world of imagination and invention that lies between abstraction and representation. This polarity attracts them now in one direction, now in the other; but they never come firmly to rest in either. Soriano, whose early work was completely figurative, remains nearer to representation than Coronel, so that his mature painting may be generally regarded as neofigurative, with cubist and expressionist derivations. Born in 1920 in Guadalajara, where he began to study art at the age of fourteen, Soriano made an early and auspicious debut as a figurative painter in Mexico City, attracting favorable attention with his seminaïve landscapes and portraits of children. He traveled in the United States and Europe, and for several years lived in Rome. There he turned toward abstraction—or rather included it as a compositional element in his hitherto figurative system. Justino Fernández has summed up these two phases of Soriano's development:

> In his work two stages may be clearly discerned: one spontaneous, ingenuous, and often intentionally commonplace, with a popular accent, that has its culmination in the large portrait of María Asúnsolo reclining on a sofa; the second—subsequent to his sojourn in Rome— has a semiabstract character and is marked by an excellent sense of color; the themes are lyrical, but with references to death and sex; the culmination of this second stage is a large canvas, The Fish (1956), with hallucinative colors.[17]

At the present time, *The Fish* may be regarded as thoroughly typical rather than culminative, in Soriano's semiabstract—and thus far definitive—phase. Now in Mexico City's Museum of Art, this painting is indeed vividly striking in its bold and original use of color, dominated by purple, blue, and green, and in its characteristic synthesis of figurative and abstract-informal elements. To the same period belong two other important semiabstract paintings, *Bird with Hallucinations* (1957) and *Skulls* (1957), both related to abstract expressionism. The second is particularly interesting because it reveals Soriano's semiabstract synthesis of

[17] Justino Fernández, *La pintura moderna mexicana*, p. 181.

a perennial theme from Mexican popular tradition, which he has elsewhere treated more realistically in *Large Death's-Head*.

In 1962, Soriano showed a series of portraits of Lupe Marín (former wife of Diego Rivera) that not only rank with his best work but also display dramatically the polarity of abstract and figurative tendencies in his mature phase. Particularly striking is a full-length portrait that veers strongly toward abstraction, in which figurative and abstract curvi-linear forms are beautifully and imaginatively blended within a richly variegated and subtle palette of colors dominated by yellows and browns. The poetic fantasy of this portrait is unmatched in recent Mexican painting.

In several canvases, Soriano applies his abstract-figurative dualism to an imaginative bestiary of fantastic fauna that seems to exist in the pictorial space with an inevitable and disturbing vitality. His bold and arbitrary use of color enhances the vivid and somewhat sinister impact of these strange creatures. A striking example is the canvas titled *Duo* hanging in the Museum of Modern Art in Mexico, depicting a head-on confrontation of two unclassifiable but possibly marine animals.

The erotic theme in Soriano's painting appears in the series on Apollo and the Muses, in which Apollo is shown as the chorus-leader with a hint of Priapus. The chorus of Muses is not one that might be expected to sing Delphic hymns, but rather the semi-nude, sexy chorus-line of a "girlie show," with large false eyelashes and eyes heavily circled with mascara. Neo-cubist and expressionist elements are effectively blended in these revitalized versions of an outworn mythology.

Pedro Coronel (b. 1923) studied at La Esmeralda School of Painting and Sculpture in Mexico City, and also with Brauner and Brancusi in Europe, where he lived from 1946 to 1952. His first one-man show in Mexico City, in 1946, was greeted with critical acclaim, particularly by the eminent writer Octavio Paz. In 1959 he won the First National Prize for Mexican Painting, and the following year, at the second Bienal Interamericana de Arte in Mexico City, he was awarded the Orozco Prize. When the Galería de Arte Mexicano had a one-man show of his work in 1964 (painting and sculpture), the well-known Mexican author Juan Rulfo wrote in his preface to the catalog: "The survival of ancient myths of humanity, conceived by indigenous inhabitants of Mexico, is the basis from which Pedro Coronel, utilizing primitive forms, succeeds in depicting the contemporary reality of man, condemned to disaster by the forces imprisoned within his own conscience." Concerning the recurrent symbol of the sun, Rulfo writes: "Pedro Coronel insists time and again on the solitude of the sun, infinitely greater than that of man. But upon transposing the space of the human mind to the region of the infinite, he assumes the magnitude of the sun in an irrational manner, since he is unable to achieve its luminosity or the motivating force of its life, but only its eclipse."

Pedro Coronel began to paint under the influence of Tamayo, an influence soon absorbed and transcended. Along with his personal style he created a private bestiary of grotesque and menacing animals, sinister and predatory, sordid and fantastic. Justino Fernández finds here "a tremendous and mysterious world in which evil beasts abound as the symbol of man bent on devouring his own kind. . . ." A masterly example is *The Wild Beasts*, which illustrates the most distinctive and powerful features of Coronel's painting, justifying the opinion of Fernández that he is "a great colorist and creator of original forms." The style is predominantly abstract but with strongly integrated semi-figurative elements. There are transfigured cubist traits in such anthropoid paintings as *Inhabitant, Woman's Head, Opaque Pain,* and *The Man of Broken Dreams*. Animal and human forms are juxtaposed in an extraordinary canvas titled *Nagual*, which perhaps contains the key to what Pedro Coronel is trying to express in his painting. The ordinary meaning of *nagual* is "witch" or "sorcerer"; but it also means "the animal that a person has as an inseparable companion."

An exhibit of thirty-six paintings by Pedro Coronel at the Galería de Arte Mexicano in the summer of 1968 confirmed the central symbolism of the sun in his metaphysical interpretation of man and the universe. There is greater emphasis on the lyrical quality of the natural world and of man's relation to nature. The poetic and metaphysical content predominates, with frequent synthesis of abstract and figurative forms. There are reminiscences of collective myths, magic rituals, the realm of the primitive and the irrational. The colors continue to be surprising, yet totally convincing. The *Wild Beasts* may be lurking in the dark woods, but here they do not disturb the flight of *Lyrical Birds* or the *Dance of the Golden Eden.*

Rafael Coronel (b. 1932), younger brother of Pedro, has chosen to stay entirely within the figurative mode, to which he has given a new aesthetic and humanistic dimension in Mexican painting. He studied with Carlos Orozco Romero and married a daughter of Diego Rivera. As in the case of Ricardo Martínez, human beings are his all-absorbing subject. When secondary objects appear in his canvases—such as the fruits and vegetables on a table in *Portrait of My Grandmother* (1965)—they are merely suggested in a semiabstract manner. The table on which the grandmother rests her arm is a dark triangle at one corner of the canvas that serves to emphasize the light, open background against which the seated figure of the old woman, carrying a fruit to her mouth, stands out starkly. Similarly, in *Girl on the Staircase* (1965), the staircase is simply a large dark area in the lower half of the canvas with the banister suggested by a diagonal above which the hunched figure of the girl peers intently at something that we do not see.

Rafael Coronel prefers to paint humble people—*The Fruit Vendor, My Grandmother in the Poorhouse, A Boy of the Market, The Nurse Waiting for the Train, The Clown*—but what he portrays is not their social class or condition or occupation but their essential humanity *as individuals.* He does not present a visual catalog of types, as Rivera did, nor a composition with figures, in which objects seem to have as much importance as people. His human beings are portrayed in their essential solitude, usually alone but sometimes two together, as in *Roland and His Wife* (1935), an aged couple depicted against a purely abstract background (a rectangle within the rectangle of the canvas). Coronel succeeds in projecting the human situation of his subjects emotionally and even with pathos through purely plastic means, not dependent on anecdotal or descriptive props.

At times Rafael Coronel uses expressionistic distortion to make his point, as in *Boy Genius at the Blackboard* (1965), where his message is not humanity but inhumanity: the precocity of man bent on self-destruction through the uncontrolled "advancement" of science. There is, indeed, an entire phase of his work that is strongly expressionist, verging on the macabre, obsessed by fear, confusion, dissolution. This phase is represented by such paintings as *Head*, *Death in the Spring*, *Death*, *The Comedian*, and *A Stain of Blue*.

Surrealism, Fantasy, and Mixed Media

André Breton, the high priest of surrealism, visited Mexico in 1938. As an aftermath of his visit, an International Surrealist Exposition was organized in 1940 at the Galería de Arte Mexicano, with various Mexican artists participating. Nevertheless surrealism, though it acquired several adherents (some only temporary), did not become a prominent movement in Mexico. Significantly, the leading exponent of surrealism in Mexican painting is an artist of English origin, Leonora Carrington, who became associated with the movement in 1936 and who has lived in Mexico since 1942. She was one of the two artists (the other was Francisco Corzas) chosen to represent Mexico at the ninth Bienal de São Paulo (1967), where she showed twelve canvases painted between 1952 and 1966, as well as eighteen recent drawings. She remains the most consistent and the most successful of the surrealist painters of Mexico. She has also done sculptures, and masks made of cement and of parchment. Among native-born artists Guillermo Meza, Benjamín Molina, and Remedios Varos have been most consistently attracted to surrealism.

Several Mexican artists, both native born and naturalized, have explored the realm beyond realism without necessarily adhering to the movement initiated by Breton. Among them are Feliciano Bejar (b. 1924) with his "Magiscopes" (a kind of Op art), Pedro Friedberg (b. in Italy, 1937) with his "fantasy furniture" (surrealist *art noveau*) and his elaborate geometrical-optical magical-symbolic "spoofs" ("One shouldn't take art too seriously," he says), and Alberto Gironella.

Alberto Gironella (b. 1929) had a Mexican mother and a Spanish father. The heritage of the Spanish masters, especially

Velázquez and Goya, is the point of departure for all of his work as
a plastic artist, whether oil painting, mixed media, drawing, engraving, sculpture, or three-dimensional object. The phrase "point of
departure" is to be taken literally; most of Gironella's work takes
off from a specific painting by Velázquez or Goya. Its trajectory
is a series of metamorphoses in various media and modes of
expression—a gradual "decomposition" of the original model and
its ultimate transformation into something that is made to appear
as the inevitable culmination of these changes.

Gironella actually began this process of plastic metamorphosis
with a non-Spanish subject, *The Countess of Uta* (1952), taking
as his model a thirteenth-century sculpture from Naumburg. In
1958 he turned to a Spanish subject with *The Boy of Vallecas*
by Velázquez, whom he eventually transformed into a dog. This
trajectory from human to animal became standard procedure for
subsequent metamorphoses. For example, Queen Maria Luisa de
Borbón Parma, as portrayed by Goya, was gradually transformed
into an owl. But Gironella lavished his most persistent and inventive transformations upon Queen Mariana of Austria, from
the portrait by Velázquez, a metamorphosis that began in 1960
and culminated three years later with her transformation into a
dog (a bitch?). Gironella was evidently so fascinated by Queen
Mariana that he undertook another series of works—paintings,
sculptures, drawings, and objects—under the collective title
Feast in the Palace, which are variations on the same theme. The
pièce de resistance of this series is a large three-dimensional
"painting/object," now in Mexico's Museum of Modern Art,
which consists mainly of a free-standing, cupboard-like piece of
furniture with a tall back. On top of the cupboard shelf there is
a life-size replica of a mastiff, backed by a real tapestry. Above
this are two pseudo-self-portraits of Velázquez, one finished, the
other unfinished; in the lower portion are two portraits of a
dwarf; in small niches are found the replicas of a head and a
hand. Here we have Gironella's basic iconography. His brilliant
virtuosity and profound vision, however, can best be appreciated
in the kinetic sequence of his metamorphoses, as in the Queen
Mariana cycle. The model undergoes every type of decomposition
and recomposition : in style, in texture, in form, in color, in

medium, and in essential being. There is metampsychosis as well as metamorphosis. There is every degree of abstraction and figuration; sometimes several degrees are combined with extra-ordinary originality and effectiveness in the same painting, as in *Red Queen* (mixed media).

As summed up by the artist and critic García Ponce,

> Alberto Gironella has evolved from a purely formalist position toward a lucid and deliberate confrontation of the possibilities of plastic traditionalism within contemporary reality, and the magical utilization of the world of objects in order to attack this reality by means of violence, of surprise and horror.... The work of Gironella maintains itself in the difficult contradiction implied by the conscious intent of making art while taking, in large measure, as fundamental theme the impossibility of art.[18]

Cuevas: Master of Pen and Ink

José Luis Cuevas was born in Mexico City in 1933. In his eleventh year he attended the Esmeralda School of Painting and Sculpture, but for one term only. His first exhibit took place in 1947 in a vacant lot in Mexico City, his first gallery show in 1953. The following year he had his first show in the United States at the Pan American Union, and in 1955 his first European show in Paris. After that he began to have numerous one-man shows, some in Mexico but more abroad. In 1959, he was awarded the First International Prize for Drawing at the São Paulo Bienal. Since 1960 he has been one of the most sought-after contemporary artists, and his illustrated books in limited editions sell at very high prices. He has remained aloof from groups and movements, and has sharply and repeatedly attacked the artistic Establishment in Mexico, the leaders of the Mexican muralist movement (especially Siqueiros, his only living target), and indeed the whole concept of nationalism and social realism upon which the "official" art of Mexico was based for about thirty years after the end of the Revolution. In "Recollections of Childhood," Cuevas tells us

[18] Juan García Ponce, "La nueva pintura mexicana: orígenes y realidad," in *Siempre*, No. 525 (July 1963).

that at school he soon became acquainted "with the Mexican trait that I most detest: nationalism." And he adds, "I think I have been an enemy of Mexican nationalism ever since that day."[19] Elsewhere he states, "What I want in my country's art are broad highways leading out to the rest of the world, rather than narrow paths connecting one adobe village with another." It was Cuevas who coined the term, "The Cactus Curtain," to signify the restrictive limitations of Mexican nationalism.

From the beginning of his career Cuevas elicited high praise from critics of many countries. Typical is this comment by Leslie Judd Portner of *The Washington Post* (1954), "His use of line is masterly, with incredible control of the smallest variation from heavy to light, wet to dry, sharp to blurred, describing the fold of drapery, the contour of a head, the push of a bone against flesh. This is draftsmanship in the best tradition."

More significant than critical acclaim is praise from artists like Alejandro Otero and Fernando de Szyszlo. In 1958, Otero wrote that the precocity and richness of Cuevas' drawings could be compared only to Picasso. De Szyszlo speaks of "the mastery of line which ... follows the most recondite intentions of the artist." All commentators agree that Cuevas is profoundly and intensely Mexican, in spite of his repudiation of nationalism. In the words of Jean Cassou, "Cuevas is as Mexican as the truest of Mexicans, and Mexican because, like them, he is exclusively possessed with a passionate, a cruel sense of truth." Cuevas is a master of "black humor," a social satirist in the tradition of Goya who shares the latter's terrible insight into the demons of the human soul. He himself has confessed that the theme of insanity was long the center of his work. He is a master of the monstrous and the grotesque. As Parker Tyler writes, "He has invented an homogenized race of goblins, sometimes humorous in inflection, sometimes sinister, but always bloblike, with large heads stuck in their torsos and preternaturally spindly legs." But whatever Cuevas creates actually *exists*: one never has the impression of merely arbitrary distortion or irresponsible fantasy.

Cuevas often produces a series of drawings that are like variations on a theme. The series of self-portraits, for example, which

[19] *Cuevas por Cuevas*, p. 188.

includes *Self-Portrait as a Sick Child* (1944), was continued over a period of many years (1944–57). Other series are *The Crucifixion* (1956), *Figures of the Renaissance* (1957), *Funeral of a Dictator* (1958), *Assaulted Woman* (1959), *Beasts* (1959), *Conquest of Mexico* (1960), and a very important series of over sixty drawings for a work titled *The Worlds of Kafka and Cuevas* (1957). This includes *Self-Portrait During a Lecture by Kafka, Portrait of Franz Kafka,* and *The Bride of Kafka.* The affinity between Cuevas and Kafka is made fully explicit in this extraordinary series of drawings.

Cuevas' own words refute the notion that he has no roots in the tradition of Mexican art. There was much that he rejected, including the work of Rivera and Siqueiros, but he was drawn to the work and personality of Orozco, "who even today I regard as the source and explanation of my work and of my artistic personality." And he adds, "I am deeply satisfied that I recognized in time the message and the greatness of José Clemente Orozco, perhaps the culminating figure in Mexican painting, and one of the artists of fundamental importance to appear in the twentieth century."[20]

Sculpture

Since 1960 there has been a remarkable growth of activity in Mexican sculpture. As one walks through the grounds of the Museum of Modern Art in Chapultepec Park, where a large quantity of recent sculpture is on display, one is impressed by the variety of style and media, ranging from traditional figurative stone sculptures to constructions of scrap metal, machine parts, miscellaneous junk, and all kinds of mixed media. One also gets the impression of a rather strenuous attempt to catch up with the international avant-garde rather than of any strongly original expression. There is, to be sure, much that attracts one's interest: Rodulfo Brito Moreno's *El Profeta*, made entirely of small pieces of rusted iron tubing; Baltazar Martínez' *Olimpia*, a seated woman with a dress of welded metal plates, her copper kerchief flying

20 *Ibid.*, p. 193.

in the wind; Pedro Cervantes' *Siren and Astronaut* (iron and wood); Jorge Angulo's *The New Old God*, made of scrap iron on a wood base; Geles Cabrera's *Pegasus* (painted iron); and a number of others, including a large construction by Brito Moreno titled *Forward*, consisting of a spiral staircase with plastic figures of men, women, and eating on one of the steps, a child (life in a low-cost housing development?).

Individually outstanding is the work of Helen Escobedo in sculpture and environments. She uses mostly bronze, though she has also worked with polyester in sound and light environments, combining sculptural forms with utilitarian ends. As described by Ramón Xirau,

> *She creates a form and a space is born to hold a television set; she invents a space that is musical and finds a place for radio equipment deep in the bowels of a fish; she outlines sharp vertical or curved shapes that are at the same time a work of sculpture and a lamp. Within the wax or bronze live structures that are converted into serviceable objects; the beauty is, here, action and art-object, a work not only for contemplation but also primarily to be experienced.*[21]

Two artists previously mentioned as painters, Pedro Coronel and Juan Soriano, have also done important work in sculpture. Both create in semiabstract modes, but Coronel has worked mostly in stone with rather monumental forms, while Soriano's usual medium is ceramic. Coronel's monumental, semiabstract figuratism is well represented in two large stone sculptures that are closely related : *Woman* and *Sorrowing*. Each represents a hooded female figure, but the "form" itself is a hollow space created by the enveloping mass of stone, shaped to the outlines of the women's robes. The way in which the hollow space is delineated by curves and masses, suggesting the face, the body, the position of the arms, projects an individual attitude and its concomitant emotion. In *Sorrowing*, the face we do not see is more moving than any traditional *Pietà* : hollow space has here the equivalent impact of silence in music. What is amazing is the expressive pathos in these hollow

[21] *Helen Escobedo: Sculpture and Environment.* Catalog of an exhibition at the Galería de Arte Mexicano (December 1966).

figures, and their sense of corporeality achieved by such simple, semiabstract means.

Soriano has done some excellent figurative sculpture, such as the voluptuous *Black Siren*, and occasionally he has worked with wood, as in *The Cage*. But above all he has accepted the challenge of ceramic—"this medium of earth and fire"—the primary artisanship of pottery, genetically related to the primitive cultures of Middle America for which Soriano feels a deep affinity. He does not reproduce indigenous motifs, but seeks rather the spirit and the symbols of these ancient cultures, as in the large stele titled *The Sun*, which is far from being an archaeological reproduction and yet looks as though it might belong to some remote and vanished culture, impossible to identify. The ceramic sculptures of Soriano, roughly finished, asymmetric, freely imaginative, though linked to organic, animal, and even mechanical forms (*The Motorcycle*), preserve their primordial, ritualistic, and symbolic character through all the permutations of time, space, and subject. What Ida Rodríguez describes as "the abstract-realistic ambivalence" of Soriano's art is reflected in his sculpture as in his painting, and with equal power and originality.

In the half-century that has elapsed since the end of the military phase of the Mexican Revolution, the plastic arts in Mexico have overcome their initial anachronism and have caught up with contemporary art. The legacy of the muralist-realist movement—a stupendous achievement when regarded on its own terms—is a historical heritage that belongs to the past. Easel painting—symbol of individual creation and subjective art—although discouraged, was not suppressed; indeed it became an important secondary medium for the masters of the "first generation": Orozco, Rivera, and Siqueiros. Tamayo led the way from muralism to easel painting as the norm of individual expression, remaining profoundly Mexican but not nationalistic. With the next generation—Ricardo Martínez, Juan Soriano, Pedro Coronel, Alberto Gironella, and others born around and after 1920—the "cactus curtain" was torn to shreds, and José Luis Cuevas scattered its last remnants with the black power of his pen and ink.

2

The Caribbean
and
Central America

*T*HE several countries of Central America and the Caribbean area—a rather loosely defined geographical entity—are somewhat arbitrarily grouped here without any claim to cultural or historical unity. The arts of Cuba and Haiti have in common an Afro-American heritage (shared in part by Panama) but in Cuba this heritage has perhaps been more prominent in music and poetry than in the visual arts (though there are, of course, some exceptions). The highly sophisticated and thoroughly modern painting of such Cuban artists as Amelia Peláez and Wifredo Lam (in spite of the latter's totemistic "jungle" themes) has nothing in common, technically or aesthetically, with the "primitive" painters who flourished in Haiti from about 1930 to 1950. A truly modern international movement in Haitian painting is just beginning to emerge. Such movements, on the other hand, have long been vigorous in the mainland countries of Venezuela and Colombia.

It might have been more logical to group Central America—and particularly Guatemala—with Mexico. Certainly the culture of Guatemala has a great deal more in common with that of Mexico than with that of Cuba, to say nothing of Haiti. In the contemporary arts this relationship is further emphasized by the dual role of the Guatemalan Carlos Mérida, an artistic leader in both Mexico and Guatemala. Yet in recent years the Central American countries, with Guatemala in the forefront, have made notable efforts to assert their cultural autonomy and to develop their own artistic activities, both national and regional. Hence it has seemed preferable to underline this burgeoning independence by separating Central America from its large and culturally assertive neighbor to the north.

GUATEMALA

According to Carlos Mérida, "The contemporary visual arts of Guatemala have only two personalities who could be called geniuses: Carlos Valenti and Roberto Ossaye." They belonged to different generations; what they had in common—besides "genius"—was death at an early age. Valenti died at twenty-two, Ossaye at twenty-seven. The latter obtained rapid recognition and wide acclaim; the former had to struggle against a stifling milieu and committed suicide after a brief period of intense productivity. Valenti's name and work might have remained in obscurity but for the admiration and affection of his close friend and youthful companion, Carlos Mérida—the best-known painter of Central America and one of the most famous of all Latin American artists.

Mérida tells how he first came to know Valenti in Guatemala City,

> I met Valenti when I arrived for the second time, from my quiet Quetzaltenango, in the capital city, in search of better moments for something that still remained confused and undefined within me; I had just reached the age of seventeen [in 1908]. I then found myself among a group of young painters who worked together closely, and whose leader was Jaime Sarbartés, a Catalan who came to Guatemala to make his fortune, a business man by accident, but an amateur of the plastic arts by nature....[1] Valenti stood out in that circle like a beacon, illuminating all about him; with a natural gift, without pretentious impositions, full of gentleness, he knew both how to guide and how to create.... His personality was attractive, in spite of his introspection and self-absorption. We all loved him, perhaps even adored him. With him I went to Europe for the first time, and there I was witness to his tragic end.[2]

[1] Sabartés became the intimate friend and biographer of Picasso.
[2] Mérida, "Carlos Valenti," in *Salon 13* (Guatemala), II, 2 (1961), p. 38.

The year was 1910; the place, Paris. For Mérida, this was the second decisive step, after his meeting with Sabartés and Valenti, in finding himself as an artist. But for Carlos Valenti (1884–1912) Paris was the end of the line; he went there not to work, but to die, a victim of his incurable neurasthenia. Hence, as Mérida observes, we must look to the work that Valenti did in Guatemala for the best of his art. For the period in which he lived, writes Mérida, his work "was of a limitless audacity; from the moment that he took up his pencil, his design was complete and definitive.... In Valenti there was always that transmutation of reality into poetic values, manifested with entire exactitude; therefore, his work is enduring, it was modern, audacious, prophetic, for its time."

Taking impressionism as his point of departure, Valenti painted landscapes, portraits, the human figure, revealing a remarkable sense of color and mastery of composition. But his real genius is revealed above all in his numerous drawings. In these he depicted humanity with the power and compassion of an Orozco, the insight and skill of a Cuevas, but with a distinctly personal style. To confirm this one has only to look at such drawings as *The Beggar Woman*, *Mother and Child*, *The Seven-Month Child*, or *The Buffoon*. His grasp of the grotesque is displayed in such drawings as *The Toast* and *The Ogre*, the latter an absolute masterpiece. For dynamic composition and force in action, *The Picador* is unsurpassed. It is true, as Mérida writes, that at the age of twenty-two Carlos Valenti "had achieved full mastery, full maturity."

Mérida and Mayan Culture

Carlos Mérida (b. 1891) himself, like most artists, had to grope somewhat before finding his own direction. During his first sojourn in Paris he painted "pathetic" subjects in the romantic vein of Picasso's "blue period." When he returned to Guatemala in 1914, at the age of twenty-three, he immersed himself in the indigenous folklore and native crafts of the country. He was now seeking an authentic "American art" through a synthesis of folklore, archaeology, and modern plastic concepts. He discarded the romantic, picturesque, anecdotal approach to native art. He perceived that the pre-Columbian cultures of America offered to the artist a source of inspiration, of vitality, of textural and visual motifs, and that this material should be treated, not romantically, but objectively, with the autonomy and freedom that Braque and Picasso had brought to their assimilation of exotic and primitive non-European artistic styles. His twofold aim was to re-establish the continuity of Guatemalan art with the ancient art of the Maya civilization, and at the same time to make the relationship valid in terms of contemporary art. Within this conceptual framework he did the *Images of Guatemala* series and other works of this period (1914–27).

The artistic climate of Guatemala was not favorable to such a difficult undertaking; in 1919, Mérida decided to go to Mexico. There, in 1920, the Academy of Fine Arts sponsored an exhibition of his Guatemalan works. In the words of MacKinley Helm, he "gave to the Mexican public its first glance at the prolegomena of a new racial movement which within two years revolutionized the character of painting in the Republic." The critic Cardoza y Aragón wrote that, "The whole problem of artistic culture in America was being debated in his paintings." Another critic, Aguilar Chacón, pointed out that in Mérida's "emphasis on the plane, on the purity of definable form, there was not only an imperative need for definition and solidity of foundation, but also an absolute fidelity to the clear mandate of a living Mayan heritage.... The painting of Mérida has an aristocracy of refined sensuality, in the formal conception as well as in the use of color." González Goyri characterizes the painting of this period as "formalistically decorative." The plane is the most prominent feature of the pictorial composition. Although Mérida used both oil and watercolor, his best works of this period are probably in the latter medium (to which he always remained partial). A good example is *Mexican Women* (watercolor, 1924), clearly figurative, yet already pointing toward the semi-abstraction that soon claimed Mérida's allegiance.

A second visit to Europe in 1927, this time for two years, brought another turning point in Mérida's development. He absorbed some of the more lyrical elements of surrealism, while at the same time moving toward ever-increasing abstraction. His forms become less geometrical, fantasy has free play, and the composition is more fluid. A good example is *Profile* (watercolor, 1928), in which almost the entire pictorial space is occupied by a distinctly Mayan head in profile, which in turn serves as background for various smaller seated figures grouped rhythmically throughout the composition in a kind of visual counterpoint. These musical analogies are not so far-fetched when one remembers that Mérida had at first intended to be a musician, until an impairment of his hearing put an end to that hope. He gave musical titles to a number of his paintings, such as *Ten Plastic Inventions on the Theme of Love* (1939). There is also a very interesting watercolor titled *Fugue*, which reveals both the surrealistic aspect of Mérida's work and its trend toward abstraction. *Watercolor No. 28*, painted after his return from Paris, is entirely abstract. González Goyri has written admirably about this phase of Mérida's work:

> He frees himself completely from the object and from all direct reference to folklore; that is to say, he discards the superficial in order to retain only the essential.... In the same way, the formal values, the plastic quality, increase: his lines become more fluid, more sensitive, his forms are simplified and reduced to an elemental design. Dynamic juxtapositions with an innate sense of rhythm are introduced into what was hitherto static. Archaeological reminiscences appear from time to time, totemic forms that have a suggestive power, magical signs, intriguing graphic elements from a primary plastic world, akin to those used by Paul Klee and Joan Miró in Europe.[3]

Mérida's most intensely abstract period was from about 1930 to 1937. Yet it is curiously revealing that during these same years he also did some of his best documentary work on Mexican folklore: two sets of colored lithographs illustrating the traditional Indian dances of Mexico and the regional fiestas. But this was a special project, sponsored by the Mexican government, which had no bearing on the personal evolution of his art. He did not remain completely bound to abstraction, any more than to

[3] González Goyri, "Carlos Mérida," in *Salon 13*, I, 4 (1960), p. 54.

figuration, but moved between both modes as suited his artistic purpose; he consistently avoided, however, any sort of naturalistic nativism or social realism. As has been so often remarked, Carlos Mérida is essentially a poet of the palette. Paul Westheim calls his painting, "music for the eyes of subtle delicacy." He is perhaps most personal and lyrical in such semiabstract, fantastically imaginative compositions as *The Message* (oil, 1944) or *Tempo in Red Major* (crayon, 1942); most brilliantly masterful in such quasi-geometrical indigenous stylizations as *The Young King* (casein on parchment, 1956), *Song to the Maya* (casein on parchment, 1956), or *Quel, Yac, and Utiah* (resin on masonite, 1964), which was shown at the New York World's Fair in 1964–65, and which reminds us that Mérida remains faithful to the spirit of Mayan forms.

There are some critics, nevertheless, who maintain that Mérida's best work is in his murals. What is certain is that since 1950, Mérida has been increasingly interested in the problem of "integrated art"—that is, in art as an integral and functional component of a larger architectural complex (see Chapter 6).

The Next Generation

Roberto Ossaye, the second Guatemalan painter whom Mérida characterized as a "genius," was born in Guatemala City on January 11, 1927. From the age of fourteen he studied at the Academy of Fine Arts with the best national painters of the time. He made a sensational public debut in 1944 with a portrait of Stalin titled *Moscow Counterattacks*, exhibited in the lobby of a local motion picture theatre. In 1945, at the age of eighteen, while still a student at the Academy—an unprecedented situation—he had his first one-man show. Endowed with charm, energy, facility, and talent, he began to produce abundantly in a variety of media—oils, water colors, murals—and was acclaimed as the great new hope of national art. Like Mérida, he endeavoured to fuse pre-Columbian elements with modernism; but unlike Mérida he also went in rather heavily, at one time, for social realism. As described by a Guatemalan art critic,

The nation was emerging from a feudal tyranny and Ossaye drew inspiration from popular sources and themes with a social content. His compositions, of great beauty and sensibility, dealt with indigenous subjects and scenes of village life. The frescoes that he painted on the walls of the National Congress depict the suffering and oppression of the natives, the exploitation of the land and the thwarted dream of its distribution—and what is more important, they affirm his clear vocation for mural painting as well as revealing a natural and well developed plastic sense.[4]

The "feudal tyranny" to which the writer refers was the despotic régime of Jorge Ubico, who ruled the nation from 1931 to 1944, when he was overthrown and replaced by a social democratic government under the presidency of Juan José Arévalo, a writer, educator, and intellectual leader.

During the 1940's, then, Ossaye knew the full measure of success. But the adulation, the facile production, the restricted artistic outlook, and the lack of stimulating challenge in his environment had their adverse effect on his work. He had reached an impasse. His lack of direction is revealed in a self-portrait of this period, in which the artist, worried and perplexed, holds one hand to his forehead within an abstract background, while two different styles of painting—the traditional and the modern— appear to solicit his allegiance. The crisis was resolved when he received, in 1948, a government stipend for foreign travel. He chose New York, where he remained, for the most part, for the next four years. He visited galleries and museums, copied the classics at the Metropolitan Museum of Art, and thoroughly assimiliated the influence of such contemporary painters as Picasso, Siqueiros, Tamayo, and Torres García, whose theory of "Universalist Constructivism" especially impressed him. As Ernestina de Aparicio observes, it was during these years that Ossaye made the transition from a gifted, intuitive, rather undisciplined young artist to the status of a full-fledged professional painter, a master of disciplined form and of various media—oils, water colors, tempera, woodcuts, linoleum engraving—using color constructively and experimenting with new techniques employing duco, casein, encaustic.

[4] Ernestina de Aparicio, "Roberto Ossaye," in *Salon 13*, I, 1 (1960), p. 27.

Ossaye gave a modern and personal interpretation to Maya mythology, and also dealt with contemporary subjects, as in the controversial painting *The American Woman*. His work remained figurative, but with a strong tendency toward abstraction and expressionism. Some of his most powerful paintings of this period, such as *Clown* and *Tragic Incident*, rank with the best neofigurative-expressionist painting done in America. The canvas titled *Poet of the Pre-Columbians*, though showing the marked influence of Tamayo, is still a strongly conceived and essentially personal work. There is great charm and poetry in his circus paintings, in which figurative, semifigurative, and abstract elements are beautifully combined. His stylized horses, modern emanations of primitive cave-paintings (as in *Primitive Manifestation of two Horses* [1950]), are among the finest examples of his work.

Roberto Ossaye returned to Guatemala in 1952. The Academy of Fine Arts sponsored a show of his works from 1948 to 1952; he also won first prize in the national salon of plastic arts. He made a brief visit to Europe and continued to work with redoubled energy. But time was closing in on him: two years later, he died at the age of twenty-seven.

When Ossaye went to New York in 1948, he was accompanied by a fellow artist who had received an official travel grant at the same time. This artist was Roberto González Goyri (b. 1924), who had studied with Rafael Yela Günther at the Academy of Fine Arts, and whose special interest was sculpture. He had worked in the National Museum of Archaeology as a draftsman and decorator, an experience that left its mark on his own work. His first one-man show was held in 1948, an exhibition of sculpture and ink drawings, including a head of the writer Miguel Angel Asturias in concrete. The next four years were spent in New York where, in 1950, he had a one-man show at the Roko Gallery; and he shared a two-man show with Ossaye at the Pan American Union in Washington. After his return to Guatemala, he also was given an exhibition at the Academy of Fine Arts. A year later two events enhanced his international reputation: he participated in the XXVII Biennale of Venice, and he won a prize in the contest for "The Unknown Political Prisoner" sponsored by the London Institute of Contemporary Arts, for which there were 3,500 entries from fifty-three countries. González Goyri was among the eighty finalists, and his model was included in an exhibition held at the Tate Gallery. Another turning-point came in 1955, when the Museum of Modern Art in New York acquired his bronze head of a wolf, *El Lobo* (1951), a powerful semiabstract sculpture "combining pre-Columbian and cubist elements." Regarding this work, the artist tells us that he did it from memory "in order the better to capture the essence of the object he wished to represent."

In June, 1957, González Goyri was appointed Director of the National School of Plastic Arts, and proceeded to carry out a vigorous plan of reorganization. But in Latin America such appointments are often short-lived, depending chiefly on political circumstances or factional rivalries. González Goyri was dismissed from his post in September of the following year. Devoting himself thereafter only to his creative activity, he produced one of his best sculptures, *Guacamaya* (tin alloy, 1958) a semiabstract stylization of the colorful Guatemala macaw, which shared the first prize in the Fourth National Cultural Competition of El Salvador in 1958. The following year he was commissioned to execute a high relief for the new building of the Social Security Institute in Guatemala City. Working with concrete, the artist depicted symbolically the history of Guatemala from the dawn of Mayan civilization to the era of independence. In 1963, González Goyri created the important monument to Tecún Umán, indigenous national hero of Guatemala.

Perhaps there has never been a finer, more imaginatively authentic or plastically convincing sculptural projection, in modern terms, of the spirit of Middle American pre-Columbian culture than the work by González Goyri titled *The Golden Age* (terracotta, 1951). It depicts two seated musicians, one playing a double end-blown pipe, the other a flute-like instrument. The work combines primitive strength and poetic evocation, in a dynamic yet beautifully balanced composition. Scarcely less impressive are *Water Carriers* (bronze), *Girl Playing with a String* (terracotta), *Cock-fight* (tin alloy, 1958), or *Rocinante* (tin alloy direct), a more expressionistic companion-piece to the earlier wolf's head in bronze.[5]

Like several other Central American artists, González Goyri continues to do outstanding work both in sculpture and painting. Notable examples in each medium are the painting titled *Impossible Dialogue* (oil in masonite, 1967) and the bronze sculpture titled *Dying Warrior* (1964 [Plate 24]). These works, together with another bronze sculpture, *The Bull* (1964), reveal the artist in his full maturity, master of a strongly expressionist style.

Roberto Mishaan (b. 1924) was born in Guatemala City, where he studied at the National School of Fine Arts. He also studied at various places in the United States, including the Art Students League and the New School for Social Research in New York; and at Syracuse University, where he specialized in textile design—a field in which he has been very active and successful. He began to exhibit collectively in 1949, in Guatemala and the United States, and in 1961 he was chosen, together with Abularach, to represent Guatemala at the São Paulo Bienal. In that same year he was given a one-man show at the Pan American Union in Washington, on which occasion the art critic of *The Washington Post*, Leslie Judd Ashlander, wrote as follows:

> *Mishaan's style has evolved from a free interpretation of pre-Columbian Indian symbols to a more abstract mode of expression exemplified by the works in the present exhibition. His abstract expressionist canvases play texture and color against dark backgrounds which give the lighter areas a great sense of luminosity and atmosphere. Sand and textural materals are applied to their surfaces and paint is piled up thickly with a palette knife against the thinly washed backgrounds. Transparent glazes of color over the textural areas give them added richness. Such a canvas as* Life Force, *outstanding in the show, attains an extraordinary brilliance of red and blue tones against the black depths behind.* Ancestral *and* Arrival *use rich glazes of color over earthly tones.*

Mishaan's brand of abstract expressionism is akin to the informalism of the French and Italian schools rather than to that of the Americans, even though he has lived in the United States

[5] See the article on González Goyri by Ernestina de Aparicio in *Salon 13*, I. 2 (1960), pp. 37–52, with illustrations.

since 1954. This can be seen in such works as *White Painting* and *Red Painting* (both mixed media on paper), which were included in the exhibition *Magnet: New York* (1964).

Younger Artists

Artists born in the 1930's have continued to sustain the creative pace set by their predecessors. Rafael Pereyra (1935–1966) produced a personal and powerful body of figurative and semiabstract work before his untimely death. Born, like Mérida, in Quetzaltenango, he was similarly attracted by the art and personality of Modigliani, whose transmuted influence may be perceived in such typically Guatemalan subjects as *Women, Children at an Exhibition* and—though more remotely—in the very strong canvas titled *The Lance Maker*, in which elements of *tachisme* are combined with well-defined figuratism. If the influence of Tamayo is also present in such works as *Tempera* (verging on surrealism) and *Primavera* (tempera), with its studied primitive quality, this did not prevent Pereyra from achieving such strongly characteristic canvases as *Doves* (Unique Central American Prize, 1960) and especially *The Conspirators* (1966), undoubtedly his masterpiece. It is a neofigurative work in which a profound atavistic feeling, fusing symbolic, telluric, and ethnic elements, is projected in strictly contemporary terms. Its latent violence is controlled by the plastic conception and the subdued use of color, with predominant grays and earth-reds.

In 1967, Rafael Pereyra was given a posthumous retrospective show by the Guatemalan Department of Culture and Fine Arts, for which a catalog-booklet was printed with an excellent essay on the artist by Robert Cabrera.

Of the Guatemalan artists born after 1930, Rodolfo Abularach (b. 1933) has achieved the most solid international reputation. His career in many ways parallels that of Ossaye. He too was precociously gifted and received public acclaim at an early age: his first one-man show was held when he was only fourteen, the second when he was eighteen. Both consisted of bullfight drawings. His paintings apparently were inferior to these drawings. He studied briefly at the School of Architecture, where he attended a course on "abstract design" taught by González Goyri, who found him to be tremendously talented but undisciplined and lacking in analytical understanding of composition. Though secure in his drawings, in his oils he was meandering in search of a style, experimenting with quasigeometrical and pseudocubist forms. Then he began to work as a draftsman in the Museum of Archaeology, copying indigenous masks. This proved to be a crucial experience. His immersion in pre-Columbian art in turn led him to an awareness of all the indigenous and folk elements in Guatemala.

Abularach's rediscovery of his national heritage was reflected in his next one-man show, in 1957, consisting of thirty oils, four temperas, and eight drawings. The themes ranged from the folk-indigenous (*The Deer Dance*, resembling Rivera repainted by Tamayo) to science fiction (*Space Ships*). Abularach had proved himself immensely gifted, impressively productive, undoubtedly successful. But he was not satisfied; like Ossaye ten years before, he felt that he was at a crossroads in his career. And the issue was resolved in the same manner: a government grant that enabled him to go to New York. The usual assiduous visits to galleries and museums followed—the best artistic education he had thus far received. This effected in Abularach what few achieve: a period of intense self-examination and reappraisal, leading to the self-imposed discipline of concentrating exclusively on drawing. In a letter to González Goyri written shortly after his arrival in New York, Abularach formulated the following self-analysis:

I believe that I am now beginning to be myself, for during the phase of earlier drawings I was too much influenced by Tamayo. Further-more, I used a great many elements in those drawings, whereas now, on the contrary, I seek only simplicity, the essential. I try to be as clear as possible so that the "message" will not be lost in an entangle-ment of rhythms. . . . I studied my drawings and was convinced that within the half Tamayo-like figures there are encrusted a quantity of simple forms that have been constants in my work since the beginning (more rarified, if you will). Therefore what I have been trying to do *is to use two or three forms; at times, only one contains my entire world.*[6]

To confirm the validity of this analysis one has only to compare the pen and ink drawing titled *Stele* (1958) with any of the drawings done after 1960, such as the *Stele* series of 1963 (wash and pen and ink). In the former, the entire foreground is occupied by an elongated creature too obviously sprung from Tamayo, with a half-moon head and a lute-like body; the background is filled with abstract forms that are completely *sui generis*, neither geometrical nor informal, neither animal, vegetable, nor mineral, at once subtle and simple, complex and clear, impersonal and evocative—a unique distillation of possible and imagined forms. In the *Stele* of 1963, the figurative factor has been totally eliminated; there is neither foreground nor background; the pictorial space actually gives an impression of infinity. Representationally, only the vertical idea of the stele is retained; dynamically, the movement is upward, from luminous radial centers toward a corona-encircled sphere symbolizing the sun. The symbolic elements of the stele are transmuted into essences.

Abularach's wide international recognition dates from 1959, when he won first prize in the Central American competition in El Salvador (with a canvas titled *Wounded Mask*); received an acquisition prize at the São Paulo Bienal (for an untitled pen and ink drawing); was given a highly acclaimed show at the Pan American Union; and had a large drawing, *Head for Ixtab* (1958), purchased by the New York Museum of Modern Art. His work was included in the traveling exhibition, *Twentieth Century Drawings*, from the Museum of Modern Art Collection (1961–63).

In Guatemala there are a number of other artists born in the 1930's who are doing fine work in painting, drawing, printmaking, and sculpture. Mario Efraín Recinos (b. 1932), trained as an engineer and architect, has also been active as painter and sculptor. He has done murals and public sculptures, and he designed the project for the new National Theater in Guatemala City. His painting is figurative, with elements of mysticism and

[6] Quoted in an article on Abularach by González Goyri in *Salon 13* I, 3 (1960), p. 48.

magic realism. He has a strong conviction that Guatemalan architecture and sculpture must reveal an affinity with, and draw strength from, the example of ancient Maya culture. In 1964 he won first prize for sculpture in the Esso Salon of Young Artists from Central America and Panama.

Roberto Cabrera (b. 1937) is another figurative painter who is even more profoundly imbued with a sense of the Mayan heritage, even though his manner is completely contemporary. His first one-man show (1960) consisted of lithographs, linoleum prints, and acquatints. Two years later he began to create a series of works based on Mayan mythology, drawn specifically from the *Popol Vuh*, a sacred book of the Maya-Quiché culture describing the origins of the world and of man. As if to reveal his versatility and the variety of his interests, at the same time he made a series of drawings (shown at the Pan American Union) based on mechanical or constructional themes, such as *Constructor of Teeth* and *Operator of a Wind Machine*. Prior to this he had evinced an interest in contemporary themes of industrial society, as in *Telephone Operator* (engraving, 1959). To these, however, he gave a certain timeless and hieratic quality, as though this telephone operator were functioning in the ancient city of Uxmal or Chichen-Itza. In 1964, he undertook a series of drawings on the Apocalypse of St. John the Divine, which brought him to a world of surrealism and intense mysticism. Some of these he also transposed to the medium of oil painting. Two of the most powerful paintings of this period are *Death of a Personage* and *Portrait of an Unknown Man*, the latter a grotesque neofigurative reworking or expressionistic metamorphosis of the portrait of the Conde Duque de Olivares by Velázquez.

In 1965, Cabrera returned to another sacred book of the Mayas, the *Chilam Balam*, for a series of drawings related to the current folklore of Guatemala and its traditional arts and crafts, including the decoration of pottery. He also used indigenous coloring materials traditionally employed by the Indians for their pottery painting, such as *nij* (an orange-like color obtained from the cochineal) and *palo amarillo* (a yellow dyestuff obtained from the coction of a certain variety of wild cane). In the words of Méndez Dávila, "The design [in Cabrera's drawings] is organic in its intention but geometric and decorative in its folk origins." The *Personages and Gods of the Chilam Balam,* as the series is titled, is a successful synthesis of ancient mythology, living folk traditions, and modern plastic techniques. This synthesis is continued, with somewhat more imaginative freedom and fantasy (verging on surrealism) in the series titled *Personages of the Solstice* (1966), drawings in ink washed with *nij.* To quote Méndez Dávila again: "This is an art that reaches from the past with a message that is ever more vivid and more ardent. . . ."

Luis Humberto Díaz Aldana (b. 1939) is a self-taught artist who has done both painting and sculpture and has also worked with mosaics. He has had six one-man shows in Guatemala and has exhibited collectively in El Salvador, Puerto Rico, Berlin, New York, Miami, Paris, and Santiago de Chile. He is a founder and co-owner of the Galería DS, the first art gallery to be established in Guatemala (1965), which became a center for the contemporary art movement in that country. In 1964, José Gómez Sicre hailed him as a "discovery" and wrote that, "Without abandoning the ancient traditional Maya forms, he has executed them in new experimental materials." The artist describes his work as "abstract figuratism," but in those paintings that I have seen the emphasis is on abstraction, as in *Mechanical Forms* (1966) and *Earthquake* (1966). Together with Efraín Recinos, Roberto Cabrera, and Marco Augusto Quiroa, Díaz Aldana was one of the artists chosen to represent Guatemala in the Fourth Biennial of Young Artists in Paris (1965).

Marco Augusto Quiroa has been referred to as a Pop artist by some local critics, but this is based on a mistaken notion of the nature of Pop Art, which makes direct use of the products of commercial mass culture, such as comic strips, product containers, and advertisements. Quiroa is a "painterly" painter who makes use of some popular themes for his art, as in *The Donald Family* or *The Lady of the Red Hearts* (based on the stylization of a playing-card design), but who treats them as pure works of art in a somewhat baroque neofigurative manner that is slightly reminiscent of what Berni has done in Argentina (no direct link is implied).

Ever since Valenti and Mérida appeared on the scene, that is to say through several successive generations, Guatemala has had a continuous tradition of notable achievement in the plastic arts, combining a deeply rooted sense of the past with an intelligent and independent assimilation of modern techniques and stylistic conquests.

NICARAGUA

Behind every art movement in the newly developing countries there appears to be a devoted and competent mentor, an artist perhaps not famous outside of his own milieu, but technically skilled, intellectually alert, and possessing personal qualities that inspire confidence and stimulate accomplishment. Such is the case in Nicaragua, where the painter Rodrigo Peñalba (b. 1908), in his many years as Director of the National School of Fine Arts, has known how to encourage and develop new talent. When I first met Peñalba, in 1957, he was making the transition from figurative to abstract painting. This was not done to be in the fashion, but rather to keep up with the times—there *is* a difference. What Ortega y Gasset calls "the imperative of one's own time" impels the artist to move in certain directions at certain moments; and if in his more recent work Peñalba has turned to a semi-abstract figuration, as in *Massacre* (1963), here again he has synchronized his own personal style with the changing shape of time. His personal and professional qualities have made Rodrigo Peñalba not only the respected mentor of the younger generations, but also their associate in the struggle to make the fledgling art of Nicaragua truly contemporary.

In 1963, Alejandro Aróstegui, one of Peñalba's former students, took the initiative, together with other graduates of the School of Fine Arts, in forming a new center for the promotion of contemporary art in Nicaragua. This was the Galería Praxis, located in Managua, which in 1964 received a subsidy from the President of the Republic. The gallery officially opened its doors with an inaugural exhibition on August 23, 1963, that included thirty-seven works by fifteen artists. Most of the canvases were abstract or semiabstract, tending toward expressionism.

The director of the Galería Praxis, Alejandro Aróstegui (b. 1935), perfected his studies in art in the United States and in Europe (Florence, 1958–59; Paris, 1960–62). In 1966 he was given a one-man show at the Pan American Union in Washington, on which occasion José Gómez Sicre wrote about his work, in the catalog of the exhibition:

> Aróstegui's compositions possess great solidarity and are highly personal in expression. As regards genre, the artist divides his efforts among figure paintings, landscapes, and still-lifes. Human loneliness is a frequently recurring theme: man is depicted either in isolation or in contrast with the power of nature. The emaciated figures occasionally suggest ancient personages of pre-Columbian mythology. Aróstegui's palette leans toward muddy, neutral hues, perhaps inspired in the colors of Nicaragua's two great lakes. Figures and landscape features are outlined in impasto, the artist making use of a textural clay to which at time he adds bones, shells, and stones, either singly or in combination. Even if there is a reminiscence of the forms of Giacometti or the textural qualities of Dubuffet—two points of departure for Aróstegui—the paintings are pervaded by the young Nicaraguan's own personality. . . .

Working mostly with mixed media on canvas, Aróstegui has given a modern dimension to themes derived from pre-Columbian sculpture, as in *Bust* (1966) and *Mask* (1966); the landscape of his native country, as in the series *Lake Scenes*; and the debris of urban life, as in the series *Dump Yards*. Living in New York during 1966 and 1967 as his country's Cultural Attaché he was, like many an artist before him, attracted by the Brooklyn Bridge, which he depicted in a "cool" composition of mixed media on canvas, *Brooklyn Bridge* (1966).

Most of the artists belonging to the Praxis group are not completely committed either to the figurative or the abstract modes of painting; they often pass from one to the other, but generally they seek a synthesis of both modes, in the direction of a semi-abstract neofiguration. Among the artists working in this area are Omar D'León, Genaro Lugo, César Antonio Izquierdo, Arnaldo Guillén, Silvio Miranda, César Caracas, Luis Urbino, and Leonel Vanegas. Leoncio Saenz and Hernando Sobalvarro, though primarily sculptors, have also worked as painters and graphic artists. Saenz is best known for his pen and ink drawings, which derive their inspiration from pre-Columbian sculpture, emphasizing mass rather than line. Like Aróstegui, he too had a one-man show at the Pan American Union in 1966.

Apart from any group is Armando Morales (b. 1927), who has traveled extensively and who, since 1966, has made his home in New York (he first visited the United States in 1957). In 1959, he went to Lima, Peru, where he had his first one-man show at the Institute of Contemporary Art. From there he traveled to Brazil by the Amazon River waterway and participated in the V Bienal of São Paulo, at which he received the Ernest Wolf Award for the best Latin American Artist. His work had previously been shown at São Paulo in 1953 and 1955, as well as at the Pan American Union in Washington, at the Museum of Modern Art in New York (1957), and at the Carnegie Institute in Pittsburgh (1958). Since 1959 he has participated in numerous international exhibitions in America and Europe, and has won many awards, including one at the Pittsburgh International in 1964. He has had several one-man shows at the Bonino Gallery in New York, and his work is in the permanent collections of the Museum of Modern Art in New York, the Solomon R. Guggenheim Museum in New York, the Institute of Contemporary Art in Boston, The Museum of Fine Arts in Houston, the Pan American Union in Washington, the Museum of Modern Art in São Paulo, the Museum of Fine Arts in Caracas, and the Institute of Hispanic Culture in Madrid. He was the only artist from Central America included in the Cornell University-Guggenheim Museum exhibition, *The Emergent Decade* (1965–66), and in the book of that title one of his paintings, *Landscape* (1964), was featured as the frontispiece in a full-page color reproduction. By 1967, as he reached the age of forty, Amando Morales was internationally recognized as one of the outstanding painters of Latin America, with a strong, characteristic style unmistakably his own, unaffected by current fashions.

Morales' painting is not abstract in the geometric or constructivist sense; that is, divorced from all associative or representational context. Animate and inanimate forms of the visible world—the latter frequently architectural (arches, walls, windows)—constitute the point of departure for many of his paintings. Examples are *Seascape* (oil, 1963), *Arcade* (mixed media, 1964), *Double Mirror* (oil, 1964), *Double Arch* (mixed media, 1964) [Plate 19], *Landscape with Walls* (mixed media, 1964), *Still Life* (mixed media, 1966), and *Sitting Manikin* (mixed media, 1966). Whether the ostensible subject is a ferryboat or a landscape, or the human figure, Morales transmutes it into his own strong compositional idiom, marked by an extremely effective use of black and white areas. Though still partial to these absolute contrasts, he has added grays, blues, and reds, always with restraint but with infallible rightness. He seeks a concordant harmony of colors within a deliberately restricted range, never the dissonance of clashing tones. In *Double Arch*, for instance, the light blue of the diagonal stripes at the bottom of the canvas is all that is needed to dramatize the black, white, and gray of the arches and to give the work a lyrical lift. In this painting, as in others since 1964, Morales has cut his canvas into the desired shapes and used the pieces in a kind of collage, also using plastic paint to heighten the interest of the surface. Morales is closer to the Spanish past than to the indigenous heritage of Nicaragua. His idols are Velázquez and Goya; among the moderns, he worships at no shrine. Almost from the beginning of his career he has known the path he was to follow: it is no small achievement to be consistently guided by one's inner vision in the midst of ever-shifting trends and quickly changing fashions.

PANAMA

There is no continuous history of art in Panama. This is not surprising, when one considers that Panama was a part of Colombia until 1903. Then, with the connivance of the United States, Panama revolted and declared itself independent. Culturally, as well as politically, Panama is one of the newest Latin American republics, and production in the plastic arts has been significant only since about 1950. Humberto Ivalfi was one of the first to bring a breath of modernism to Panama, and his pupil Alfredo Sinclair (b. 1916)—who perfected his studies in

Buenos Aires—was the first contemporary Panamanian artist to win wide international recognition, beginning with a one-man show at Buenos Aires in 1950. He participated in the Bienal Americano of Mexico in 1958 and 1960, and in the São Paulo Bienal of 1961, obtaining an honorable mention. Of his work, Gómez Sicre has written, "Alfredo Sinclair turns to the chiaroscuro of the stained glass window and applies impasto to his paintings in accordance with the medieval enamel tradition." He has done abstract work, but more recently has turned to neofiguratism.

Alberto Dutary (b. 1932), who studied both drawing and painting in Madrid and has done outstanding work in both media, is another artist who has made the transition from pure abstraction to neofiguratism. Like many of the Latin American artists who studied in Madrid, his work shows the influence of Goya. Typical of his dynamic, semiabstract expressionism is the oil painting titled *Juke Box*, exhibited at the New York World's Fair in 1965.

Justo Arosamena (b. 1929), who studied in Montreal, New York, and Madrid, was one of the first adherents of abstract expressionism in Panama—a style that has also been adopted by such younger artists as Antonio Alvarado (b. 1938) and Constancia Calderón (b. 1937).

Guillermo Trujillo (b. 1927) has done some of the most fascinating work to come out of Latin America in recent years. Trained as an architect at the University of Panama, he studied painting, drawing, and landscape gardening in Madrid under a grant from the Institute of Hispanic Culture from 1954 to 1958. It is evident that he also studied the works of Goya and of Hieronymus Bosch, and that the pre-historic cave paintings at Altamira did not fail to impress him. What is surprising is that after five years in Madrid he was not captivated by the rather sterile abstract informalism of the new Spanish school. He came fairly close to it in such canvases as *Urban Landscape* (1957) and *Composition in Blue* (1960). But even in his more abstract works, the objective form—the presence of animate and inanimate objects—was always latent, and the future direction of his painting is clearly indicated in the semiabstract figuration of such canvases as *Hunting Scene* (1959) and *The Wedding* (1960), in which the figures seem to emerge from, and at the same time merge with, the abstract elements. In a painting like *Musicians* (1962)—where the musicians are playing African-type drums—the figuratism is accentuated by strongly-drawn contours with a dynamic, expressionistic context. The paintings of the 1960's—such as *Holy Family, Mystics, Salutation* (all 1963), and *End of the Feast* (1965) [Plate 15]—are in the expressionistic, neofigurative vein, but without extreme distortion. The humans depicted by Trujillo— generally in a state of nudity—are often grotesque and sometimes monstrous, but seldom hideous or repulsive. These naked people, whether at a religious ceremony or a cocktail party (wearing elaborate hats), simply illustrate familiar phases of the human condition under a somewhat unusual aspect. This is social satire, biting, even devastating at times, but without rancor. The artist creates a modern mythology, peopled by politicians, viragos, bikini bathers, socialites, and bureaucrats, while taking traditional mythology to pieces and bringing it down to earth. "The old mythology is dead," says Trujillo, and he has written its necrology on canvas, with paint and brush. In the words of R. M. Koster (art critic of *El Mundo de Panamá*), "Venus cannot fecundate the sterile landscape where she now resides watched over by plaster saints [*Venus in Custody*, 1965]. Circe ruminates stoically while no longer finding any relish in her enchantments, discouraged by her success in upsetting the process of evolution, while Paris is bored by his judgment. Homer . . . yields to the *Beauty Parlor*, where common mortals talk of their empty vanities with pathetic seriousness."

In his "new mythology" Trujillo creates his own visual world, solidly based on plastic values, which is a commentary on human nature and on the social order, while simultaneously affirming the autonomy of art through the personal vision of the artist and the integrity of his medium. Whether in his *Homage to Thomas Jefferson*, his *Anthropomorphic Landscape*, or his *Landscape of Tomorrow* (all 1965), the paintings of Trujillo achieve a remarkably successful synthesis of abstract and figurative elements. Then there are his drawings, in which he proves himself a worthy emulator of Goya and Cuevas. We should mention also the mosaic murals executed by Trujillo for various public buildings in Panama, such as the one for the Social Security Hospital, based on a stylized abstraction of pre-Columbian motifs.

CUBA

Contemporary Cuban painting began to emerge around 1925 with the work of a number of artists who were born near the turn of the century: Eduardo Abela (1891–1965), Victor Manuel García (b. 1897), Fidelio Ponce de León (1895–1949), Carlos Enríquez (1901–1957), Amelia Peláez del Casal, and Wifredo Lam. Abela was not only a painter but also a powerful political cartoonist who wielded pen and pencil against the dictatorship of Machado. As a painter he is best known for local scenes (*The Guajiros*, 1942), although in later works, such as *The Cow* and *The Toast*, dating from the early 1960's, he achieved a rather interesting kind of quasi-expressionist figuratism. It was above all through the work of Amelia Peláez and Wifredo Lam—two artists presenting a complete contrast in their backgrounds, subjects, and styles—that Cuban painting first acquired its prestige in the modern art of Latin America.

Amelia Peláez

Amelia Peláez (1897–1968) was the first to take Cuban painting out of its aesthetic provincialism and into the mainstream of contemporary art. She personally plunged into the cross-currents of Parisian art circles in the 1920's and 1930's, as did many other Latin American artists. What is remarkable about Amelia Peláez is not merely her venture into new realms of plastic expression, but above all her independence from the fashionable modernism of the Ecole de Paris. In the words of Gómez Sicre, "She had no desire for a new academicism disguised as radicalism." She evidently decided that she would rather be right than radical. This involved a determined search for a style that would be at once modern and personal, as well as Cuban.

Amelia Peláez began to study art at the age of fifteen, and a few years later attended the San Alejandro Academy in Havana. In the summer of 1924, she worked at the Art Students League in New York. In 1927, she went to Paris on a grant from the Cuban government and worked for a while at the Grande Chaumière. She rejected the teaching of two currently fashionable painter-pedagogues, André Lhote and Amédée Ozenfant, because she thought that studying with them was simply an easy way of learning to be superficially "modern." When the Académie Moderne opened in 1930, she attended classes in scene designing and color dynamics given by the exiled Russian artist Alexandra Exter, whose teaching proved decisive in developing her own sense of color and design. Among the painters of the Paris School, she felt the strongest affinity for Picasso and Juan Gris. She traveled extensively in Europe and showed a special interest in Gothic architecture. In 1933 she had her first individual show at the Galerie Zac in Paris, which received high praise from the critics. In 1934, she returned to Havana, where she remained except for occasional trips abroad.

When Amelia Peláez returned to Cuba in 1934, dictator-president Machado had recently been ousted and a series of short-lived provisional governments were creating a situation of chronic instability until the appearance of a new strong man, Fulgencio Batista, in 1940. The artistic situation was also unstable and transitional, torn between tradition and innovation. Two of the most gifted younger artists, Wifredo Lam and Mario Carreño, were living in Spain. Others were barely beginning to be known. When the first National Salon of Art was held in 1935, Peláez sent some of her work and received a prize. But her first individual show, earlier that year, had passed virtually unnoticed. At the second National Salon, in 1938, she felt that the judging was unfair and as a protest she retired to the tranquility of her home, where she devoted herself to the steady production of the paintings and drawings, and later the ceramics, that eventually brought her wide recognition. Through all the years she remained devoted to her home and her craft, avoiding artistic circles and personal publicity.

In general terms, the painting of Amelia Peláez evolved from monothematic unity and chromatic austerity to an almost baroque complexity of design and a tropical exuberance of brilliant colors. As described by Gómez Sicre,

> Little by little the tables and fruits began to find a continuation in colonial stained-glass windows, and to these were added embroidered tablecloths, capitals, wickerwork, tufts, and fringes in an infinite interweaving sketched in a continuous line that involved the whole picture, now widening, then narrowing, leaving zones of solid, brilliant color in a many-colored mosaic. Blue had always dominated her palette; now she used every possible shade of it. The lines,, thick or thin, gave the tones unaccustomed brilliance, so that they seem to be stained glass. The effect is of a chunk of tropical vegetation seen through a baroque iron grating with wide black rails. Whether it be glass or grating, Amelia Peláez has carried this baroque resolution of the picture to its highest point.[7]

Typical of the earlier style is *Still Life in Red* (oil on canvas, 1938), in the New York Museum of Modern Art, which is about as close to bidimensional abstraction as Peláez ever came. A transitional canvas is *Still Life* of 1940 in the San Francisco Museum of Art, in which dynamic curvilinear designs begin to appear. The decorative patterns derived from architectural details, become more prominent in such canvases as *Hibiscus* (1943) and *Fishes* (1943) [Plate 17]. As a rule, Peláez was more partial to still lifes—especially the Cuban fruits that she loved—than to the human figure. There is, however, a delightful watercolor, *Girls* (1943), which combines neo-Picassian figuration with the baroque intricacy of wrought iron gratings and rounded architectural forms. There is also a charming *Portrait of the Artist's Nephew* (gouache, 1945), showing a boy holding a small bird, which is almost naturalistic but has strong semiabstract elements in the background, derived from stylizations of tropical vegetation. In another medium—ink drawing—the *Botanical Forms* (1956) reveals the sureness of her compositional mastery in the bidimensional arrangement of these forms. If to these achievements we add her work in ceramics, including the splendid ceramic tile

[7] *Four Artists of the Americas.* Pan American Union, 1957, pp. 55–56.

murals for various buildings in Havana, we can begin to compre-
hend the artistic stature of this self-effacing woman joyfully
immersed in her creative and domestic tasks.

Wifredo Lam

Wifredo Lam (b. 1902), the second Cuban artist to achieve
wide international fame, derives his style in part from Picasso,
like Amelia Peláez, but otherwise his painting offers a complete
contrast to that of the older artist. Peláez is the painter of
domesticated tropical exuberance: her flora and fauna are there
to adorn a patio. Her art, in spite of its genuine modernism, is
spiritually rooted in the *criollo* tradition of Spanish-American
provincial life. Wifredo Lam is a painter of the jungle, of tropical
exuberance untamed, teeming with the fetishistic forms of
primitive cults and strange animistic symbols. What he learned
from Picasso, from West African and Oceanic sculpture, he
related to his own Afro-Cuban heritage. From this synthesis
emerged his best-known work, *The Jungle* (gouache on paper
mounted on canvas, 1943), which has long been prominently
displayed in the foyer of the Museum of Modern Art in New
York [Plate 7].

After a brief time at the Academia San Alejandro in Havana,
Lam went to Europe for further study, chiefly in Spain. His first
one-man show took place in 1928 at the Galería Vilches in Madrid.
In 1937, he went to Paris with a letter of introduction to Picasso
from the sculptor Manolo. Befriended by Picasso, he had a one-man
show at the Galerie Pierre in 1939, then exhibited jointly with
Picasso at the Perls Gallery in New York. In 1940, he joined a
group of surrealists in Marseilles, among them Max Ernst, André
Masson, and André Breton (whose book, *Fata Morgana*, he
illustrated). He accompanied Breton and Masson to Martinique,
thence made his way to the Dominican Republic and finally back
to Cuba.

One of Lam's early influences (along with Picasso and surrealism) was the work of Matisse. This influence is reflected in
such a work as *The Chair* (oil on canvas, 1943), with its vase of

flowers on a garden chair and its lush tropical garden. The contact with surrealism is strongly evident in a gouache of the same period, *Satan* (1942), with its overt eroticism. But the most characteristic works of this period are undoubtedly those of Afro-Cuban inspiration in which Lam applied all the technical resources that he had assimilated to evoking the primitive forces and the powerful deities of the *vodun* cults, which are seen as monstrous personifications of dark stirrings within ourselves. Distorted and fragmented semi-human forms blend with the lush vegetation and the symbols of primeval rituals in *The Jungle*, the masterpiece of this period, in which both the formal complexity and the subtly varied range of colors are realized with impressive virtuosity—none strident, but giving a mysterious and sinister effect. For neoprimitivism in a contemporary idiom, there is no painting to match this in Latin American art.

Other Cuban Painters

Of the Cuban painters of the next generation, the most prominent are Felipe Orlando, René Portocarrero, Mario Carreño, and Cundo Bermúdez. Orlando (b. 1911), self-taught, is closer to the line of Peláez than of Lam, with his domestic interiors (*Yellow Interior* [oil, 1942]), brightly-hued still lifes (*Two Dead Roosters* [oil, 1952]), architectural themes (*The House of the Cuyá Trees* [oil, 1943]), and local flora and fauna (*Flora and Fauna* [oil, 1957]). He has also done some neo-Picassian portraits (*Woman with Mirror* [oil, 1952]).

Although René Portocarrero (b. 1912) studied briefly at the Academia San Alejandro, he too is mainly self-taught in art. This did not prevent him from becoming a teacher at the Eduardo Abela Free Studio of Painting and Sculpture in 1939. He has traveled in Europe and America. At the VII São Paulo Bienal (1963) he was represented by no less than fifty-eight works, of which nineteen belonged to a series titled *Carnival Figure*. Portocarrero lived in the Colonial quarter of Havana, *El Cerro*, from which he has drawn many of his subjects, such as *Girl of El Cerro* (oil on wood, 1943) and *Interior* (watercolor, 1943). His work is figurative, and he shares with Peláez a love for baroque exuberance of detail. "In his paintings," writes Gómez Sicre, "reality and fantasy are blended in an exquisite plastic interplay." It is precisely this "exquisite plastic interplay" that characterizes an extraordinarily fine painting titled *Cathedral in Yellow* (1961), in which infinitely varied colors are blended with an amazing wealth of structural detail in a composition that is both harmonious and dynamic. The element of fantasy is evident in such paintings as *Santa Barbara* (1962) and *Small Devil* (1962), relating to Afro-Cuban tradition. The combination of reality and fantasy is prominent in a remarkable series of drawings and watercolors titled *Angels* (1941), many of which are in the New York Museum of Modern Art. These angels are *sui generis*, without specific religious geneology or mystical divinity, with butterfly or gadfly wings, quietly going about their duties as guardians of mankind. In one of these drawings a naked man sits on a bed dreaming of a woman, as one angel taps him on the shoulder and another floats gently over the floor.

Mario Carreño (b. 1913) studied at the Academia San Alejandro and, from 1932 to 1935 in Madrid. After a brief sojourn in Mexico, he lived in Paris from 1937 to 1939. He then returned to Cuba, but from 1944 to 1948 he was in the United States as professor of painting at the New School for Social Research. In 1958 he settled in Chile. The New York Museum of Modern Art has two of his paintings: *Tornado* (oil on canvas, 1941) and *Vase of Flowers* (Duco on composition board, 1943). His recent work is represented by *Petrified World* (ink and watercolor, 1965), included in the exhibition *Latin American Art since Independence*, and by his murals for various buildings in Chile (see Chapter 6). These later works are abstract.

Cundo Bermúdez (b. 1914) is a figurative painter who has concentrated on popular scenes with a bravado use of bright colors. Two of his paintings, *The Balcony* (1941) and *Barber Shop* (1942) are in the Museum of Modern Art in New York. Concerning the former, Edward Alden Jewell (former art critic of *The New York Times*) remarked that it "demonstrates that color propelled to brazen pitch can, when kept in hand, be made to accomplish capital results." In 1967, Bermúdez left Cuba and came to the

United States. The most recent of his paintings that I have seen, *La Gusanita* (oil, 1967), shows a Matisse-like interior with neocubist touches (in the face of the woman and in various objects), but has an indubitable charm and tropical flavor of its own.

Of the same generation is Raúl Milián (b. 1914), who has specialized in drawings—first nonobjective, then expressionistically neofigurative. In 1956, he showed seventeen ink drawings representing both styles at the Pan American Union, including among the neofigurative works *Man in Red, Blue Face, The Couple,* and *The Oracle.* In the Museum of Modern Art in New York may be found *Composition* (colored inks, 1951) and three untitled works in watercolor and ink (1959–60). At the VII São Paulo Bienal he exhibited a series of five ink drawings titled *Horizon.* Carmelo González (b. 1920), the outstanding print-maker, specializes in woodcuts with strong national and socialist-realist tendencies. He was represented at the VII São Paulo Bienal with thirty *xilogravuras.*

Hugo Consuegra (b. 1930), who also studied architecture, represents the emergence of purely abstract concepts in Cuban painting (and collage and drawing), even though he still gives associative titles to his canvases: *Against Ourselves, Looking at Africa, The Montagues and Capulets,* and *Vanquished Afternoon,* all dating from the mid-1950's. In works such as these he has generally followed informal tendencies with a marked lyrical character in the fluid forms and flowing lines. But in some canvases like *Child Playing* (oil, 1959), he follows a semiabstract figuration with a rather subdued range of colors. At the VII São Paulo Bienal (1963) he was represented with five paintings.

Among the sculptors, Tomás Oliva (b. 1930) cultivates a somewhat violent expressionist style in his abstract iron sculptures with allusive titles: *Tension, Specter, Blockade, Movement.* He showed twenty-eight sculptures at the VII São Paulo Bienal.

There are many other Cuban artists who might be mentioned if space permitted. For example, the exhibition *A Panorama of Cuban Art Abroad,* organized by the Pan American Union at the end of 1964, included works by thirty artists (of whom the best-known was Felipe Orlando). In January–February 1968 an exhibition of contemporary Cuban painters and graphic artists was held in Mexico City, jointly sponsored by the National Institute of Fine Arts and the Organizing Committee of the XIX Olympiad, with the cooperation of the National Museum of Art of Havana. The dates of the works exhibited ranged from 1924 to 1963. The artists represented were Victor Manuel García, Eduardo Abela, Fidelio Ponce de León, Carlos Enríquez, Jorge Arche, Wifredo Lam, Marcelo Pogolotti, Amelia Peláez, René Portocarrero, Mariano Rodríguez, Luis Martínez Pedro, Raúl Milián, Angel Acosta León. The abstract works of Milián, such as *Abstraction* (ink, 1959) and *Horizon* (ink, 1962) are especially interesting.

HAITI

In spite of its disastrous political and economic situation, Haiti—the Black Republic of the Caribbean—has produced one of the most original and flourishing art movements of Latin America. It is gratifying to note that this occurred largely as the result of interest and support, both personal and official, from the United States. In 1930, an artist from Chicago named William Scott went to Haiti and began to paint local scenes. His example stimulated several Haitians who were artistically inclined but had no means of effectively developing their talents. One of these was Pétion Savain, a lawyer and teacher who had been doing some photography and drawing in his spare time. By following Scott around and observing him at work he picked up sufficient knowledge to begin his own career as a naïf painter in the manner of the Douanier Rousseau. From 1931 to 1939 Savain had some eight exhibits of his work. His style gradually veered toward greater realism, as in *Market in the Country* (1938), which was chosen to represent Haiti in two international exhibitions organized by the IBM Corporation. Encouraged by this success, Savain went to the United States in 1940 and enrolled in the Art Students League of New York, where he studied tempera and graphic arts. He had one-man shows in New York and Washington. By this time he was no longer a "primitive." As an "educated" artist he had other problems, and was not entirely successful in solving them. The writer Thoby-Marcelin regards Savain as the dominant figure in Haitian art from 1931 to 1944; when he returned to Haiti in 1946, the emphasis was on popular art (the terms "popular," "primitive," and "naïf" are used interchangeably to describe this phase of Haitian art). Indeed, by that time extraordinary developments had taken place in the artistic life of Haiti.

What proved to be the decisive event was the arrival in Port-au-Prince, early in 1943, of an American artist named DeWitt Peters. He had come as one of a group of teachers of English sent by the United States government in pursuance of the Good Neighbor Policy. As an artist, Peters began to wonder, "Why, in this haunting city of 150,000, rich in history, literally shimmering with color, is there no single art gallery, no art shop, not even a nook where a painting can be hung for people to see?" He decided to do something about this situation; with support from the Haitian government and the American Embassy he was able to create the Centre d'Art in Port-au-Prince, which was officially opened in May, 1944, with a pioneer exhibit of contemporary art. As Peters told the story,

We waited tensely for public reaction. Suddenly it was there, a tumultuous response, almost overwhelming us. Excited crowds packed the galleries.... A country, tiny and poor in monetary wealth, learned, to its astonishment, that twenty-three pictures had been sold for more than $500, down here a truly fabulous sum.[8]

This was the beginning of a period of intense activity and of a new and golden era for Haitian art. According to Thoby-Marcelin, "at the end of its first year, the Centre d'Art had had fifteen exhibits with the participation of sixty painters, four sculptors, and twenty-one children." Painters from abroad, especially from Cuba, came to the Centre as visiting teachers. The fame of the Centre and its artists spread far and wide: exhibitions were held in many places throughout the Americas and in Europe, always with acclaim and financial success. Museums, as well as private collectors, began to buy Haitian paintings. In 1948, the writer

[8] "Haiti's Primitive Painters," in *Harper's Bazaar*, (January 1947), pp. 104–5, 159.

Selden Rodman opened the Haitian Art Center in New York and at the same time published his influential book, *Renaissance in Haiti: Popular Painters in the Black Republic.* Who were these "popular painters?" What kind of work did they produce?

Philomé Obin (b. 1892), is called "a popular realist" by Rodman. He comes from the North, where the principal town is Cap-Haïtien; he and his brother Séneque and son Antoine constitute the nucleus of what has been called the *Ecole Primitive du Nord.* In 1944, Philomé Obin sent a painting to the Centre d'Art titled *Roosevelt's Arrival at Cap-Haïtien* (Franklin D. Roosevelt went there in 1934 to mark the end of the nineteen-year military occupation of Haiti by the United States). The painting was quite realistic, painted with careful attention to detail, and yet with a certain attractive naïveté. DeWitt Peters wrote Obin an encouraging letter and paid him a good price for the painting (he had never before sold a picture for more than a dollar!). According to Rodman, Obin's "admitted ambition [was] to leave behind him a documentary record of the appearance and principal historical events of Haiti...."[9] In this enterprise he succeeded to an impressive degree: the evidence is in such paintings as *Toussaint l'Overture receives a letter from the First Consul* (1945), *The Cacos of Leconte* (the *cacos* were the guerrilla fighters against the U.S. Marines), and *The Funeral of Charlemagne Péralte* (a guerrilla leader). Social themes are no less effectively depicted in *Prisoners Returning from the Woods, Mardi Gras,* and *Dance at the Home of Fédermé Valcourt.* Obin's strong points are color, composition, and detail; yet in spite of so much detail his pictures are never cluttered, but retain plenty of open space.

One of the most famous Haitian painters was Hector Hyppolite (1894–1950), regarded by Thoby-Marcelin as "the authentic genius of the Haitian movement." After being apprenticed to a shoemaker, he managed to travel widely during 1915–20, visiting Cuba, New York, and Africa. Like his father and grand-father, he became a *vodun* priest, but gave this up after achieving success as an artist; yet there are many *vodun* themes and symbols in his work (*Vodun Gods, Black Magic, Papa Ogoun and Papa Zaca, Macanda*). One of the first to buy his pictures was the

9 Rodman, p. 33.

Cuban painter Wilfredo Lam, who, according to Rodman, "bought five at eight dollars apiece to take to Paris." Hyppolite soon became celebrated and rich but refused to change his style of living in order to conform to bourgeois standards of success; he preferred to live in a *caille* (African-type thatched hut) near the water-front of Port-au-Prince.

Unlike Obin, Hyppolite made no attempt at realism. Fantasy was his forte, decoration his delight, color his joy, and poetic expression his aim. All these qualities are evident in such a painting as *A House in the Country*, wherein most of the pictorial space is filled by a highly colorful and intricately decorative pattern of birds and flowers (including fledglings in their nests). In *Nude Woman* the central figure is entirely surrounded by stylized decorative patterns, including three landscapes inserted in small medallions. In *Vodun Gods*, the objects associated with the *vodun* rituals are displayed on a round table so that they become both decorative and functional. There is expressionistic distortion in such paintings as *Spirits at the Crossroads* and *Macanda*. But it is perhaps in such a painting as *Composition*, with its central nude female figure surrounded by vivid tropical birds, butterflies, and plants, that the poetic charm of Hyppolite's art is most effective.

Some of the popular artists of Haiti, like George Liautaud (b. 1899), specialize in metal sculpture. A blacksmith by trade, Liautaud was discovered by DeWitt Peters in 1953. Six years later he had a special display of ten sculptures at the V São Paulo Bienal, and in 1960 he had his first New York exhibit jointly with the painter Antonio Joseph. His one-man show at the Pan American Union later that year was very successful—all the works were sold. Many of his tin sculptures are flat vertical structures decorated with circular perforations and flower motifs, with both abstract and figurative motifs, the whole strongly influenced by the traditional popular sculpture of Haiti, particularly that associated with the *vodun* rituals. Joseph Jasmin (b. 1923), an illiterate peasant who was discovered by the American sculptor Jason Seeley (a teacher at the Centre d'Art) in 1948, also won rapid recognition as a sculptor (more recently as a painter, too).

Space does not permit discussion of the individual work of the many popular or primitive painters of Haiti, among them Rigaud Benoit (b. 1911), Louverture Poisson (b. 1914), Micius Stéphane (b. 1912), Wilson Bigaud (b. 1931), Prefete Duffaut (b. 1923), Pauleus Vital (b. 1918), Gabriel Alix (b. 1930), Sisson Blanchard (b. 1929), Fernand Pierre (b. 1929)—and dozens of others who have contributed to this amazingly prolific movement. But something should be said about the nonprimitive painters of Haiti.

Nonprimitive Painters

In 1950, a schism occurred in the art movement of Haiti: an important group of painters broke away from the Centre d'Art and created the *Foyer des Arts Plastiques*. One of their main grievances against the Centre d'Art appears to have been what they considered an excessive emphasis on the popular or primitive phase of Haitian art. One of the dissenters, Dieudonné Cédor (who had begun as a primitive) expressed the view that the younger artists should be given the opportunity for professional training and should be encouraged to make the transition from primitive experience to the new forms of artistic expression. Some Haitian artists had already begun to make this transition. In 1948, Luce Turner (Haiti's outstanding woman painter) and Maurice Borno received grants from the Rockefeller Foundation that enabled them to study in New York and Paris, respectively. The ex-tailor Antonio Joseph (b. 1921) received a Guggenheim Fellowship in 1952 (later renewed) that enabled him to spend a year in the United States. Having already had seven one-man shows at the Centre d'Art, he was given a one-man show at the Pan American Union in 1954, consisting of twenty paintings collectively titled *Impressions of the U.S.A.* In 1960, he was given a one-man show in New York. His work is figurative but not naturalistic, because he introduces some distortions and semi-abstract elements. He is more concerned with flat vertical structure than with depth or perspective (cf. *Uptown New York* [1954]).

An older artist, Lucien Price (b. 1914), studied in Paris and became professor of drawing (his speciality) at the Centre d'Art. He had his first one-man show in 1947, but his career was brief, for in 1951 he was committed to a mental asylum in Haiti and since then has produced no new works. A retrospective exhibit of his drawings was held at the Pan American Union in 1962. Although they have descriptive titles, he actually worked in a semiabstract style akin to informalism. The semiabstract painter Max Pinchinat received a grant from the French government, and his first show in Paris (1953) was favorably noticed by the critics (as was Luce Turner's Paris show in 1955). In short, while the United States has shown much enthusiasm for the Haitian primitives, the chief encouragement for the nonprimitives appears to have come from Europe. In this country, the view seems to prevail that, "properly speaking, the 'Haitian' artists are the popular painters. The others are international artists."[10] It is significant that Luce Turner, Max Pinchinat, and Roland Dorcely—three of the leading "international" painters—have for many years resided in France. Yet I venture to say that the future of the plastic arts in Haiti depends on these international artists. A deliberately naïf or primitive art movement leads eventually to a dead-end—or to the souvenir counters of the tourist bazaars.

Encouraging evidence of support and recognition for the contemporary artists of Haiti is found in the important exhibits of their work organized by the Foyer des Arts Plastiques for the VII and VIII São Paulo Bienal (1963 and 1965). In the 1963 Bienal twelve painters and one sculptor were represented; in that of 1965, there were fourteen works by nine painters, among them Emmanuel Jolicoeur (b. 1928), René Exumé (b. 1929), Wilson Jolicoeur (b. 1932), Alfred Dujour (b. 1938), and George Hector (b. 1938). According to Wilson Jolicoeur, there is great interest in art among the youth of Haiti. He cites as evidence the participation of twenty-five ceramists in the Exhibition of Negro Arts organized by Howard University in Washington, D.C. (1965), and the participation of twenty-five artists under the age of forty in the Esso Salon of Young Painters. The aim of most Haitian artists today is to identify themselves with the modern art movement.

[10] Private communication from Prof. Richard A. Long, College Museum, Hampton Institute.

VENEZUELA

The first great figure among Venezuelan painters of the twentieth century was Armando Reverón (1889–1954), an eccentric recluse who filled his studio with large rag dolls stuffed with sawdust, which he used as models. Born in Caracas, his early years were spent in Valencia. In 1904, he returned to the capital to begin his studies at the Escuela de Artes Plásticas. His first exhibition took place at Caracas in 1911, jointly with Rafael Monasterios. A stipend granted in 1914 for travel in Europe enabled him to visit Paris, Barcelona, and Madrid. At this time it was the Spanish painters who influenced him most strongly. Yet he also absorbed the lessons of the French impressionists, particularly in their preoccupation with light, which was to become his own obsession after his return to Venezuela in 1921.

Shunning the capital, Reverón settled in Macuto, a small town on the coast. There, in a hut-like house surrounded by a stone wall, he lived in a solitude shared only by his wife and model Juanita, and by the objects that he made to fill his private dream world: the large rag dolls (for which he made clothes and hats, furniture, pianos, violins, telephones) and the wire skeletons, complete with sex and biceps, that hung on the walls or the rafters. Whether as a result of an illness now thought to be encephalitis, or from some other cause, Reverón began to show signs of progressive mental derangement from 1943 (the year in which his mother died), and after 1945 he spent frequent periods at a sanatorium in Caracas. It was there that he died, on September 17, 1954. The Museum of Fine Arts immediately organized a memorial exhibition. The "Hermit of Macuto" had become a national glory. His fame had spread abroad too: in 1956, the Institute of Contemporary Art in Boston organized a retrospective exhibition of his work that traveled to various cities in the United States. Gone was the indifference with which his first one-man show (in 1931) had been received by the public of Caracas. In 1964, the tenth anniversary of Reverón's death received wide attention in the press. The Caracas daily, *El Nacional*, published on its front page a reproduction in color of Reverón's painting *The Cave*, for which he used as models two of his rather plump rag dolls, one nude, the other seminude, in his own, highly personal Caribbean version of *Naked Maja* and *Robed Maja* (Goya was one of the painters whose influence he had felt in Spain).

The same newspaper devoted its entire art section to Reverón, reproducing the celebrated photograph of the artist taken just before his final illness, with his long, unkempt hair falling on either side of his face, and his large white beard, equally unkempt, falling over his robust torso.[11] One of the writers for *El Nacional* even hailed Reverón as a precursor of Pop art, long before that term was invented. Without taking this claim too seriously, we may readily admit that Armando Reverón was in all respects an extraordinary person. That he was also an extraordinary artist is what mainly concerns us here. In the words of Clara Diament de Sujo,

Space between objects, light itself as an object, emphasis upon atmosphere and light at the expense of the depiction of objects, found their ultimate expression in Armando Reverón. The diaphanous, tremulous, vibrating light of the coastal region permeates his work from 1924 on—a blinding light which imparts hazy outlines to beaches, vineyards, streets, brooks, huts, coconut groves.... This light dazzled and obsessed him for ten years, throughout his blue, white, and sepia periods, imposing upon him a rigorous artistic asceticism.[12]

This distinguished Venezuelan critic thinks that the painting titled *Light Behind My Arbor* (1926) represents most vividly the use of light in Reverón's work: "White, piercing light is the very subject of the picture. It transmits the vibration of the atmosphere outside, it suggests the landscape fading into the distance, even when transformed into shadows in the shelter of the hut [that served Reverón as a studio]."

Armando Reverón left more than three hundred canvases and upwards of one hundred drawings. A remarkable example of his drawing style is the mysteriously illusive but marvelously delineated *Nude* (charcoal on canvas), posed from a live model.

[11] A similar photograph, magnificently reproduced in color—one notes the deep bronze of the sunburnt torso—can be found in Messer and Capa, *The Emergent Decade.*
[12] *Art in Latin America Today: Venezuela*, Pan American Union, 1962, p. 8.

Somewhat similar are two nude figures in the painting titled *Daughters of the Sun* (oil on burlap). *The Mechanics' Workshop* (oil and charcoal on canvas, 1943), reveals a highly impressionistic approach, poeticizing the Industrial Age while at the same time showing a strong contrast between the static architectural features and the dynamic attitudes of the workers. *The Wake of the Cross,* a popular religious observance, shows how completely the artist could identify himself with local scenes while avoiding any trace of commonplace *costumbrismo*. Reverón was incapable of banality.

Semiabstract and Neofigurative Painters

Escape from banality can scarcely be imputed to the usual crop of conventional landscapists and academic figurative painters, found in Venezuela as elsewhere during the first half of the present century. Some of these figurative painters nevertheless achieved a measure of distinction within their self-imposed or inevitable limitations: Antonio Edmundo Monsanto and Marcos Castillo as followers of Cézanne; Pedro León Castro and Manuel Cabré as skillful landscapists and effective colorists; Armando Barrios and Hector Poleo as explorers of formal relationships, the former along quasigeometrical lines (as in *The Weavers* [1958]. Of these, the one who has had the most interesting evolution is probably Poleo.

After completing his studies in Caracas, where he was born, Hector Poleo (b. 1918) received a grant to study mural painting in Mexico. From there he went on to New York, where he lived for two years (1946–47). In 1947 he was awarded a Guggenheim Fellowship that enabled him to work in Paris. Returning to Venezuela in 1952, he continued to paint in a somewhat stylized but essentially naturalistic manner (*The Wedding* [1957]), and also executed a mural for the new Ciudad Universitaria. In 1958 he returned to Paris. After participating in important international exhibitions, such as those of São Paulo and Venice (Acquisition Prize, 1956), and after numerous one-man shows, his international reputation was well established. During 'the 1960's he turned toward a kind of semiabstract, expressionist, neofigurative painting, as revealed in the works that were shown in the Second Córdoba Bienal of 1964: *Evening, From the Earth to the Earth,* and *Re-encounter.* In this fusion of abstract expressionism and figuratism there is no trace of the influence formerly exerted on him by the Mexican muralists.

The neofigurative movement in Venezuelan painting continues to be important, mainly because of the powerful originality of its leading representative, Jacobo Borges. But others who follow this trend are by no means negligible: among them are Angel Luque, Louisa Richter, José Antonio Dávila, and Luis Guevara Moreno. Moreno won the National Prize for Painting at the Official Salon of Caracas in 1959. His *Composition* (1957), showing two horsemen taming a bull, reveals a deliberate interplay of abstract and figurative elements, used as contrasting factors in the composition. The canvas that he sent to the Dallas exhibition, *South American Art Today,* titled *Group* (1959), clearly delineates two women carrying a placard through the streets; but their message remains an abstraction, a mystery. The theme is not *a* protest, but the act of protest itself.

Angel Luque (b. 1927), a native of Córdoba, Spain, who has lived in Venezuela since 1955, was active in Madrid as a member of the group called Artists of Today. In 1961, he won the National Prize for Engraving at the Official Salon in Caracas. Some influence of De Kooning is revealed in the expressionistic, semiabstract canvases that he exhibited in the Second Córdoba Bienal (1964): *Long Live Painting, Long Live Sensorial Vitality,* and *Project for a Robot* which has the merit, or at least the novelty, of being completely unmechanistic and inefficient.

Louisa Richter (b. Germany, 1928), who also settled in Venezuela in 1955 (with some subsequent sojourns in Europe), has adhered rather closely to abstract expressionism, with only slight traces of figuration, as in *Figures Emerging from the Landscape,* one of the three canvases that she exhibited in the Second Córdoba Bienal (the others were *Apocalyptic Animal and Behind the Door*). A *Landscape* (1964), included in the exhibition *The Emergent Decade,* is a good example of her "informalist" tendency.

Jacobo Borges (b. 1931) is a master of what Thomas Messer calls "strong, semifigurative contemporary expressionism." After study at the Escuela de Artes Plásticas in Caracas, Borges was awarded a fellowship for further work in Paris (1952). He participated in the biennials of São Paulo (1957) and Venice (1958), and, in 1963, was awarded the National Prize for Painting at the Official Salon in Caracas. Two years later he received the Armando Reverón Biennial Award for Painting. His strongly expressionistic canvas *Personage of the Coronation* (1963) was included in the exhibit *The Emergent Decade.* At the Córdoba Bienal of 1964, Borges exhibited three powerful neofigurative canvases: *The Gangster, At the Fiesta,* and *The Show Goes On* (triptych).

Guillermo Heiter was born in Czechoslovakia and his formative years, before World War II, were spent under the influence of expressionism. From 1933 to 1937, his drawings and canvases were exhibited in Prague, Paris, and Vienna. In 1949, he emigrated to Venezuela and became a naturalized citizen. Thereafter he worked toward achieving a synthesis of expressionism and cubism. Into this synthesis he also assimilated Venezuelan racial types, and both the urban and rural landscapes of his adopted land. He was interested in the constructive and compositional possibilities of cubism, which he explored in such a painting as *Players* (1957), which shows four women playing cards. The faces are Picassian, but the racial types are Caribbean, and the color and composition, a dynamic interplay of circular, diagonal, and rectangular planes, are entirely Heiter's own. What is also remarkable in this painting is the psychological perception and projection of a particular cultural milieu, not only through the obvious physiognomy but also through more subtle nuances of attitude, movement, and tone. Another striking synthesis, this time of Van Gogh and Picasso, is achieved in the canvas titled *Harlequin*, where we see a neocubist Harlequin giving an olive branch to a dove against a swirling expressionist sky.

If we detect a certain affinity with Rouault in some of Heiter's religious paintings, the artist himself gives us a helping hand by calling one of his major works *Homage to Rouault.* This is a triptych, the three parts of which are titled *Divinity, Agony, Humanity.* It is in oil on canvas but painted in the style of a stained glass window. The central panel is the most expressionist;

but it is curious that, in this triptych too, we find a marked cubist influence, concentrated especially in the praying Harlequin (who represents humanity) in the third panel. Heiter's religious paintings are among the strongest that have been done in modern Latin America: for example, the expressionist *Christ on the Cross* (Planchart Prize, 1956), and the extraordinary *Descent*, with its utter economy of means to express the desolation of death and the resigned acceptance of man's implacable destiny. There is nothing here of Christian hope and faith; both life and death are seen as parts of the same tragedy. The inert body of Christ is carried under the shoulders and under the knees by the two somberly hooded women against the pitiless background of a cold sun and a hard sky that envelope the entire canvas with a swirling impasto of luminous browns mixed with white.

In other paintings of religious subjects, on a different plane of feeling and perception, such as *Rome MCMLV*, *Cardinal*, and *Two Nuns*, Heiter is more concerned with color as a compositional element (the rich red of the Cardinal's robe; the white habits of the nuns, cubistically projected, contrasting with the two dark faces). Composition with color is also the essence of *Rome MCMLV*: three black seminarians with their black broad-brimmed hats, white collars, red mouths and robes, and black capes.

Heiter has painted many rural and urban scenes of Venezuela, but always with a tendency toward abstraction. His rural shacks (ranchos) either become elements in a neocubist composition or are treated as studies in textural and linear contrasts. This can be seen also in *Stockade Fence* (1953) and in *Suburb*, where the functional elements are used purely for their textural and compositional qualities, emphasized by the total absence of the human figure. Nevertheless, though the human factor is absent, it is not excluded but rather implied, as a latent presence: one feels that these dwellings and suburbs are inhabited. The same holds true of an industrial urban scene, as in *Cranes*, with its semiabstract buildings in the foreground and the high, vertical, stylized shapes of the cranes in the background. There are no workers in sight; yet one feels that this is not just a semiabstract composition in verticals and horizontals: it is also the presentation of an *idea*—the industrial development associated with Venezuela's great resources in petroleum.

Similarly, in another context, in *Ravine*, the idea of a deep opening in the earth, with its exuberant tropical vegetation, is presented in abstract terms, through the dynamism of colors and shapes and textures. Even in a purely abstract canvas, like *Composition in Relief*, one recognizes the striated surfaces of the ranchos and their stockade fences. For Heiter, the transition from the objective to the abstract and back again is never forced or arbitrary. Whatever his subject—and he has done many fine portraits (including one of Marcel Marceau)—he is always composing with color, with design, with form, with texture.

Abstract Expressionism and Informalism

Informalism and abstract expressionism have an extensive following in Venezuela. Besides Louisa Richter, leading exponents of informalism are José María Cruxent, Mercedes Pardo, and Maruja Rolando. Cruxent (b. 1915), by profession an archaeologist before he took up painting, has been influenced by the primitive forms and textures that he has unearthed, as well as by vegetable forms encountered in his explorations in Africa and Guiana. As Clara Diament de Sujo writes, "His painting seems to evince a fascination with processes of disintegration." Mercedes Pardo (b. 1922) has lived in Paris and Chile, and has executed murals and stage sets as well as oils. Her *Composition over Gray* (1959) and *Composition in Red* (1960) reveal her vivid use of color and her formal freedom. Her paintings of the 1960's, to judge by those she exhibited in the Córdoba Bienal of 1964, are characterized by a more extreme informalism and by a heightened metaphysical intent: *Weights Traversed by the Transit of Wings, You No Longer Love even the Shadow that You Despoil*, and *Be the Enclosure of Our Nocturnal Trances*.

It is difficult to establish a distinction between informalism and abstract expressionism, and many critics do not even attempt to make the distinction. The former term is usually preferred in France and Latin America, the latter in the United States. Hence the painters discussed here are closely akin, aesthetically, to those mentioned in the preceding paragraph. Angel Hurtado, Humberto Jaimes Sánchez, Victor Varela, Oswaldo Vigas, and a number of other Venezuelan painters have worked within the orbit of abstract expressionism without necessarily regarding it as the ultimate phase of their creative evolution. Jaimes Sánchez, for instance, has recently done some semi-Pop figurative painting, such as *I Love Your Crazy Years*, with a small target in the upper left-hand corner that might be construed as a tribute to Jasper Johns.

Humberto Jaimes Sánchez (b. 1930) studied at the Escuela de Artes Plásticas in Caracas from 1947 to 1950, and a few years later he received a stipend for further study in Paris and Rome. He received the National Prize for Painting at the Official Salon of Caracas in 1962. During the 1950's his work reminds us chiefly of De Staël, with its "large, well-composed patches of color."[13] A good example is the *Composition in Blue* (1959) that he sent to the Dallas exhibition, *South American Art of Today*. The paintings that he exhibited in the second Córdoba Bienal (1964) are quite different; instead of the well-composed blocks of color, there are wide horizontal areas that serve as background for a dominant geometrical form—the circle. Such is the composition of *After 1913*, which is further characterized by informal abstract elements placed within the circle. Thus, the combination of geometrical and informal elements appears to characterize the work of this period. This particular painting is one of a chronological trilogy that includes *Before 1913*, and *1913*.

According to Clara Diament de Sujo,

Jaimes Sánchez locks himself in to paint, and paints for days and weeks without a break. When he comes out of his studio, it is hard for him to accustom his eyes to a world which, by contrast with the colors he has been using, seems absurdly gray. He then looks for new color relationships in the light and atmosphere, much as if he were beholding the earth on the first day of creation. The color he seeks, however, is not external and visible; it is something he feels within, which his fingers and brush can put on canvas.[14]

[13] Paul Damaz, *Art in Latin American Architecture*. Reinhold Publishing Corp., 1963, p. 62.
[14] *Art in Latin America Today: Venezuela*, p. 17.

With such a compulsive drive toward subjective expression, the painting of Jaimes Sánchez may take directions not at present predictable from his past work. He is an artist in constant renewal.

Like Jaimes Sánchez, Angel Hurtado (b. 1927) lived for a number of years in Paris, where he became interested in making art films. During the 1950's he painted in a strongly articulated caligraphic style, somewhat in the manner of Soulages. In the 1960's he abandoned these linear articulations in favor of an informal type of abstract expressionism centered around dynamic clusters, as in *The Milky Way* (1961) and *Nuclear Matter* (1962). A subjective and introspective personality, his metaphysical searchings are directed toward intuitive rather than logical perceptions of meaning. Two of his paintings, *Day* and *Night* were acquired by the Museum of Modern Art in New York in 1958.

Oswaldo Vigas (b. 1928) is a self-taught painter who received a degree in medicine from the University of Caracas. He held his first one-man show in 1952, and participated in the exhibition *South American Art of Today* in Dallas with a quasigeometric painting titled *Composition in Black and White* (1957). This is similar to *Imposing Symbol* (1956), which is in the collection of the Pan American Union in Washington; but the work titled simply *Composition* (1961) reveals a shift toward a completely fluid and open type of informalism, with color as the chief compositional factor.

Elsa Gramcko (b. 1925) is an artist who cannot be placed in any single category. Her work of the mid 1960's concentrates on surface textures (doors, walls) and their related functional objects (handles, locks). At the same time, she gives conceptual, metaphysical titles to these paintings, as though insisting on the presence of some mystery behind the surface appearance. This metaphysical approach is made explicit in a trilogy sent to the Second Córdoba Bienal wherein the physical object (in this case a door—or is it simply a wall with a door knob and a hinged lock, the semblance of a door?) serves as a point of departure for three permutations of "inside and outside." The three paintings are titled, respectively, *To Be Outside is the Same as To Be Inside, Inside and Being Outside, What Is Inside Is Also Outside.* Very similar is *The White Castle*, where the main textural elements are a brick wall, a vertical board, a wide horizontal band of burlap, and three hinged locks. The symbolism of the white castle remains a mystery; but the painting stands firm and compels our attention.

Elsa Gramcko has passed through quasigeometric and informalist phases. She has used all kinds of textures and materials, including found objects. Yet her work does not strike the viewer as being without direction: the motivating force is her creative energy and integrity. In the dialectical confrontation between the material object and the metaphysical meaning, she has found another dimension for her painting.

There are many other followers of informalism in Venezuela, among them Albert Brandt, Mary Brandt, Lía Bermúdez, Teresa Casanova, Daniel González, Fernando Irazabal, Gabriel Morera, Manuel Quintana Castillo, and Renzo Vestrini.

Geometric Abstraction: Otero and Soto

The two most famous Venezuelan painters of today have followed entirely different paths. They are Alejandro Otero and Jesús Soto, both of whom turned to abstract constructivism.

Alejandro Otero (b. 1921) studied at the Escuela de Artes Plásticas and worked in Paris from 1945 to 1952 (also again from 1960 to 1964). During the 1940's he cultivated a semi-figurative type of painting that was very close to informalism in its very free evocation of such material objects as coffee pots (his favorite subject for a time). Around 1949 he made the transition to pure and complete abstraction, eliminating all traces of subject matter and of composition with color. On a background of white he placed a single patch of color or a few small lines. He did not exhibit these paintings, but went on to develop a new type of geometric-kinetic art that he called "Colorrhythms," the first of which were shown in 1955. These consist of rectangular, vertical wood panels to which Duco is applied with an air-brush. The Colorrhythm effect is obtained by the contrast between a static element—the parallel vertical lines running from top to bottom of the panel—and a dynamic element created by a variety of color-forms asymmetrically placed "behind" the vertical bars. In the long series of *Colorrhythms* that he executed during this period, Otero devised many variants of space-form-color combinations based on this simple but highly effective principle.

But Otero is not the kind of artist who remains tied to a single concept, however valid and fruitful it may be. During the 1960's he turned to collage, using old manuscripts glued to an austere background of one or two subdued colors. Two works of this type were included in the exhibition *The Emergent Decade: In Manuscript, Brown and Silver* (1963) and *In Manuscript and Silver*. Another painting of this type, shown at the Second Córdoba Bienal, takes its title from the dateline of the manuscript (in this case, a letter), *Pisa, 8th Oct. 1821*. The background here is figurative, in that it shows the panel of a door to which the manuscript is affixed. Other paintings take their titles from the colors used, as in *Gray, Oxide, and Silver*. Is this just another phase for Otero? Very probably. Yet to emphasize the successive phases of Otero's work—figurative, semi-figurative, abstract, geometric—is to risk underestimating the fundamental integrity of his technique and the rightness of his style in whatever he undertakes. He is not a follower of fashions but a creator of forms stamped with his own style.

Other aspects of Otero's work should be mentioned, such as his mosaic and aluminum mural for the Public Amphitheatre in Caracas, his *Vertical Elements in a Gasoline Station* (aluminum, 1958), and his ornamental metal screen for a bank in Caracas. In the words of Paul Damaz, "Otero is the Venezuelan artist who has shown the strongest interest in integrating his work with modern architecture." As we shall see later (Chapter 6), he has worked closely with the famous Venezuelan architect Carlos Raúl Villanueva.

Jesús Soto (b. 1923) also studied at the Escuela de Artes Plásticas (1942–47) and then became director of the School of Fine Arts in Maracaibo (1947–50). Since 1960 he has lived in Paris. He participated in the São Paulo Biennials of 1957 and 1959, in the Venice Biennials of 1958 and 1960, and in 1964 was awarded the Gran Premio Bienal Americana at Córdoba (Argentina). The three paintings that he exhibited at Córdoba, *Inversion, 1 Blue 15 Blacks, Black and Silver Manuscript*, are in the geometric constructivist style from which Soto has never departed in his mature work. Yet, because of Soto's preoccupation with kinetic values and light vibrations, this style is nearer to the aims of the Groupe de Recherche d'Art Visuel than to orthodox constructivism. The best description of Soto's experiments with multi-dimensional space and light energy is that of Clara Diament de Sujo:

> Beginning in 1955 he [Soto] started to use sheets of plexiglass placed a short distance from the background panels. The lines he drew thereon, in varying juxtaposition with the intervening blank spaces, produced "vibrations" of changing and unexpected appearance. These works show how the artist acquired an intuition of movement or energy in space—energy with attributes of light and color, capable of aesthetic expression. About 1957, Soto abandoned plexiglass for other means of conveying vibration. On a paper background he traces a line in absolute freedom, breaking it off, crossing it, and treating it in the same fashion, in which his fingers twist, break, solder, knot, bend, and tangle a thin thread of wire which, placed in a very short distance from the panel, gives off vibrations that run in changing rhythms over the surface of the composition. vibrations that escape to the walls, floor, and ceiling. Soto has delved intensely into the possibilities of expression contained within different materials, each of his black or white panels representing a new experiment. In some he makes use of clots of glue under the layers of color; in others nails have been hammered into the panel; in still others thick threads have been scattered over the surface, beneath the base color, so that the pen which draws lines thereon is interrupted upon encountering them. The thin black or white wire behaves in widely varying fashion. Blue, red, or green accents, bright blue spots or disconcerting reflections, a network of shadow which is but a twisted wire—all these color the whites and change the effect of the blacks. For the Exhibition of Movement which took place in Brussels in 1961, Soto created a mural in the room devoted solely to his work, using a fishnet, a withered tree, and a few sticks. In another mural he had used a few rolls of barbed wire, wire fencing, and random pieces of scrap iron, all in a search for vibration....[15]

A work from Soto's plexiglass period is the swirling *Spiral* (1958), in which the background consists of plaka and ink on wood, with four capped iron rods protruding at each corner. One of his uses of fine iron wire, in this case horizontally affixed on

[15] *Art in Latin America Today: Venezuela*, p. 14.

masonite in a solid area, combined with plaka, is illustrated in *Vibration* (1961). Soto has also done important work in sculpture, and like Otero has collaborated with the architect Villanueva, notably with his *Metal Construction* in the Carlos Villanueva Garden in Caracas (1956).

Soto feels at home in Paris: "In this city, even if you have no name but people know that you are an artist, there is warmth." At first he made his living by playing the guitar in Left Bank night clubs. He came to "Optical Vibration" in his art by studying the work of Mondrian and Calder,

> I saw how Calder integrated time and movement in sculpture and I wanted to do the same thing in painting. . . . I tried to make Mondrian's elements move on canvas. . . . I have great respect for Mondrian, for Kandinsky and Malevitch. They prepared us for Optical Art, eliminating visual concepts of the classical Greek and of the Renaissance. I believe that my contribution consists of having integrated movement in painting, using the vision of man as the motor.[16]

Although Soto is married to a Parisienne and considers Paris his home, he has not forgotten Venezuela or the city of his birth, Ciudad Bolívar: "I have grown closer and closer to Venezuela because of the interest there in my paintings. Now I have a plan to create a museum in my home town, Ciudad Bolívar, filled with my own work and that of other avant-garde artists."

Soto's *Vibration* (1965), included in the *Emergent Decade* exhibition, shows his use of fine wire elements in rectangular patterns of the utmost symmetry, with small metal rectangles as contrasting elements. A painstaking craftsman as well as an inspired artist, Soto aims at perfection in every work that comes from his studio.

Since mid-century, geometric abstraction has held the center of the stage in Venezuelan painting and sculpture. Besides Otero and Soto, its adherents include Armando Barrios, Carlos Cruz Díez, Omar Carreño, Mateo Manaure, Carlos González Bogen, Pascual Navarro, and Victor Valera, who is both sculptor and painter. Cruz Díez (b. 1923) has lived in Paris since 1960, where

[16] From the profile of Soto by Cornell Capa in Messer and Capa, *The Emergent Decade*. Cornell University Press, 1966, p. 137.

he came under the influence of the Op art movement. During the 1960's he executed a long series of works that he calls *Fisiocromias,* in which the kinetic optical effect is obtained through the juxtaposition of closely spaced vertical lines and overlapping spheroidal forms.

Sculpture: Marisol

The Venezuelan sculptress Marisol Escobar (b. 1930) is one of many Latin American artists who have chosen to live and work in New York. True, she has always led an international life, for she was born in Paris, raised in Venezuela, and has traveled extensively since she was a girl. Marisol (as she is always called) began to sculpt in 1954 with wood carvings that often represented family groups (*Family,* painted wood, 1956). Prior to that she had studied painting in New York with Kuniyoshi and Hans Hoffman. According to Jacqueline Barnitz, it was after seeing an exhibition of pre-Columbian sculpture that Marisol adopted that medium in preference to painting. Furthermore, "William King influenced her to do painted wood sculpture and Robert Rauschenberg gave her the idea for mixing media. The monumental size of her work was a 1960 development due to a chance visit to the East Hampton home of her friends, the Marca-Rellis, where she found a bag of hat forms suggesting life-size sculpture."[17]

The completely personal synthesis of these influences is evident in such large, three-dimensional, free-standing sculptures as *Woman and Dog* (1963) and *The Party* (1965–66)—both painted wood and mixed media. The latter work is actually an "environment" consisting of fifteen figures and requires an entire room for its display. *The Party (Fiesta)*—Marisol's most famous work to date—reveals the most characteristic features of her style.

It combines the repetitive motifs that suggest Op art, the basic geometric simplicity of minimal sculpture, theatrical props, assemblage, realistic painting, and ... the Marisol masks. A headdress which sits

[17] Jacqueline Barnitz, "The Marisol Mask," *Hispanic Arts,* I, 2 (1967), p. 45.

like a crown on top of the central figure is a sort of animal-vegetable composite of shapes resembling the baroque terracotta compositions she did in the fifties. . . . A small working TV set is built into one of the guests' forehead. The figures stand rigid and elegantly gowned in real or painted dresses. Some wear archaic Egyptian hairdos, a familiar shape in Marisol sculpture. All hide safely behind a social mask.[18]

The importance of the mask in Marisol's sculpture is also revealed in such a work as *Mayflower* (1961–62, mixed media), a vertical panel six feet high consisting entirely of three-dimensional masks depicting almost every variety of human expression. Her block-like *Baby Boy* (wood and mixed media, 1962–63) and *Baby Girl* (mixed media, 1962–63) reveal her unique gift for combining the grotesque and the pathetic. *The Mural* (wood and mixed media, 1963), showing a group of five musicians, is an example of her virtuosity in composition and quasi-realistic representation. The fantastic and grotesque aspects of her work, verging on surrealism and with erotic implications, are present in such pieces as *Women Sitting on a Mirror* (wood and mixed media, 1965–66) and *Couple* (mixed media, 1965–66).

Marisol is doubtless the most contemporary of all Latin American sculptors, the one who has most completely identified herself with the materials, tools, techniques, and aesthetic concepts that are typical of this particular moment in the twentieth century. At the same time there is a solidity, a profundity of feeling, a classical quality of workmanship in her creations that will probably make them immune to the changing fashions of one of the most volatile periods in the history of art.

COLOMBIA

Just as in Venezuela the international prestige of Otero and Soto tends to place major emphasis on geometric and optical abstraction, so in Colombia the fame and influence of Alejandro Obregón and Fernando Botero tend to emphasize the importance of neofigurative painting. Not that abstract art is unimportant in Colombia—the work of Ramírez Villamizar in painting and

[18] *Ibid.*, p. 37.

of Negret in sculpture would preclude such a hypothesis—but by and large, at least up to about 1965, Obregón and Botero have been the two giants of contemporary painting in Colombia, the artists whose influence has been most widely felt.

Alejandro Obregón

Obregón, the older of the two, was born in Barcelona, Spain, in 1920 (his mother was Spanish, his father Colombian). He was raised in the seaport of Barranquilla, on the Caribbean coast of Colombia, and it is there that he continues to live and work. He studied art in Spain and at the Boston School of Fine Arts (1937–41). His first one-man show was held in Bogotá, in 1947. In 1958, he received the Guggenheim Prize for Colombia and, in 1964, a first prize at the second Bienal of Córdoba (Argentina). His work was included in the exhibition *The Emergent Decade* (1965–66). According to Cornell Capa, "Obregón consumes life, love, and liquor in generous quantities. They burn in him with scorching flames, searing all who are near him. But out of this fire also come his paintings."[19] Obregón described his own painting as "the obsession for a solution of that which one can never solve." He is a man driven by a fierce compulsion to transform the world about him into images of his own making. In the words of Thomas Messer, "His condors, and his semiabstract seascapes, his coloristic analogues of the opulent Caribbean flora, are, to be sure, extracted from the world of observed experience. But it is his apprehension of the form language of his generation— a private version of abstract expressionism—that renders his shapes and images alive and meaningful."[20]

Modern painting in Colombia begins with Obregón, even though his was not a modernism of *le dernier cri*. His earlier works were overtly figurative, but with strong injections of cubism, and a palette showing the influence of Gauguin, to whose Tahitian style he also paid tribute in *The Gray Cloud* (1949), but with his own particular brand of distortion. The gigantism of the nude female

[19] Messer and Capa, *The Emergent Decade*, p. 105.
[20] *Ibid.*, p. 102.

figure (upper body only shown) is emphasized by the yellow coloring and by the disproportionate smallness of the head; this strange woman with staring, slanted eyes and large, sensual lips fills almost the entire canvas, leaving but little space for a cloud that is merely a slab of dark gray near her head.

During the 1950's, Obregón developed and perfected his own style in spite of the influence of Tamayo in such a canvas as *Still Life in Gray* (1954). His *Souvenir of Venice*, painted in the same year (and acquired by the New York Museum of Modern Art), reveals him in masterful command of the entire space of his canvas, from which depth has been banished in favor of a flat pyramidal structure of horizontal planes, dominated at the top by a towering Venetian church and at the bottom by the stylized roosters and doves that figure, along with the condor and the eagle, in so many of Obregón's paintings. With *Cattle Drowning in the Magdalena* (1955), Obregón is in full possession of the powerful, semiabstract, expressionist style that he has continued to develop in all his subsequent work. The elements of his subject are decomposed, broken down into separate components, then reassembled and recomposed according to the demands of a purely pictorial organization of forms, figures, and colors that is both controlled and fired by a painterly imagination.

The strength and communicative power of Obregón's canvases derive in part from the tension between abstraction and representation. This tension enables him to convey a direct emotional involvement in a specific human situation while maintaining the complete autonomy of his artistic style. There are, for example, two canvases, both painted in 1956, that have death as their theme: *The Wake* and *Mourning for a Dead Student*. The former is more overtly figurative: the dead body on the crude table, with a bottle of wine and fruit beside it, the cock crowing, the symbolic flora. The second painting uses some of the familiar symbols—fruit, flower, bird—but is much more abstract and hermetic, as though the injection of a social theme (the death of a student in Latin America is almost certain to have sociopolitical implications) demanded a counterbalancing abstraction to prevent intrusion of the anecdotal, the descriptive, the merely pathetic.

In the mid 1960's, without abandoning any of his tutelary

symbols and images (in particular the omnipresent condor of the Andes) Obregón incorporated his fauna and flora, the condors and cocks, the bulls and iguanas, in paintings as commandingly beautiful as they are unmistakably personal and contemporary in style. Such are the three canvases that he sent to the second Córdoba Bienal: *Bullcondor* (uniting his two most powerful images), *Iguana Devoured by a Tiger*, and *Escape from the Alcatraz*; and the two splendid paintings included in *The Emergent Decade*: *The Baroque Garden* and *The Last Condor* (both 1965).

Concerning Obregón's obsession with the condor, Cornell Capa writes, "He is a huge bird, brave, solitary, soaring high above the others. He is also gullible, easily trapped, and on his way to extinction." Perhaps Obregón has painted the epitaph as well as the apotheosis of the condor.

Botero: The Apotheosis of Rotundity

Fernando Botero, master of "inflated images," was born in Medellín in 192. He had his first one-man show in Bogotá in 1951, and the following year went to Madrid, where he studied at the San Fernando Academy. During 1953–55 he was in Paris and in Florence, studying fresco technique in the latter city. His return to Colombia was followed by a year in Mexico (1956–57), after which a one-man show at the Pan American Union in Washington, D.C. established the basis of his growing reputation in the United States. Since then he has participated in many international and American exhibitions including two traveling shows organized by New York's Museum of Modern Art in 1969: *The Portrait in Contemporary Art* and *Inflated Images*. From 1960 he made his home in New York.

In the words of Marta Traba, "Botero returned to forms their full power of expression. . . . For Botero, painting was simply a form, enormous and grotesque. Space, color, design, existed as a function of form. The exaggeration of the concept of form implied a true creation, belligerent and daring."[21] In his obsession with form, Botero was attracted by rotund objects (such as the

[21] As quoted in *ibid.*, p. 116.

lute) whose shape made them especially apt for depicting fullness combined with curvilinear contours (*Still Life* [ca. 1957], *Black Lute* [1959]). But he soon found in the human figure itself the rotundity and amplitude that, by a process of exaggeration that became his hallmark, he could use to fill almost the entire space of his canvas with a single form. It was thus that, in 1959, he painted his now celebrated portrait of *Mona Lisa, Age Twelve* (Museum of Modern Art, New York), whose huge head, with puffed-up cheeks, occupies nearly the whole pictorial space, while arms and hands are disproportionately small. The enigmatic smile is still there, but it reminds us more of the Cheshire Cat than of the Mona Lisa.

Botero has continued to rework the old masters in a whole series of grotesquely exaggerated portraits, conspicuously macrocephalic. There is, for example, the portrait of *The Cardinal Niño de Guevara* (1964, after El Greco), whose bloated face, with its gimlet eyes, has the aspect of a bearded and bespectacled rodent. Again the tiny hands serve to emphasize the exaggeration of the huge head. In *The Wife of Rubens* (1963), there is the same discrepancy between the enormous head and the tiny hands and body; but a further touch of caricature is provided by the contrast between the vast expanse of fleshy face and the small mouth and minuscule nose. There is a delightful parody in the parallel between the large globular earrings and the twin globes of the ample bosom. Withal, there is an air of bravura and elegance about this portrait—which is not so much the caricature of a person as of a style—evident in the rakish tilt of the feathered hat, the large mass of reddish hair, the opulence of the dress and the richness of the coloring. During the 1960's, Botero continued this series of portraits of "Mrs. Rubens," with slight variations (see Plate 8).

The disquieting achievement of Botero's parodies of the old masters is that they create grotesque doubles of some of the most famous paintings of the western world, which nevertheless appear to have an independent and ineradicable authenticity.

In an important exhibition of his recent work at the Center for Inter-American Relations in New York (March–May, 1969), Botero demonstrated the versatility of his talent and the adaptability of his style to a wide variety of themes, both historical and contemporary. He reaches toward the past in the portrait of *St. Rose of Lima According to Vázquez Ceballos No. 3* (1968), after Gregorio Vázquez Ceballos, the most famous Colombian painter of the Colonial period; and in the gloriously inflated image of *Our Lady of Colombia* (1967), with the Child Jesus holding a miniature Colombian flag in one hand, while at the bottom corners of the canvas the tiny figures of a politician and a prelate hold up the ends of a runner bearing the legend, *Libertad y Orden.* Botero continues in the vein of political and social satire with such canvases as *Prelates Bathing in a River, The Presidential Siesta, Chief of Police, The Family,* and *Picnic* (all 1968). His *Adam* and *Eve* (both 1968) are well-padded middle-class Colombians, posing self-consciously—perhaps rather smugly—for their portraits in the nude. The "theory of rotundity" is systematically applied not only in these portraits of people, but also in such still-life paintings as *Sunflowers, Fruits on the Table,* and—most impressively—*Still Life with Pig's Head* (all 1968).

Other Semiabstract Painters

Among the many Colombian artists who have felt the influence of Obregón, the most notable is probably Enrique Grau (b. 1920). Born in the old fortified seaport of Cartagena de Indias, he studied art in Bogotá and then received a stipend from the Colombian government to study at the Art Students League in New York (1940–43). He lived for a time in Italy, mostly in Florence, and in 1964 returned to live and work in New York. In 1957, he was awarded the First Prize in Painting at the Tenth Salon of Colombian Artists. He participated in the biennial exhibitions of Barcelona (1955), Venice (1958), São Paulo (1959), and Córdoba (1964).

Picasso was the dominant influence on Grau's work during the 1950's, as can be seen in such works as *Figure* (oil), *Still Life* (crayon), and *Still Life and Skull* (crayon), all dating from 1957. Another painting of the same year, *Elegy to a Martyr,* is also quite Picassoesque, and is interesting to compare with Obregón's

Mourning for a Dead Student. It is clear that at this time Grau had not yet come under the influence of Obregón; this was to occur after 1957, and is adumbrated in such a work as *Woman with Flower Vase* (oil, 1959). Yet, by 1963, he had completely freed himself of this influence too, as revealed in the works that he sent to the second Córdoba Bienal: *The Model, Serenade No. 2,* and *Still Life.* A comparison of the last-mentioned with the still lifes of 1957 shows that Grau has taken possession of an entirely different pictorial world. There is no straining toward abstraction, either cubist or expressionist; instead, an apparently random but pictorially precise representation of "real" objects realistically depicted. Yet it is evident—or so it seems to me—that the aim of the painting is not realistic. Why these particular objects— vases, pitcher, cups, bowl, bird-cage, looking-glass, spectacles, toy blocks, knives, etc.—in this particular order, arranged on the four shelves of a wooden cupboard? One recalls a much earlier figurative painting by Grau, *A Glimpse at Your Future* (1954), which depicts a carnival barker selling tickets for a fortune-teller's side-show (*Una mirada en su porvenir,* reads the legend on his ticket-seller's stand). The fortune-teller's face in a kind of arched niche, the details of the ticket stand, the blending of the exotic and the commonplace, seem to prefigure such a work as the *Still Life* of 1964, with its feeling for the mystery and pathos of every-day objects in arbitrary juxtaposition.

David Manzur (b. 1929), like Grau, studied in the United States, as well as in Bogotá and Spain. He was awarded two consecutive Guggenheim Fellowships (1961–63), and received in 1964 the John F. Kennedy Memorial Award Fellowship from the Pan American Union. His rather densely organized semiabstract canvases are figurative only by allusion: *Landscape with Instrument, Geometry of the Sun, For Velázquez* (all shown at the Córdoba Bienal of 1964).

Alberto Gutiérrez (b. 1935) is another artist who studied in the United States (at the University of Florida and in New York) as well as in Europe (Amsterdam and Paris). In 1964, he obtained the First Prize for Painting at the Fourth National Art Festival in Cali, Colombia. At this time he was painting a series of canvases collectively titled *Summa,* combining abstract expressionism with figurative interpolations, including graffiti. Two of these paintings were included in the 1964 Córdoba Bienal (Nos. II and V), and two others (Nos. VI and XI) in *The Emergent Decade* (1965–66). Together with such a work as the powerful *Three Days in May* (1964), these paintings place Gutiérrez in the front ranks of the neofigurative movement in Latin America.

Sculpture: Negret

Edgar Negret, called by Marta Traba "the only contemporary sculptor of Colombia to assimilate and make his own the convictions that nourish modern sculpture," was born in Popayán in 1920. He studied at the School of Fine Arts in Cali, where he had his first one-man show in 1943. Others soon followed: in Bogotá (1946), New York (1950), Paris (1951), Madrid (1953), Washington (1956). From 1951 to 1955, Negret lived in Europe, then in New York for the next eight years. For a time he taught at the New School for Social Research in New York and made a study of indigenous American art with a research grant from UNESCO. Since 1945 he has participated in many national and international exhibitions, including the São Paulo Bienal (Silver Medal, 1965), the Venice Biennale (David Bright Prize for Sculpture, 1968), and *Documenta IV* (Kassel, 1968). In 1967 he was awarded the Grand Prize for the Arts at the XIX National Salon of Colombia.

Until about 1953, Negret's work was largely eclectic, an assimilation of many contemporary styles. His early work was representational, as in *Virgin* (1944) and *Girl at the Window* (1947). But already, as Marta Traba has observed, one notes the tendency to subordinate representation in favor of formal and abstract elements, particularly "the isolating, selecting, and organizing of planes."[22] He was working with metal, stone, wood, and plaster, later adding fine wire as a contrasting factor. His commitment to abstraction is fully evident in the *Saint Sebastian* (plaster and wood, 1951), where the theme of the saint's martyrdom is reduced to its simplest elements: a vertical molded slab pierced by pieces of wood.

The sulpture titled *Traffic Signal* (polychromed iron, 1953) utilizes Negret's favorite medium and signals a very important aspect of his work, which might be called the "industrial phase," characterized by freely imaginative interpretations of mechanical objects and industrial constructions. Another example from the same period is *Sign for an Aquarium* (polychromed iron, 1955), in which open curvilinear forms define a composition that is both dynamic and graceful.

During the 1950's, Negret also created a series that he titled *Magic Apparatus*, which Paul Damaz has aptly described as "combining precise geometric construction and mysterious poetry."[23] The first of these inventions in metal dates from 1954; No. 16 was done in 1958. This series might be regarded as the obverse of Negret's industrial phase. We have here the illusion of functionalism: tubes, cylinders, pistons, wheels—all kinds of plausible mechanisms transformed into marvels of impracticality by the artist's imagination. In *Magic Apparatus*, the artist is an illusionist, which is another name for magician.

During the 1960's, Negret continued to work with polychromed iron, in a further development of his industrial phase. He remained partial to strong primary colors, as in *The Bridge* (*Homage to Paul Foster*, 1968), painted bright red. Negret uses his theme as a sort of reservoir of ideas, form which he extracts structural elements that enable him to create variations on the theme. There are, for instance, several contrasting though related versions of *The Bridge*, as also of *Tower* (1968). In works of this period Negret tends to avoid strictly horizontal or vertical planes. *Tower No. II*, for example, looks like a modern industrial version of the leaning tower of Pisa. *The Bridge No. II* is cantilevered at an angle to convey the idea of a thrust into space. In terms of contemporary sculpture, Negret's recent works are not large (*The Bridge* is 59 inches long; *Tower No. II* is 38 inches high). Gigantism is no part of his aesthetic ambition. His gift is for the poetic vision translated into a precise construction: metal and mystery.

[22] *Art in Latin America Today: Colombia.* Pan American Union, 1959, p. 9.
[23] Paul Damaz, *Art in Latin American Architecture.* Reinhold Publishing Corporation, 1963, p. 64.

3

Nativism
and Modernism
on the
West Coast

PERU

*P*ERU, Bolivia, and Ecuador, with their large Indian populations, have been deeply affected by the heritage of the indigenous cultures that flourished before the coming of the Spaniards. Peru was the center of the Incan empire as well as the seat of the most important Spanish Viceroyalty in South America. This twofold and essentially antagonistic heritage has created a cultural dichotomy that manifests itself in many phases of Peruvian intellectual life. It is customary, for example, to divide Peruvian historians and national exegetes into two camps, the *indigenistas* and the *hispanistas*, those whose interpretations stress the values of indigenous culture and those who emphasize the importance of the Spanish heritage. While the dichotomy can be exaggerated and is not always applicable to individual cases, it nevertheless has been a significant factor in the Peruvian search for a national identity. There is no doubt that certain intellectuals, such as José Mariátegui and Luis Valcárcel, have placed more emphasis on the Indian culture and have virtually repudiated the Spanish heritage.[1] Others, like Ricardo Palma, glorified the latter. Others,

[1] Cf. Luis E. Valcárcel: *Ruta cultural del Perú* (Mexico, 1945).

again, like José de la Riva Agüero, attempted to reconcile the two cultures, and to seek national unity through a synthesis. Riva Agüero was the first modern Peruvian writer to travel extensively through the Indian communities of the cordillera and to report what he saw in a remarkable book, called *Paisajes peruanos (Peruvian Landscapes)*, written in 1912–15. While Riva Agüero drew attention to the "human geography" of Peru and stressed the necessity of incorporating the indigenous population into the national life, a younger and more radical writer, José Mariátegui, combined Marxism with nativism in a brilliant and very influential book titled *Siete Ensayos de Interpretacion de la Realidad Peruana (Seven Essays for Interpreting Peruvian Reality)*, published in 1928.

The title of Mariátegui's book epitomizes the dominant theme of Peruvian thought since the final decades of the nineteenth century; more precisely, since Peru's disastrous defeat by Chile in the War of the Pacific (1879–83), which aroused the country's leaders from their complacency, embarked them on a long process of "national reconstruction," and involved them in a persistent and often polemical search for the "reality" of Peru as a nation rather than as a depository of past glories. Racial, cultural, and geographical factors had contributed to the fragmentation of Peru, its division into relatively isolated sectors. Millions of Indians spoke their native tongues and lived in extremely primitive conditions. At the same time, the grandeur of the Andean setting and of certain ancient ruins (such as Machu Picchu and Sacsahuaman); the continued use of the llama as a beast of burden; the retention of "native" costumes, festivals, dances, and musical instruments (though often mixed with European elements)—in short, the whole panorama of an indigenous culture in an immensely imposing natural environment—exerted an irresistible attraction not only on poets and other writers, but most especially on the visual artists, the painters and print-makers and sculptors, who saw in all this an inviting blend of the picturesque and the grandiose, of the traditional and the novel, of the familiar and the sublime. For many of them, this became the "Peruvian reality" that everyone was seeking to discover. No wonder, then, that the first strong movement in Peruvian painting of the twentieth century was compounded of nationalism and nativism.

Prior to about 1920, Peruvian painting had been strictly academic and derivative, even though some painters, notably Francisco Laso and Teófilo Castillo, occasionally turned to local subjects. Castillo (1857–1922), like his literary contemporary Ricardo Palma, author of the celebrated *Tradiciones peruanas*, was attracted by the picturesque and romantic aspects of the viceroyal period. After a trip to Europe in 1909, Castillo discovered impressionism, and the results can be seen in one of his best paintings, *The Burial of Santa Rosa* (1912). In 1919 he left Peru, deeply hurt by his failure to be appointed director of the newly-founded National School of Fine Arts The post was given to a more strictly academic painter, Daniel Hernández. Of more consequence was the work, mostly in watercolors, of the popular artist Pancho Fierro (1803–1879), a self-taught mulatto who depicted in a vivid and often humorous manner the types, the trades, the festivities, the dances—in short, the everyday life—of Peru in the nineteenth century. Because he created a personal style nourished on the vernacular, his work is still very much alive.

The artistic situation of Peru from about 1920 to 1930 was somewhat similar to that of Mexico, though with important differences. What they shared were nationalism, nativism, a trend toward Marxism, and a tendency to accept the doctrine of the decadence of the West. To these should be added a rejection of extreme innovation, as reflected in Mariátegui's declaration that, "Futurism, Cubism, Dadaism—pirouettes of the decadent bourgeoisie—would never arise in Peru." The cultural review *Amauta*, founded and directed by Mariátegui, was far to the Left politically but not artistically. The atmosphere was receptive to the ideas and the example of the Mexican nationalist movement. The Peruvian artist through whom that influence was most strongly exerted in Peru was José Sabogal.

Sabogal and the Indigenistas

José Sabogal (1888–1956) was born in Cajabamba, in northern Peru, a region of strongly indigenous character, as reflected in the many place-names of Indian origin: Sayapullo, Ositacocha, Cachachi, Olucmapampa, Uticyaco, Yamaluc. It is located between the Central and the Eastern Cordillera of the Andes, in the midst of a grandly imposing lanscape, remote and isolated. Part Indian himself, Sabogal grew up in this region where native customs and traditions persisted, and where the overwhelming beauty and power of the landscape were bound to make a deep impression on him. He early displayed artistic inclinations, but not until 1910, when he was twenty-two years old, did he receive any systematic training in art. This was in Buenos Aires, where he worked for three years at the School of Fine Arts. Upon his return to Peru, he spent some time in the ancient Incan city of Cuzco and its environs, painting local landscapes, scenes, and types. Some of his best canvases are from this period: for example, *Street in Cuzco*, *Elections in the Sierra*, *Carnival in Rilcara*. During this time he was observing clearly and attempting faithfully to depict—within his technical limitations, which he never completely overcame—the characteristic features of an environment that he knew and loved. His peril was that he too often came under the spell of the merely picturesque.

In 1909, while on a visit to Europe, he came strongly under the influence of the Spanish painter Ignacio Zuloaga, who specialized in "local color," replete with popular scenes and characteristic types, and who influenced many Latin American painters besides Sabogal (among them Diego Rivera). Without either Zuloaga's talent or technique, Sabogal could apply only the most superficial aspects of that master's art to his own search for the pictorial reality of Peru. Then, in 1922, on another visit abroad, Sabogal received the impact of a much stronger influence: he went to Mexico for the first time and saw the work of the Mexican muralists. True, their work was still in its incipient stages, but their doctrines—nativism, nationalism, social realism, and the rest—had already found militant expression (for instance, in the 1922 Manifesto of the Syndicate). Sabogal eagerly imbibed these doctrines. He returned to Peru a dogmatic indigenist and a doctrinaire nationalist, obsessed with the notion of creating a national school of Peruvian painting based on the exploitation of native themes. He placed increasing emphasis on descriptive content, to the detriment of technique and formal construction. It was then, in the words of the Peruvian critic Juan Acha, "that he lost his promising use of impasto and the humility and freshness of his earlier works." But he became a national figure, important and influential, the recognized leader of the *indigenista* movement. When, in 1933, he was appointed director of the National School of Fine Arts (he held that position until 1943), his power and influence greatly increased, and he and his followers dominated the scene for a long time. But he remained a controversial figure, politically as well as artistically, and his ouster came as the result of a quarrel with the Minister of Education. Thereafter, his prestige rapidly declined, owing not only to his fall from power but also to the pressure of new currents in the artistic life of Peru.

The type of painting advocated by Sabogal and his followers might be described as Spanish *costumbrismo* (depiction of local scenes and customs) transported to the Andes, with an admixture of social realism imported from Mexico, and some elements of heroic allegory from the same source. On the positive side, Sabogal helped to arouse interest in the native arts and crafts of Peru, past and present, with his careful and loving study of indigenous artifacts, textiles, and ceramics—a study that particularly influenced his work after 1940, in his so-called "adobe style." If his inspiration had equaled his aspiration, and if his technique had equaled his inspiration, he might have been at least the Diego Rivera of Peru. As it was, the vast pictorial record contained in his painting is for the most part neither inspired nor inspiring. As Acha observes, "Composition in all his works is extremely simple: a figure or a central group is surrounded by pictorial padding."[2] His prints, especially his woodcuts, are the best of his work. In this medium he achieved an individuality and a technical skill too seldom present in his paintings.

[2] Juan Acha, *Art in Latin America Today: Peru*. Pan American Union, 1961, p. 8.

Withal, Sabogal's historical place in Peruvian art cannot be discounted. He became an institution, he had a national following. In 1957, the year of his death, a retrospective exhibit of his work, containing some 320 items, was held in Lima. It summarized not only his life's work, but also the aspirations of an era, the persistent search for the reality of Peruvian culture. Shortly before he died, Sabogal summed up his artistic creed by saying, "Art is the translation of man and nature, the capturing of an authentic and enduring essence in the national soul; it is the immediate obligation of every Peruvian artist." This creed is perhaps no longer valid: the national soul is out of fashion. Yet the translation of man and nature remains an important function of art; the crucial question may be what is meant by "an authentic and enduring essence."

The painters who were the closest followers of Sabogal have been called *indigenistas sabogalinos* to distinguish them from the independent nativists. These *indigenistas* include Julia Codesido (b. 1892), Ricardo Flores (b. 1893), Camilo Blas (b. 1903), and Enrique Camino Brent (b. 1909). Of these, the most interesting is Julia Codesido. In spite of a visit to Mexico in 1935, she has never subordinated aesthetic values to any doctrinaire ideology. If the influence of Siqueiros is only too evident in some of her canvases, there are many others, such as *At the Church Door*, in which she achieves compositional strength with a semiabstract treatment of the pictorial elements: a tree, a wall, a fountain, the hooded figures of women crossing a square. Especially effective is her handling of architectural forms in counterpoint with the human figure.

Of the independent nativists, the most interesting was Jorge Vinatea Reinoso (1900–1931), from Arequipa. Juan Ríos said of him that he was "gifted with a pictorial sense of the picturesque." There is no "padding" in his canvases, nothing static. He painted the usual typical scenes; but the Indians, the llamas, the churches, the *chicherías* (taverns), the mountains, the dancers, are all *inside* the painting. They occupy the entire pictorial space in a dynamic relationship of each part to the other. The landscape, instead of being merely a background, is brought *into* the space of the canvas. It is a pity that Reinoso's promising career was so untimely cut off by death.

A place apart belongs to Mario Urteaga (1875–1957), a self-taught painter from Cajamarca with no academic pretensions. Without being exactly a "primitive," his approach to art was relatively naïve, and he was able to preserve the freshness, the spontaneity, the directly captured vision, and the plastic quality that is lacking in the work of many official *indigenistas*. In such a painting as *The Fight*—depicting a street brawl—there is a genuine projection of emotion as well as a vividly observed reality. Urteaga was probably closer to the Peruvian vernacular than any other artist since Pancho Fierro.

Sérvulo Gutiérrez (1915–1962), self-taught painter and sculptor, one-time boxer, was influenced by Picasso, Portinari, and Siqueiros. He tried to maintain his identity as a Peruvian artist while avoiding the localism of the doctrinaire indigenists. To accomplish this he relied heavily on the symbol, the metaphor, the power of association suggested by a title. In a painting titled *The Andes* (1943), the peaks of the cordillera in the background are dwarfed by the gigantic female figure in the foreground, awkward, vulnerable, exposed to the elements, shielding her face with folded arms and huge hands. What is the message? Is it allegory, personification, symbolism? The artist has substituted metaphor in place of anecdote—doubtless a step in the right direction. Yet the "message," the theme, is still outside of the painting itself. Shortly afterwards, Gutiérrez went to Buenos Aires (1944), where he came under the influence of the painter Pettoruti. As a result he began to strive for a mastery of form, for the achievement of a plastic quality, even though his work continued to be figurative. His portraits and still-lifes done after 1945 proved that Sérvulo Gutiérrez was capable of continuous growth.

Beginnings of Modernism

Juan Manuel Ugarte Eléspuru (b. 1911) is an accomplished painter who at one time was much influenced by the Mexican muralists, especially Rivera. He undertook an ambitious mural project in the former church and convent of Santo Tomás (now a school), consisting of a large historical-allegorical fresco, elaborately organized and highly detailed, depicting the Past, the Present, and the Future of Peru. But there was no continuous support or demand for large-scale mural painting in Peru; hence Ugarte Eléspuru, like most of his fellow-painters, turned mostly to easel painting, in which he has done distinguished figurative work. One admires, for example, the quasiexpressionistic force of *The Little Saint* (oil and tempera, 1951), and the disciplined skill of a still-life such as *The Black Dish* (oil, 1959).

Some contemporary currents had been reaching Peru even during the heyday of indigenism, notably in the work of the experimental painter Macedonio de la Torre (1893–1965), who absorbed and reflected almost every style known during his lifetime, from surrealism to *tachisme* ("action painting")—not forgetting his own brand of nativism, concentrated on landscapes of the lowlands rather than the *sierra* that held such a strong attraction for the *sabogalistas*. Talented and adventurous as he was, he lacked direction and discipline, so that his efforts failed to counteract the influence of Sabogal. That task was achieved by a painter of completely different temperament, an artist whose work developed logically from one premise to another, guided by the strictest discipline and capacity for self-criticism. This was Ricardo Grau who, in the words of Juan Acha, "familiarized the public with pictorial quality and re-established its importance."

Ricardo Grau (b. 1908) spent his formative years (1926–37) in Paris, at first under the influence of Cézanne, later working in the ateliers of André Lhote, Othon Friesz, and especially Fernand Léger, who impressed him most deeply and lastingly. In Europe he also became friendly with the surrealist painters, notably Salvador Dali and René Magritte, and made the acquaintance of Breton and Eluard. These associations drew him for a time into the realm of surrealism, both in oil paintings and drawings, but without any deep or enduring conviction, since at heart his main interest was in the purely formal aspects of painting. He has always tried to remain aloof from any elements not inherently a part of the plastic composition, and particularly from all anecdotal or literary allusions.

When Grau returned to Peru in 1937, he found the folklorism and regionalism of the *indigenista* movement at its apogee. This he regarded as a deviation from true artistic values, and he accordingly reacted against it, not so much by polemics as by the example and prestige of his own work. As Juan Ríos wrote, Grau was the first Peruvian painter effectively to occupy an aesthetic position equally removed from the "monotonous recipe of the nativists, the routine academic formulae, and the sensational exploitation of novelty." In Acha's opinion, Grau's presence was "decisive" in the transition of Peruvian painting from a local to an international outlook. The first concrete step in that direction was the exhibition of Grau's work after his return to Lima, in 1937. The next and very important step was Grau's appointment as Director of the National School of Fine Arts in 1945. Assisted by such progressive painters as Manuel Ugarte, Sabino Springett, Alberto Dávila, and Carlos Castillo, Grau brought about much-needed reforms, and above all succeeded in establishing complete autonomy for the faculty—not always an easy task when educational institutions are financed by the government. And indeed, this happy situation came to an end with the accession to power of General Odría in 1949, which also terminated Grau's tenure as Director. But in 1956, after the restoration of democratic government, Ugarte Eléspuru was appointed Director of the School of Fine Arts, continuing the measures for reform and making it one of the best institutions of its kind in the Americas.

At the time of his first exhibition in Lima, in 1937, Grau's work was entirely figurative, consisting of still-lifes, portraits, nudes, landscapes, and some urban scenes, including several of Lima itself. All these were done with a skilled professionalism and a technical proficiency not hitherto known in Peru. During the 1940's came Grau's surrealist ventures, and during the 1950's he turned to abstract painting. This was a natural development of his life-long concern with pure form and with plastic values in art. He began by painting without a model and gradually the figure disappeared completely. It was in 1959 that he exhibited his abstract work in a one-man show at the Institute of Contemporary Art in Lima, receiving wide attention. He had achieved his own abstract style through a long process of self-examination, partly by assimilating and reworking pre-Columbian elements and partly by developing a personal vocabulary of colors and forms, all strongly articulated and dynamically organized. He aimed at cleanness of execution within a geometrical framework on a flat surface. In 1959, his show included some objective work, but since then all his work has been nonobjective. He has preferred to work with larger canvases, up to about six by eight feet in size, and recently his main concern has been with chromatic effects over a large surface. He has used all media except engraving: oil, gouache, watercolor, pencil, charcoal, pen and ink. In all his work he has unswervingly pursued an ideal of purely plastic and chromatic expression.

The Rise of Abstract Expressionism

The first exhibition of purely abstract painting in Peru took place in 1949, at the Galería Lima, with a show by Enrique Kleiser, which passed virtually unnoticed. It took another painter's one-man show, held two years later, to provoke a polemic and arouse general interest in the issue of abstract versus representational art. The painter who achieved that distinction, and who gave the opposition no quarter, was named Fernando de Szyszlo.

Szyszlo, born in Lima in 1925, attended the School of Fine Arts of the Catholic University there, studying with the Austrian-born Adolfo Winternitz who had founded the school in 1939. He completed his studies in 1946, and the following year had his first one-man show at the Peruvian-American Cultural Institute in Lima. At this time his painting was figurative; it was only after further work and observation in Europe that he turned to abstraction. Upon his return to Peru in 1951 he showed his abstract work. When it was received with some hostility the artist reacted vigorously. As he told Cornell Capa many years later, "The more common adjectives applied to my work then were 'decadent', 'un-Peruvian', 'immoral', and the like."

The fact is that Szyszlo, far from simply following international trends for the sake of being up-to-date, was seeking a deeper and more meaningful identification with Peruvian culture. He found in pre-Columbian art a kind of abstraction—autonomous, powerful—that appealed to him both spiritually and technically. He loved "the solid, perennial, earthy quality" of the adobe structures of the ancient Peruvians. He began to study the textiles, the ceramics, the ruined temples and cities, and also the history, the legends, the languages and lore of pre-Hispanic peoples of Peru—not as an archaeologist, but as a creative artist possessing a strong affinity for his cultural environment. As a result of all this he developed a style that might be called "abstract nativism," not directly utilizing any specific indigenous elements—designs, symbols, pictographs—but attempting to express in abstract forms and colors his own subjective feeling, both emotional and lyrical, for the grandeur and mystery, the splendor and tragedy, of this vanquished civilization that has left so many and such extraordinary traces in the Andean region. In 1963, Szyszlo summed up his aesthetic position by saying, "I believe that if some day we are to achieve our identity, both as painters and as a human group, this will come to pass in the degree that we commit ourselves not only to our individual and collective destiny, but also to the heritage of our past and to our present reality."[3]

Those words were written at a time when Szyszlo had just completed a series of paintings inspired by a Quechua elegy on the death of the last ruling Inca, Atahualpa, treacherously executed by the Spaniards in Cajamarca. The date of its composition is not known, but it is considered an authentic expression in the tradition of Quechua lyrical poetry, of the suffering, humiliation, and spiritual strength of a people whose destiny is symbolized in the tragic fate of the Inca Atahualpa. The thirteen paintings of the series are firmly situated within the context of the elegy, with each painting identified by a line, a phrase, or an image taken from the poem. The title of the first painting, for example, is taken from the opening of the poem, "What rainbow is this black rainbow that rises?" (Szyszlo uses the Quechua text for his titles, though in this series he also provides a Spanish translation.) And the last painting of the series takes its title from the penultimate verse, "Fortified with this vision." The

[3] In catalog of exhibition, *Serie sobre el poema "Apu Inca Atawallpaman,"* Instituto de Arte Contemporáneo (Lima, 1963).

series *Apu Inca Atawallpaman* is a continuation of the style that Szyszlo had begun to develop some ten years earlier, with the *Cajamarca* series, the *Yawar Fiesta* series, and a large number of individual paintings, such as *Black Sun* (1959). He further explored this vein in the *Machu Picchu* series (1964), and in other paintings of the 1960's. By 1966 he had unquestionably succeeded in creating a new nativism, which had the immense advantage of being as thoroughly contemporary as it was deeply rooted in the Peruvian past.

Thomas M. Messer has written very perceptively about Szyszlo's art:

> *What seems most important to me in Szyszlo's work is the intensive presence of content with definable visual, literary, and formal components. The visual element comes to the fore in Szyszlo's landscape allusions, which at times are traceable to a particular reminiscence of the Peruvian landscape. The literary component, always present in cultivated minds, tends, in Szyszlo's case, to focus upon indigenous themes, which then strengthen the native timbre already contained in the visual allusion. Finally, the formal component, evolving from cubism and deriving its initial momentum from Tamayo, furnishes the channel through which visual and literary allusions can be brought to the surface.... Szyszlo's is not an art that can be separated from the palpable reality of the observed world, nor does it imitate such reality. Rather, it would seem, are we viewing formal analogies, parables if you wish, whose ideated transformations read like memories of the observed. From this act of mutation comes the evocative power of Szyszlo's forms, which contain a reality substance far exceeding in meaningfulness the observed fact or the literary plot from which they ultimately derive.... It is rare to see the unique personal and the generally valid, the indigenous motivation and the international common denominator, so intensely interlocked....*[4]

The line of abstract nativism, within the general tendency of abstract expressionism, has been followed by a number of other Peruvian painters, including some who, like Sabino Springett (b. 1914), made the transition from overt, representational nativism to the symbolic, nonobjective expression of indigenous values. Carlos Aitor Castillo (b. 1913) and Alberto Dávila (b. 1914) have also worked within this domain, though one has the impression

[4] Messer and Capa, *The Emergent Decade*, p. 88.

that they are not so deeply committed to the indigenous theme as to the postulates of abstract expressionism itself. The latter statement would appear to be true also of some of the younger painters, such as Milner Cajahuaringa, Arturo Kubotta Carbajal, Fernando Vega, Venancio Shinki Huaman (all born in 1932), Enrique Galdos-Rivas (b. 1933), Manuel Jiménez (b. 1935), and Daniel Yaya Arias (b. 1936). Some of these painters prefer purely abstract titles, while others tend to make specific geographical or literary allusions, as in Yaya Arias' *Of the Black Heralds*, which refers to a book by the Peruvian poet César Vallejo. Who, however, can specify the locus of Castillo's *Landscape of a Memory* (1964)? And the sceptic may ask, "Does it matter?" Perhaps only to the artist himself—and to those who still believe that it is the task of the artist to express the "soul" of his own country.

That such a view still has force in Peru is proved by an open letter written to Thomas Messer by the Peruvian art critic Carlos Rodríguez Saavedra in 1965. According to this writer,

> The best of Peruvian painters are probing the soul of Peru. Adhering to an international standard, therefore, is not their true goal. I am sure that this adherence will develop in some instances, but only incidentally, when the essence of the Peruvian soul has become part of the artists' work. . . . Some artists . . . have demonstrated remarkable insight into the essential values of Peru. Their insight has stimulated our painters to follow suit, to search out and decipher the true nature of our country.[5]

If this point of view is valid, then the "search for Peruvian reality" proclaimed by Mariátegui in 1928 continues in the realm of art some forty years later; and this, in turn, would indicate a continuity of purpose, though not of method, between the *indigenismo* of Sabogal and the abstract nativism of today. While not denying validity to this view, one may question its exclusivity, and the dogmatic assertion that the *best* Peruvian painters are necessarily those most concerned with "probing the soul of Peru."

For my part, I fail to detect any evidence of national soul-probing in the work of two of the most original and gifted of contemporary Peruvian painters, Emilio Rodríguez-Larraín and Jorge Piqueras.

[5] *Ibid.*, p. 91.

Rodríguez-Larraín (b. 1928) studied both architecture and painting in his native city, Lima, where he had his first one-man show in 1950. Two years later he went to Paris for further study, and in 1956 he traveled in the United States. Since 1957, he has participated in many international exhibitions, including the Venice Biennials of 1960 and 1964. He now lives in Paris. George Staempfli states that Rodríguez-Larraín's art is "very personal and very abstract, in spite of close metaphoric relations to realistic subjects." This painter likes to give metaphoric, literary, or allusive (and sometimes cryptic) titles to his paintings: *Luna plus la lune* (1961), *Momaie du Pape-Duchamps* (1962), *Paracentèse de l'Homme Cheval* (1963–64), *Go to Hell* (1964), and a series titled *The Young Girl and Death* (1962). To be sure, there are some titles alluding to Peru: *Ancestral Memory* (1960), *Ancestral Landscape* (1960), *Viceroy* (1961), and one canvas called simply and unequivocally *Peru* (1961). But this last happens to be one of his purely abstract paintings, consisting of a large square (segmented at the top) against a solid black background. It is possible that the series titled *My Geologic Reconciliation* (1961) refers to Peru. For that matter, does the *Anonymous 7* (1960), with its gold shapes against a background of dark blue, refer to the gold of the Incas? These are matters of speculation—idle or otherwise—but what can be perceived with certainty is the quality of these paintings, which create their own universe of images, colors, and perceptual relationships. Working with a mixture of oil, tempera, and wax colors, Rodríguez-Larraín—particularly in his paintings since 1963—has achieved a kind of personal surrealism, at once decorative and demonic, flowing with fantasy and freedom, yet always fully realized as an integrated vision.

Jorge Piqueras (b. 1925) has also chosen to live in Paris—which may not necessarily mean that he has forgotten Peru. But if he has encrusted any fragments of the Peruvian soul in his paintings, they remain a mystery to the beholder. I agree with the French critic Alain Jouffroy that, "The pictures of Jorge Piqueras are very beautiful." I also admire the critic who dares to use an old-fashioned term from the traditional vocabulary of aesthetics to describe the work of a young painter of today. The usual terms for describing recent and current art trends scarcely apply to these paintings; they are abstract, but neither geometric nor expressionist, neither hard-edge nor *tachiste*. They use geometrical forms, to be sure, but also nongeometrical forms. There are neofigurative elements—strange little anthropomorphic and vegetable shapes floating like fantastic figments in the space between the strongly delineated rectilinear or curvilinear areas. Borders that at first sight seem to be purely decorative are soon perceived to be swarming with hallucinatory configurations issuing from the realm of the irrational. Yet these paintings *are* very beautiful—we must insist on the appropriateness of the semiobsolete term. They are beautiful in design, in form, in composition, and in their extraordinary color harmonies—*Mistaken Reflections* (1963), is a striking example.

Alain Jouffroy sees the paintings of Piqueras as a confrontation of the rational and the irrational,

> *They give an impression of perfect mastery, balance, and control; but on close examination we discover the delirium—the dreams, the boxed fury—that they contain.... The "monsters" we make out in the background of his pictures look like larvae; but these larvae are imprisoned on all sides; the squares, the rectangles, ovals and rhomboids confining them impose on them an order which is not their own but which they cannot avoid.... Piqueras has created a language of forms for himself, and all his work clarifies the articulation of that language.*[6]

As of 1968, neofiguratism had very few adherents in Peru. Its two principal representatives, Juan Manuel de la Colina (b. 1917) and Gerardo Chávez López both happen to be residents of Paris. Of the two, only Chávez López paints in the somewhat violent, expressionistic manner of the current Latin American neofigurative painters, who are most strongly represented in Argentina. The three paintings that he sent to the third Bienal de Córdoba in 1966, including *Images Disconnected from Appearance*, reveal the metaphysical, quasisurrealist tendency of his present work.

Luis Arias (b. 1932) is an exponent of Pop art specializing (during the 1960's) in postal covers. At the third Córdoba Bienal he exhibited five paintings, each titled simply *Envelope*, with a corresponding number. He lived in Buenos Aires for ten years

[6] Catalog of Piqueras exhibition, Staempfli Gallery, New York (1963).

(1953–62) and studied there with Rosa Frey. Jaime Dávila puts his faith in geometric designs, but with a blend of informalism that keeps him oustide the camp of the constructivists. Emilio Hernández Saavedra (b. 1940) appears to strike the same sort of balance between informalism and Pop art in such paintings as *Sandwich Box* and *Tic-tac Box* (both 1966). José Tang is an exponent of Pop art.

Thus, in 1968, Peruvian painting represented a fairly standard cross-section of contemporary trends, but with the major emphasis on abstract expressionism and informalism. This emphasis, as well as the process of national soul-searching, will doubtless diminish during the coming decades, when the artists born after 1930 take over the center of the stage.

Sculpture: Roca Rey

The leading contemporary sculptor of Peru—and one of the foremost of Latin America—is Joaquín Roca Rey (b. 1923). After an early naturalistic phase he evolved toward a semiabstract style, with open forms, strongly influenced by Henry Moore. From the time of his first one-man show in 1948, he has consistently developed a personal style and a mastery of diverse materials, though his preference is for working with metals (bronze, aluminum, steel). He began to exhibit individually in Europe in 1951 (Florence, Madrid, Paris) and later had one-man shows in Rio de Janeiro (1957), São Paulo (1959), and Washington (Pan American Union, 1959). He participated in the Bienal de São Paulo three times, and in many other international exhibitions. His work has been acquired by a number of museums in the United States, including the Dallas Museum of Fine Arts and the Milwaukee Art Center. His bronze sculpture, *Project for a Monument to the Unknown Political Prisoner* (1953) is in the permanent collection of the Pan American Union. Other works of the 1950's are the graceful *Butterfly Hunter* and the massive *Maternity* (both in aluminum), the latter making a complete break with all traditional representations of this familiar subject; it is an abstract representation of the act of birth. Toward the end of the decade, Roca Rey began to experiment with more complex, neobaroque steel structures, in which colors and textures are important compositional elements.

As professor at the National School of Fine Arts in Lima, Roca Rey has proved to be an excellent teacher who has trained a number of promising young sculptors, among whom may be mentioned Alberto Guzman, Varela Neyra, and Victor Aldave.

ECUADOR

As might be expected the contemporary art movement in Ecuador presents close parallels with that of Peru. In each country there was a derivative academic tradition, a strongly articulated nativist movement, and an eventual transition to international styles and contemporary modes of expression. The first Ecuadorian painter who can be identified with the contemporary scene is Manuel Rendón (b. 1894), who was born in Paris of Ecuadorian parents (his father was a distinguished diplomat, physician, and judge of the World Court at The Hague). He was educated in Paris, where he began to exhibit in 1916 and where he continued to live and work until 1937. In that year he went to Ecuador, living and painting for the next ten years in Cuenca, absorbing the mountain landscapes, the native folkways, and the local scenes. After 1947, he divided his time between Paris and Ecuador, with exhibits in Europe, Latin America, and the United States. His works have been acquired by the Musée d'Art Moderne of Paris and the San Francisco Museum of Art. During the 1950's, Rendón turned to abstract expressionism in the manner of the New School of Paris, with particular reference to the style of Nicolas de Staël.

The academic painter Camilo Egas (b. 1895) was influenced in his search for a national expression with social implications by the Mexican muralists. He also took some tips from surrealism, as in *Dream of Ecuador* (oil, 1939), which is evidently to be interpreted as an allegory of despair. It depicts the abject poverty and misery of peasants in a desolate mountain setting, the whole dominated by a large, emaciated female head projecting through the "roof" (merely a rough hide covering) of a miserable hut. The message is obvious; but so, unfortunately, is the influence of Salvador Dali.

During the first half of the present century, a number of Ecuadorian nativists or *indigenistas* went in search of local color, among them Leonardo Texada (b. 1902), Luis Alberto Heredia (g. 1909), Diógenes Paredes (b. 1902), Eduardo Kingman Riofríos (b. 1911), Jorge Levoyer (b. 1912), and Atahualpa Villacres (b. 1914). Heredia deliberately adopted a primitive manner, painting "in the style of the popular votive pictures executed for the villages and small towns" (as Lincoln Kirstein wrote). A typical example is his oil painting, *Plaza at Pomasqui*. Local color often appears along with social content in the work of these painters. For instance, in *Threshers* (tempera on cardboard, 1942), by Paredes, there is a sense of oppressive labor that emphasizes the economic plight of the Indian.

Of the painters in this group, Eduardo Kingman Riofríos has recently become especially important. From his native city of Loja, he went to Quito to study at the National School of Fine Arts. Later h⁀ studied with Camilo Egas in New York, where he was commissioned to do some paintings for the Ecuadorian Pavilion at the 1939 World's Fair. Returning to Ecuador the following year, he founded and directed the Caspicara Art Gallery in Quito, named for an Ecuadorian artist of the eighteenth century, Manuel Chili, who was called "Caspicara." For a while he was on the staff of the San Francisco Museum of Art (1945–46), but in 1947 was appointed Director of the National Museum of Art in Quito and Director of the National Artistic Patrimony. Besides oil paintings, he has also done woodcuts and illustrations.

Kingman's first important recognition came in 1936, when he obtained his country's highest artistic award, the Mariano Aguilera Prize. He then left the School of Fine Arts in order to live and paint among the Ecuadorian people, identifying himself completely with the nativist movement. He was, indeed, much influenced by the writings of Mariátegui and by the example of Sabogal in Peru, as well as by the Mexican muralists. He painted the local scene assiduously and for a long time was the leading exponent of indigenism in Ecuador. During the 1950's, however, we find him turning toward more abstract concepts, as in the oil painting titled *Submarine Dwelling* (1959), which shows a tendency toward free form with surrealist elements.

Oswaldo Guayasamín (b. 1919), is doubtless the Ecuadorian painter whose work is best known abroad, especially in the United States, where a traveling exhibit of his paintings was sponsored by the Department of State following his first one-man show in Quito. His oil painting on wood, *My Brother* (1942), was acquired by the New York Museum of Modern Art. It is a rather conventional portrait. Although Guayasamín studied for seven years at the School of Fine Arts in Quito, his strongest influences were Picasso and the Mexican muralists, especially Orozco. His style may be said to have resulted from the attempt to reconcile these two rather contradictory influences. The Colombian art critic Marta Traba accused him of having "sacked the most facile and obvious resources of the great Picassian repertory" in order to create what she disparagingly calls "americanismo picassiano." If so, he was not the only one to attempt such a feat; but perhaps he did it more conspicuously than most. The method might be described as a shot-gun wedding of modernism and nativism, "blessed" by social realism. Allegory, monumentalism, and emotionalism are its products, as displayed, for example, in *Days of Wrath* (1940), an allegory inspired by Malraux's *Le temps de mépris*. The painting titled *The Road of Tears* (1952) is literally a global tear-jerker, since it depicts the lamentation of the underprivileged masses who weep over their sad fate. If the sorrow were individually characterized, as in Portinari's portrayals of human suffering, it would be more convincing. A representative exhibition of Guayasamín's work was included in the IV Bienal of São Paulo, in 1957. In the exhibit *South American Art Today* (Dallas, 1959), he was represented by a canvas titled *Bull and Condor* (oil, 1959), which has a certain forceful dynamism. In addition to his easel paintings, Guayasamín has executed frescoes and other murals in Quito and elsewhere.

In 1965 the Grand Prize of the Municipality of Quito was awarded to the painter Aníbal Villacis (b. 1927), who was born in Ambato and began to draw and paint at a very early age. In 1948, he received a travel grant that enabled him to go to Paris and Madrid, where he studied at the Academia de San Fernando.

He lived for a while in Caracas, then traveled in Colombia, Brazil, the United States, and Europe again, before settling in Quito. During the 1950's, he was combining native themes with semi-abstract configurations remotely derived from cubism (*Still Life with Mask* [oil, 1957]). By the 1960's, however, his nativism remained explicit only in his titles, and the objects to which these referred served merely as a point of departure for abstract compositions in the manner of the Spanish informalists (*Interior of a Colonial Church, Dancer, Interior, Tropical Archtype*). Other canvases have cosmic connotations: *Image of Time, Dynamic Space*. All of these paintings are also identified simply by number (*Painting* 1, 2, 3, and so on), as if to emphasize their abstract imagery. Villacis was represented with eight paintings in the II Bienal of Córdoba (1964).

Oswaldo Viteri (b. 1931) studied architecture and became Professor of Art in the School of Architecture of the Central University of Quito. His art studies were with Jan Schreuder of Holland and Lloyd Wulf of the United States. In 1960, he obtained the Mariano Aguilera Prize in Quito and, in 1961, the first prize of the Salón Bolivariano de Pintura in Guayaquil. He also won honorable mention at the VI Bienal of São Paulo (1961), and was represented with six paintings in the II Bienal of Córdoba. His canvases in the latter exhibit, identified simply by number, were abstract expressionist, with emphasis on large contrasting areas in the manner of Franz Kline.

BOLIVIA

The important exhibition *Art of Latin America since Independence*, which circulated widely in the United States during 1966, included a painting by the Bolivian artist Arturo Borda (1883–1955), titled *Leonor Gonzálvez and José Borda* (1920). This is a double portrait of the artist's mother and father, seated; in the background is an imaginary landscape dominated by a large tree, with small figures of adults and children dispersed around it. The painting is certainly impressive, but it might have passed relatively unremarked in such a large collection (more than 400 works) had not the art critic of *The New York Times* selected it as "the most interesting" in the entire show and reproduced it in the Sunday art section of that widely read newspaper. This started a Borda revival, resulting in a retrospective exhibition of his work (La Paz; June, 1966), co-sponsored by the American Embassy; the theme: "A forgotten Bolivian artist rediscovered in the United States."

Arturo Borda left about five hundred paintings, which are owned by his brother Héctor. Self-taught in art, he was also a prolific writer and a social activist who, in 1921, organized a national confederation of workers. But, discouraged by lack of progress toward the ideal socialist society of which he dreamed, he lapsed into alcoholism, and the rest of his long life dragged out in poverty and obscurity. In the words of John Canaday:

> He painted everything from genre groups in the academic manner to surrealist fantasies with socio-aesthetic allegorical arguments like the curious Criticism of Modern Art. He painted imaginary landscapes of the Andes.... He painted Crucifixions, an Allegory of Progress, a despairing The Demolishers showing naked men in a domestic interior destroying the symbols of science and progress ... and portraits of his family and friends.[7]

Borda was a surrealist *malgré lui*, for he loved beauty and hated what he called the modern "crudities" of the futurists, the cubists, and the surrealists. Though his own work is uneven, it should no longer be ignored.

The Development of Nativism

The art movement in Bolivia resembles that of Peru and Ecuador in its development from figurative to abstract nativism. Cecilio Guzmán de Rojas (b. 1900), an academic painter trained in Spain, cultivated conventional nativism, following the example of Sabogal. Jorge de la Reza studied at Yale University, and has

[7] *The New York Times*, June 19, 1966, D 21. Includes a reproduction of Borda's *Criticism of Modern Art*. The portrait *Leonor Gálvez and José Borda* is reproduced in *Art of Latin America Since Independence* (Plate 85).

specialized in Indians and Andean landscapes, chiefly in tempera. Armando Pereira Pacheco (b. 1910) was strongly influenced by the didactic nationalism of the Mexican muralists. To an interviewer in 1948, he said, "The artist can educate his people in the history of their country by presenting it to them colorfully and graphically in murals and other paintings." Pacheco's *Maternity* (oil, 1946) is an essay in the monumental Mexican style. Like Rivera in Mexico, he has painted a whole gallery of Indian types, often strongly delineated, as in *The Ferryman* (of Lake Titicaca), *The Newsvendor* (an Indian woman), and *Indian Couple* (two women fording a stream). The transition from overt, figurative nativism to semiabstract and abstract nativism was achieved in the work of two fine painters: María Luisa Pacheco and Jorge Carrasco Núñez del Prado.

María Luisa Pacheco (b. 1919) studied in her native city of La Paz and, during 1951 and 1952, in Madrid with Daniel Vázquez Díaz. In 1956, she went to the United States, and since then has made her home in New York. She was three times awarded a fellowship by the John Simon Guggenheim Memorial Foundation, and has won numerous national and international awards. She has utilized cubist, expressionist, and abstract elements to project themes of her native land. There are cubist influences in such paintings as *Colonial Town* (1955), *Idols* (1956), and *White Figure* (1959). One of her most powerful canvases, *Palliri* (1958), depicts a woman miner who kneels in a distorted attitude of suffering—a figure almost subhuman in its anonimity, a symbol of despair. Here the approach is expressionist and reminds one of De Kooning. Another powerfully conceived female figure, more poetic in its semiabstract symbolism, is that of Antawara (*Twilight*; oil 1955). Semiabstract figuration is present in many of the paintings of the 1950's such as *Composition with Figures* (1957), *Seated Woman* (1959), and *White Figure* (1959). The paintings of the 1960's have moved toward a completely abstract expressionism, as in *Tihuanacu I* (oil and mixed media on canvas, 1964) and *Construction* (oil, 1962). The *Tihuanacu* series may be compared to the work of Szyszlo in Peru, in that both artists have used the resources of abstract expressionism to convey a telluric and spiritual identification with their native environment.

Jorge Carrasco Núñez del Prado (b. 1919) studied at the School of Fine Arts in La Paz where, in 1952, he was appointed professor of painting. From 1943 to 1963 he had thirty one-man shows in America and Europe. He has also worked as an illustrator. He has cultivated abstract expressionism with freely symbolic associations in such paintings as *Cosmic Crystalization, Large Universe,* and *Painting at 4,000 Meters* (the approximate altitude of La Paz), all shown at the Second Córdoba Bienal in 1964.

The line of abstract expressionism with associative connotations has also been followed by Moisés Chire Barrientos (b. 1930) in such paintings as *Tin-mining Shaft, Mineral Deposit,* and *The Enigmatic Stairs of Tihuanacu,* all dating from 1964. Various types of abstract expressionism are represented by Oscar Pantoja (b. 1925), Antonio Mariaca Arguedas (b. 1926), Alfredo La Placa (b. 1929), Antonio Llanque (b. 1935), and Alfredo Da Silva (b. 1936). Da Silva displays a strong telluric feeling in many of his paintings, for example *Andean Cosmogony, Genesis, Cosmos,* and *Spirit of the Earth* (1964). When he was given a one-man show at the Pan American Union in 1961, a commentator wrote: "His compositions suggest mineral forms, slabs of stone, or ancient monoliths, rendered with a sensitive feeling for color." One of his most striking works is titled *Homage to John F. Kennedy* (oil, 1964). In 1959, Da Silva was awarded the First Prize for Foreign Artists at the National Salon of Painting in Buenos Aires, and in 1962 he received a fellowship from the Pratt Institute of Art in New York. His paintings of the 1960's suggest views of the earth seen from a space capsule; he appears to be more concerned with cosmology than with ecology.

Among the younger Bolivian painters who have adhered to figurative painting are Lorgio Vaca (b. 1930), Gil Imaná Garrón (b. 1933), and Luis Zilveti Calderón (b. 1941). Of these Gil Imaná is the most overtly figurative, both in his landscapes and in his representation of local types. Lorgio Vaca tends toward semiabstract composition in his reinterpretation of familiar native themes, such as *Women in the River* and *Musicians.* Zilveti Calderón inclines toward expressionist neofiguratism in paintings like *Bird* (1964) and *The Bride* (1966). A list of his works reads like the usual nativist repertory—*Old Women, Burial, The Virgin of Copacabana*—but his neofigurative approach gives them a new spiritual and technical dimension. Another young artist, Domingo Parada (b. 1941), who studied for a year with Ivan Serpa in Rio de Janeiro, has brought to Bolivia a kind of free (not strictly geometrical) constructivism (*Construction 5* [1966]), combined with metaphysical aspirations (*Interior Universe* [1966]). Both Parada and Zilveti Calderón were well represented at the third Córdoba Bienal.

Sculptress of the Andes

Marina Núñez del Prado (b. 1910), whom Archipenko called the "sculptress of rolling curves and volumes symbolizing the Bolivian Indian," ranks high among contemporary artists of Latin America. In her distinctive sculpture she employs "spectacular native materials"—basalt, black granite, comanche granite (from the name of a local river), guayacán wood, white onyx—and with her semiabstract plastic rhythms she gives new life and dynamic form to the familiar themes of the nativist vocabulary. Working within the Brancusi–Arp tradition, she achieves forms that are both monumental and lyrical. Her work has been described as "stylization pushed to the point of abstraction." Her use of white onyx to suggest the female body is wonderfully effective. She cuts all the stone herself, by hand.

Among her sculptures with indigenous themes are *Dance of Cholas* (walnut, 1937), *Work Dance* (mahogany, 1937), *Huaka-Tokori* ([fertility ritual dance] wood, 1937), *Llamas* (walnut, 1943), *Andina* ([female Indian head] basalt), *Indigenous Group* (granite), *Alpaca* (basalt, 1950), *Mother and Child* (guayacán wood, 1958), *Black Venus* (basalt, 1958), *Spirit of the Cloud* (white onyx, 1959), and *White Venus* (white onyx, 1960). The last three are among the most beautiful of her sculptures.

In an interview with Geneviève Tabouis, Marina Núñez del Prado spoke of her work as follows,

The aim of my life as a sculptor is to interpret the ancient soul of

my country and our great Indian ancestors.... My works are inter-
pretations of the Bolivian soul, marked by the joys and sorrows of
our Indian forebears. In the expression of the three Indian miners
you see the spirit of revolt against the social injustice which marks
the times, and in the group Flowers of the Andes *[three Indian women,*
in wood] you see the poetic soul of the Bolivian Indian of today.[8]

CHILE

The turning-point of the contemporary art movement in Chile
occurred in 1928, when Pablo Ramírez, the Minister of Public
Instruction, ordered the National School of Fine Arts to be closed
for two years. His purpose was to achieve an artistic renewal,
to break away from the outmoded aesthetic atmosphere, and to
make a fresh start in terms of contemporary values. He sent some
thirty of the most promising young artists to Europe on government grants, to study, to work, and to absorb the latest artistic
currents. Then, in 1930, Ramírez created the Faculty of Fine
Arts in the University of Chile, staffed it with some of the artists
who had returned from Europe, and gave it authority to organize
the official Salon for annual exhibitions of Chilean painting. Thus
did modernism entrench itself in Chile—or, more accurately, in
Santiago, the capital, which dominated the cultural scene.

But this "modernism" was relative: by no means did it represent *le dernier cri* of 1930. Its leading representatives were the
members of the Montparnasse Group, most of whom took Cézanne
as their point of departure—without ever radically departing
from the model. In the words of the Chilean art critic Antonio
R. Romera, their creative principle consisted of "a compromise
between external reality and its translation into purely figurative
forms and signs." But in Paris they *did* learn to think and work
in terms of plastic values, to compose a picture as a *painting* not
as anecdote, description, or representation. The original members
of the Montparnasse Group were Julio Ortiz de Zárate (1885–
1946), Manuel Ortiz de Zárate (1887–1946), Camilo Mori (b. 1896),
Luis Vargas Rosas (b. 1887), and José Perotti (b. 1898). To these
should be added the name of the older painter, Pablo Burchard

[8] *Pour La Victoire,* January 20, 1945.

(1873–1960), who did not accompany the group to Paris (in fact, he never left Chile during his whole, long life), but who was actually their leader and mentor at home. He was also the most important Chilean painter of his generation, the first to assimilate creatively the lessons of the European innovators, and the one who was able to renew himself throughout many decades of activity, so that his latest works are in many ways his best— "marvels of artistic purity," as Romera calls them. The *Portrait of Pablo Burchard* (1908), by Pedro Lira, shows him as the artist of distinction, with his fine forked beard, imperial moustaches, and wide-brimmed felt hat worn at a rakish angle.

Of the former members of the Montparnasse Group still active in the 1960's, Camilo Mori has moved toward a semiabstract neofiguratism, as revealed by the three paintings that he sent to the first Biennial at Córdoba in 1962. José Perotti has displayed a restless and diversified activity not only in painting, but also in engraving, enameling, ceramics, and sculpture.

The next significant group of Chilean painters, known as the Generation of 1940, turned largely toward the vivid colors and strong contrasts of fauvism, as exemplified in the work of Israel Roa (b. 1909), whose painting; *The Painter's Birthday* is in New York's Museum of Modern Art; Carlos Pedraza (b. 1913); Raúl Santelices (b. 1916); and Sergio Montecino (b. 1916), who likes to paint the marvellous landscapes of southern Chile with predominantly blue and green tones.

But on the whole, academic modernism had become the established order in Chilean painting, and it was time for another renewal, a more profound revolt against accepted values and methods than had been previously experienced. The leaders of this new rebellion against official art where Roberto Matta Echauren, Nemesio Antúñez, and Enrique Zañartu. Significantly, none was a graduate of the National School of Fine Arts. Matta and Antúñez had both studied architecture, and both worked with Stanley W. Hayter at his Studio 17 in New York for several years. Of the three, only Antúñez chose to live and work in his homeland; Matta and Zañartu made their home in Paris. They belong to the international scene.

The Expatriates: Matta and Zañartu

Roberto Matta Echauren (b. 1912) graduated from the School of Architecture of Santiago in 1933 and then went on to work with Le Corbusier in Paris for three years (1934–37). Finding himself more strongly attracted by painting than by architecture, he began to paint in the surrealist manner in 1937, and three years later had his first one-man show at the Julien Levy Gallery in New York. He remained for several years in New York, but after the end of World War II settled permanently in Paris. In 1957, the Museum of Modern Art in New York organized an important retrospective exhibition of Matta's painting. By that time he was generally recognized as one of the Latin American painters whose place in the history of art was secure. Although related to the aesthetic of surrealism, his style is unmistakably individual, unreal in its arbitrary images yet capable of projecting ideas about "the real world." This was demonstrated in a series of six mural-size canvases exhibited at the Alexander Jolas Gallery in New York in May, 1966, representing controversial issues of the 1960's—namely *Vietnam, Santo Domingo,* and *Alabama* (all 1965). In these topical canvases, the symbolic violence latent in many of Matta's earlier paintings becomes explicit in the stylized forms of modern weapons of destruction and in the explosive brutality of racial strife. Yet the essential style remains unaffected either by changing art fashions or recurrent political-social issues. Matta has not turned himself into a painter of social realism simply by a public display of his social conscience. Whatever his ideological message may be, it is to the painter who created a world beyond realism that we look for an enduring revelation of artistic values.

Matta's painting is essentially metaphysical. He once said: "If you ask me what I seek, I shall reply that I am trying to discover the morphology of the psychic processes. Or rather, I am seeking a microscope with which I can scrutinize the spirit of man." The Chilean critic Antonio Romera discerns in Matta's work "a faultless technique and a vision in which fantasy seems to burst forth in sparks and explosions of extraordinary suggestive power." An American critic, Hilton Kramer, has written perceptively about Matta's style:

> *Matta is a consummate constructor of imaginary worlds, meticulously designed cosmologies that combine the atmosphere of a science-fiction fable with some of the lurid feeling of an erotic nightmare. . . . Into a deep luminous space he projects an imaginary and highly metaphorical spectacle of bizarre objects and structures. Everything contained in this pictorial space seems to be in motion—indeed, at the point of violent collision or collapse—and the space itself is imbued with an eerie, liquid color that confers a further element of menace to the objects it illuminates.*[9]

These qualities are exemplified in such paintings as *The Unthinkable* (1957), *Under the Flames of Delusion* (1958), *To Cover the Earth with a New Dew* (1959), and *Untitled* (1962–63), which was included in *The Emergent Decade* exhibit of 1965–66.

Another Chilean expatriate, Enrique Zañartu, was born in Paris in 1921 and has lived there since 1949. His formative years, however, were spent in Santiago, where he began to paint, and the Chilean landscape has left its indelible mark on much of his work. From 1944 to 1947 he worked with Stanley Hayter in New York, and then spent two years in Havana before settling in Paris. According to Antonio Romera, Zañartu has described himself as a "realist"—but certainly not in the conventional sense. Zañartu claims that he is "a realist according to my own way of seeing things, a realist for whom reality is what I feel within myself." There are neofigurative elements in his work, along with elements of surrealism and abstract expressionism. He creates a mysterious confrontation between dream and reality, between fantasy and objectivity, between the subconscious and the rational. His *Beachcomber* series (1955) is frankly surrealist, but during the same period he was painting such semiabstract canvases as *The Sower* (1954) and *The Forester* (1955). Abstract expressionism predominates in the *Paris* series (1959–63).

[9] *The New York Times*, May 15, 1966, D 19. Includes a reproduction of *Vietnam* (1965).

Antúñez and Neorealism

Nemesio Antúñez (b. 1918) shares the surrealism of Matta and the abstractionism of Zañartu—as well as the former's eroticism—but his most recent phase is a kind of neorealism derived from magnifying minute aspects of real objects. An important phase of his work consists of the "abstract landscapes" inspired by the sensational natural scenery of Chile, such as *Inside the Cordillera, Vertical Volcano, Andean River, Volcano in the Sun*, and *Sun on the Water* (all painted in the early 1960's). Trained in architecture, Antúñez also worked for a number of years with Stanley Hayter in New York. Upon returning to Chile, he was appointed Director of the Museum of Contemporary Art in Santiago. He also organized the Workshop 99 for engraving. His influence on contemporary painting in Chile has been great.

The combined influence of Matta, Zañartu, and Antúñez has given rise to various forms of "unrealism" (to borrow the term used by Romera), in which artists are guided primarily by their inner vision, a kind of metaphysical ordering of chaos. Such is the work of Jaime González Barahona and Rodolfo Opazo, whose *Inner Landscape* (1959) may be regarded as a paradigm of this trend. To this may be added two other paintings by Opazo: *Woman Smelling Flowers from the Tree of Two Heads* and *The Sacred Cow* (both 1962). Enrique Castrocid (b. 1927) has developed along somewhat similar lines in *Reincarnation, Dead People*, and *Natural Speed* (all 1961). Although Carmen Silva (b. 1930) studied with both Antúñez and Zañartu, she cultivates a neorealism in the depiction of everyday objects that has moved from a high degree of abstraction, as in *Kitchen-Bathroom* (1958), to overt figuratism, as in *Washstand* (1964).

Then there are the members of the Grupo Signo, consisting of Gracia Barrios, José Balmes, Alberto Pérez Martínez, and Eduardo Bonatti. They are essentially abstract expressionists.

Ricardo Yrarrázaval (b. 1931) studied in Rome and at the Académie Julien in Paris (1952–53). Returning to Santiago, he had his first one-man show there in 1954. His abstractionism derives from de Staël but has developed also under the influence of pre-Columbian ceramics and of the artist's own work as a ceramist. He resembles Fernando de Szyszlo in that he uses abstract form symbolically to evoke the indigenous past of America, as in the painting titled *Ancestral Presence* (1964), with its very subtle and beautifully harmonized use of color as a formal component. The Chilean critic Jorge Elliott finds an underlying figuration in Yrarrázaval's abstractions, "simplified into elementary forms earthy as Chimu pots, or striped liked Indian textiles."

The "return to reality" is represented in the work of Ernesto Barreda (b. 1927, in Paris), whose training in architecture at the Catholic University of Chile is reflected in his predilection for painting doors, walls, and other architectural features. The human element is generally absent from his paintings; his urban playgrounds and squares are usually deserted, though now and again a child will appear in some distant doorway or lonely alley.

In our survey of contemporary art on the west coast of South America we have not attempted to delineate any regional profile. But perhaps some distinction could be drawn between those countries of the central Andean region—Ecuador, Peru, Bolivia—and those occupying the two extremities (Colombia to the north and Chile to the south). This in turn implies a different kind of relationship to the indigenous cultures, both of the past and the present. As we have seen, the indigenous factor has had considerable importance in the central Andean countries, and indeed gave both origin and name to one of the strongest artistic movements in that area: *indigenismo*. The trajectory of the contemporary arts in those countries might be described as leading from nativism to modernism—and the "agony" of this movement was for a long time defined by the problem of how to achieve the latter without entirely sacrificing the former. The work of Fernando de Szyszlo illustrates the most successful pictorial solution of that agonizing problem.

In spite of (or possibly because of) its isolated geographical position, the contemporary art movement in Chile is characterized by a cosmopolitanism comparable to that of Argentina and Uruguay, two countries with which it has always had traditional cultural ties. In this connection it is significant to note that the two most famous contemporary painters of Chile, Matta and

Zañartu, are both expatriates. It has been argued that the spirit or "essence" of Chile is present in their work, and such metaphysical interpretations are not without interest. But again they raise the question: What *is* Latin American art?

In the case of Colombia, which faces toward the Caribbean as well as the Pacific, we have likewise an essentially cosmopolitan situation, reflected in the neofigurative expressionism of Obregón, the geometrical abstraction of Ramírez, and the abstract mechanistic sculpture of Edgar Negret.

4

Argentina and Uruguay : Cosmopolitan Currents

ARGENTINA

*B*UENOS AIRES and Mexico City may be regarded as opposite points determining the axis of modern art in Spanish-speaking Latin America. Whereas nationalism, muralism, and social realism have been paramount in Mexico, they were negligible factors in Argentina. There was no impressive pre-Hispanic culture in Argentina to be incorporated in the national heritage. The Indian population, never large, was virtually eliminated. Although the grasslands of the *pampa* and the legendary figure of the *gaucho* acquired the status of national symbols, the nation was over-whelmingly dominated—culturally, politically, and economically —by its capital city, Buenos Aires, with a population vastly greater than any other city. With its large influx of immigration during the second half of the nineteenth century (especially from Italy) and the close contacts of the élite with French culture, Buenos Aires quickly became a cosmopolitan city. It is the only city in Latin America that has a world-famous opera house, the Teatro Colón, with an unbroken history of national and international operatic performance drawing on top international talent (though in that respect it has somewhat declined from its former prestige).

The norm of artistic activity in Buenos Aires has been high technical accomplishment in easel painting and the graphic arts, with a few really outstanding talents in sculpture. Artists have kept in close touch with current developments in Europe, art galleries have flourished, many *avant-garde* groups were formed (and dissolved), and art has been considered as the privilege of a cultivated minority. The tendency has been to value art for its own sake rather than as an expression of social realism or a vindication of political convictions.

Argentina owes its priority and prestige in the modern art movement of Latin America largely to the pioneer work of Emilio Pettoruti in painting and Pablo Curatela Manes in sculpture.

Argentine Cubist

Emilio Pettoruti (b. 1892) was the first abstract painter of Latin America to develop a consistently modern style that was both personal and contemporary. Unlike Diego Rivera, who simply imitated all the European styles that were fashionable between 1907 and 1920, Pettoruti, who also went to Europe at an early age, assimilated elements of cubism, futurism, and (to a lesser degree) expressionism, while forging a personal style that was evident almost from the beginning and that followed a consistent line of development throughout his entire creative career, which has been long and productive.

Pettoruti was born in La Plata, capital of the Province of Buenos Aires, an administrative and university city founded only ten years before his birth. His youthful talent was recognized by the provincial legislature, which awarded him a grant for study in Europe. Thus, in 1913, at the age of twenty, Pettoruti found himself in Florence, where he was to remain, with sidetrips to Rome and Milan, throughout World War I and for several years thereafter. He quickly joined the group of avant-garde artists and writers who frequented the Caffè delle Giubbe Rosse—Café of the Red Shirts. The chief influence was that of futurism, a movement launched by Marinetti in 1909, calling for a complete break with the past. Shortly after Pettoruti's arrival in Florence the futurist painters, among whom were Balla, Boccioni, Carrà, and Severini, held a large exhibition at the Galeria Gonelli. The young painter from La Plata went there daily, meeting the artists and absorbing the theory of "dynamism," or kinetic figuration, that formed the basis of futurist painting. The experience was stimulating, but it did not sweep him off his feet or cause him to repudiate the past. He assiduously studied the Italian masters of the *quattrocento*, and was especially attracted by their flat surfaces. When his teacher urged him to use the spatula, he refused, objecting that this was not necessary in order to paint well. He also wanted to learn the techniques of fresco and mosaic, and this he did by working as an apprentice to masters in those media.

During 1914, Pettoruti participated in three group shows, and in July, 1916, he had his first one-man show at the Galeria Gonelli. It included both figurative and nonfigurative works, oils, drawings, and mosaics. In the same year he sent his first work, an abstract painting titled *Harmonies*, to the National Salon in Buenos Aires. It was accepted—for the section of "Decorative Art." When he sent a painting to the National Salon in 1921, it was rejected. Pettoruti's first purely abstract work was a charcoal drawing entitled *Centrifugal Force*, done in 1914. This was followed by *Lights in the Landscape* (oil, 1915) and *Light-Elevation* (oil on cardboard, 1916). The first two were based on circular motion; the third on rectangular structures. By combining curvilinear and rectangular forms, Pettoruti, in the following year, produced such semiabstract paintings as *A Friend* and *Woman in the Café* (both oil on cardboard, 1917). He continued his semi-abstract quasigeometrical portraits with *The Philosopher* (1918), *The Teacher* (1918), *Woman in the Green Hat* (1919), and *The Painter Xul Solar* (1920). He also applied the same technique to landscapes: *Sunshine and Shade* (1917), *The Park* (1918), and *Environs of Milan* (1919).

Pettoruti did not agree with the futurist idea of depicting motion figuratively (an exception is the painting titled *The Dancers*, dating from 1918). Many years later, Pettoruti explained that he had been brought to abstraction in his early work by the desire, on the one hand, "to obtain movement, velocity, dynamism, according to my imagination, nonfiguratively," and on the other hand, by his desire "to copy the classics in their constructive lines and not in what their pictures represented."[1] Pettoruti's work is essentially a dynamism of constructive lines enhanced by color as an element of composition. The critic Córdova Iturburu has observed the various ways in which Pettoruti's painting of this period departs from the orthodox manner of cubism,

> It does not have that geometrical disarticulation of the different profiles of the figure—the visible and the invisible—and their simultaneous presentation on the plane of the canvas, which is such a characteristic trait of cubism. Nor is there the typical assertion of bidimensionality through the abolishment of spatial depth, and the structurization of the figure on the surface instead of in volume. Nor does his color, so classically Venetian, with half tones dominated by purples, dull reds, warm browns, sumptuous yellows and grays, present the traits of the cubist palette, inclined to pure tones. . . .[2]

Pettoruti's painting developed along the general lines of cubism, with special reference to Braque and Gris, but with an independence determined by his own sense of structure, composition, and color. He actually did not see cubist paintings until 1923, when he went to Berlin and Paris prior to returning to Argentina. In Paris he became friendly with Juan Gris, whose influence is apparent in such works as *Cherries* (sand and oil on canvas, 1924), *Woman with Green Fan* (1925), *A Silent Corner* (1926), *Goblet on the Table* (1930), and *Photograph of Maria Rosa* (1931). Perhaps one should speak of affinity rather than influence, since these paintings represent a logical development from the premises of Pettoruti's earlier works.

When Pettoruti returned to Argentina in 1924, he found a climate of aesthetic revolt, that had been brewing since the beginning of the decade and that reached its culmination with the appearance of a review called *Martín Fierro* (after the great gaucho epic of the nineteenth century by José Hernández). Founded in February, 1924, this review and the group of artists and writers identified with it signalled a turning point in the

---

[1] Quoted in Córdova Iturburu, *Emilio Pettoruti* (Buenos Aires, 1963), p. 52.
[2] *Ibid.*, p. 52–53.

artistic life of Argentina. Its fourth issue contained the *Manifesto de Martín Fierro*, which announced the presence of "a new sensibility" in the arts, called for the aesthetic exploration of the contemporary world, and declared that a modern steamer trunk from a department store was more valuable than a sedan chair from the period of Louis XIV. The traditionalists, or *pasatistas*, as they were called, reacted furiously to this attack on consecrated values. It was in this controversial atmosphere that Pettoruti held his first one-man show in Buenos Aires, at the Galería Witcomb, in October, 1924. His exhibition immediately became a rallying point for the avant-garde, a target of vituperation for the *pasatistas*. The transition from words to blows was inevitable, and more than one aesthetic dispute ended in the police station. When the dust of battle settled, it was clear that a radical change had occurred in Argentine art. The contemporary current had reached the River Plate.

During the next twenty-eight years that he was to remain in Argentina (1924–52), Pettoruti's art gained many adherents, he established a very successful studio, and he achieved an unparalleled prestige. But he was frowned upon officially for many years. In 1930, he was appointed director of the Museum of Fine Arts of La Plata, but soon afterwards a federal "Interventor" fired him. Reappointed later, he was again removed, this time by the Perón government, in 1947. It was then that he established his atélier in Buenos Aires, in order to have a regular source of income. In 1941, Pettoruti received two concurrent invitations to visit the United States, one from the Committee for Inter-American Artistic and Intellectual Relations, the other from the San Francisco Museum of Art, which organized a traveling exhibition of forty of his most important paintings. Pettoruti spent eight months in the United States, visiting museums and universities. The Museum of Modern Art in New York acquired his painting titled *The Gray-green Goblet* (1934). The critic of the New York *Herald Tribune* hailed him as "one of the masters of abstract art."

In 1952, Pettoruti returned to Europe, going first to his beloved Italy, where he exhibited in Milan, Florence, and Rome. The following year he went to Paris, where he remained for several years and exhibited frequently, with a large one-man show in

1958. In 1960, he had a one-man show in London; in 1962, the National Museum of Fine Arts in Buenos Aires at long last honored him with a retrospective exhibition. In 1957, he was invited to participate in the first Guggenheim International Exhibit, representing South America. By 1962, he was the subject of twelve monographs and innumerable articles, essays, catalog introductions, and literary references, in many languages. His famous painting *The Quintet* (oil on plywood, 1927) was included in the exhibition *Latin American Art Since Independence* (1966).

One of Pettoruti's best-known paintings is *The Improvisor* (oil on canvas, 1937), which is in the National Museum of Fine Arts in Buenos Aires. Representing three musicians dressed as Harlequins, it is the major work in a series of Harlequin paintings that constitute an important and highly characteristic phase of Pettoruti's production. These include *The Singer* (1934), *Strollers* (1935), and *Romantic Serenade* (1938). In spite of a superficial family resemblance, these Harlequins are actually not Picassian. The fact that Pettoruti's *The Improvisor* depicts three musicians, as in Picasso's celebrated cubist painting of 1921, has often led to false comparisons, based on the subject rather than the style. As Julio Payró observed, "The differences to be noted are that Picasso's figures are static, of two dimensions, and of symphonic coloring, without chromatic modulations, while those of Pettoruti are dynamic, three-dimensional, and of tonal coloring with subtle modulations in all the parts." *The Improvisor* is neither abstraction nor cubism, but an eloquent and moving masterpiece of contemporary humanistic art.

In some of his more recent works, Pettoruti has returned to the pure abstraction of his earliest works, but with much greater formal flexibility and a stronger visual dynamism. The purest of these abstractions is perhaps *The White Bird* (1959), which has the economy and elegance of a sculpture by Brancusi. The optical manipulation of the plastic elements is prominent in some of these later paintings, with their superimposed forms and intersecting planes. Their titles also imply a metaphysical bent not present in the earlier work: *A Child's Dream* (1954), *The Last Hour of a Day* (1955), *Quietness of the Beyond* (1957). Two paintings of the next decade, *Viper's Grass* and *Bird of Light*

Plate 2. *José Clemente Orozco. "Modern Migration of the Spirit"
(Fresco, 1933). Fourteenth panel, Dartmouth College Murals,
Hanover, N.H.*

Plate 3. *Diego Rivera.* Temptations of Saint Anthony *(Oil on canvas, 1947).* Collection, National Museum of Modern Art, Mexico.

Plate 4. *Alberto da Veiga Guignard.* Ouro Preto: St. John's Eve *(Oil on plywood, 1942). Collection, The Museum of Modern Art, New York. Inter-American Fund.*

(OVERLEAF) **Plate 5.** *José Clemente Orozco.* Zapatistas *(Oil on canvas, 1931). Collection, The Museum of Modern Art, New York.*

Plate 6. *Rufino Tamayo.* Girl Attacked by a Strange Bird *(Oil on canvas 1947). Collection, The Museum of Modern Art, New York. Gift of Mr. and Mrs. Charles Zadok.*

Plate 7. *Wifredo Lam.* The Jungle *(Gouache on paper mounted on canvas, 1943). Collection, The Museum of Modern Art, New York. Inter-American Fund.*

Plate 8. *Fernando Botero.* Mrs. Rubens (No. 5) *(Oil on canvas, 1968).* *Photo: courtesy Ferdinand Boesch.*

Plate 9. *Rómulo Macció.* Emplacement *(Oil on canvas, 1965).* *Photo: courtesy Peter Moore.*

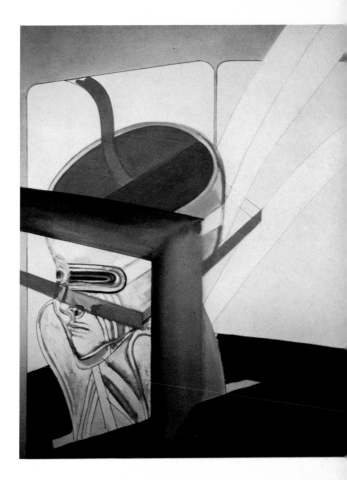

Plate 10. *Oscar Niemeyer. National Congress (above) and Ministry of Foreign Affairs (at right), Brasília, Brazil (1967). Photo: courtesy of Marcel Gautherot.*

Plate 11. *Félix Candela (structural design and construction) and Mario Pani (architect). Band shell, Santa Fé, D.F., Mexico (1956).*

(OVERLEAF) **Plate 12.** *Carlos Raúl Villanueva. Olympic Stadium, University City of Caracas (1950). Photo: courtesy Paolo Gasparini.*

Plate 13. *Carlos Raúl Villanueva (architect) in collaboration with Alexander Calder. Aula Magna, University City of Caracas (1952). Photo: courtesy Paolo Gasparini.*

Plate 14. *Roberto González Goyri. Concrete Reliefs for Government Building in Guatemala City (1964). Photo: courtesy Ricardo Mata.*

Plate 15. *Guillermo Trujillo*. End of the Feast *(Oil on canvas, 1965)*.

Plate 16. *Joaquín Torres García. Untitled work (Oil on canvas, 1943). Rose Fried Gallery, New York.*

Plate 17. *Amelia Peláez.* Fishes *(Oil on canvas, 1943). Collection, The Museum of Modern Art, New York. Inter-American Fund.*

Plate 18. *Cândido Portinari. "The Mining of Gold" (Tempera, 1941). Panel of mural in the Hispanic Foundation, Library of Congress, Washington, D.C.*

Plate 19. *Armando Morales*. Double Arch *(Mixed media, 1964).*
Photo: courtesy of O. E. Nelson.

Plate 20. *Gyula Kosice. Detail from* Divi All the Time *(Plexiglass and water, 1967). Photo: courtesy Peter Moore.*

Plate 21. *J. A. Fernández Muro*. Shot in the Back *(Mixed media, 1963). Photo: courtesy O. E. Nelson.*

Plate 22. *Marcelo Bonevardi. Detail from* "Sun Wheel" *(Painting-Construction, 1966). Photo: courtesy Peter Moore.*

Plate 23. *Alicia Peñalba.* Small Winged Object *(Bronze, 1965).*

Plate 24. *Roberto González Goyri.* Dying Warrior *(Bronze, 1964). Collection, General Director of Fine Arts, San Salvador, El Salvador. Photo: courtesy Sittler.*

(both 1961), revive, though in different terms, the fusion of abstract and natural elements that characterized such very early works as *Sunshine and Shade* and *The Park*. From first to last, Emilio Pettoruti has remained unswervingly true to his artistic faith, "an abstract innovator who paints like a classic" (Alberto Sartoris).

An Original Personality

When Pettoruti went from Florence to Milan in 1917, he was accompanied by a fellow artist from Argentina who called himself Xul Solar, whose portrait he painted in 1920, whose work he greatly admired, and with whom he formed a lifelong friendship. Oscar Agustín Schulz Solari (1887–1963), born of German and Italian parents who had migrated to Argentina, began to call himself simply Xul Solar when he gave up his government job and decided to become a spiritual voyager in the world of the imagination. This circumlocution is used deliberately instead of "artist," not only because of Xul Solar's many-sided spiritual and intellectual quests and ventures in astrology, mysticism, linguistics, musical notation, and other esoteric realms, but also because he was never a painter in the strict professional sense of making a career from his creative efforts. He exhibited infrequently, and then only a few works; he never sought prizes or awards; when visitors came to his studio to purchase his paintings, he did his best to dissuade them. When Aldo Pellegrini called Xul Solar "one of the most original personalities ever to appear in the history of Argentine art," he was stating an incontrovertible fact. Yet it was not mere originality alone, much less what might pass for sheer eccentricity, that characterized the work and personality of Xul Solar. An artist who could arouse the unstinted enthusiasm of such a perceptive and exigent writer as Jorge Luis Borges—to mention only the most famous of his discriminating admirers—must surely have had something exceptional to offer. Writing of Xul Solar's work, Borges said, "His paintings are documents of the ultraterrestrial world, of the metaphysical world in which the gods take on the imaginative forms of dreams. The passionate architecture, the felicitous colors, the numerous circumstantial details, the labyrinths, the angels and homunculi, unforgettably define this delicate and monumental art."[3]

Xul Solar began his spiritual voyage into the unknown by the symbolic act of shipping as a sailor aboard a freighter bound for Hong Kong. Perhaps because he was more of a mystic than a seaman, he found himself set ashore on the coast of Italy. From there he went to Paris, to London, to Berlin, and back to Paris, where he remained during World War I. In 1920, he had his first show, in Florence, introduced by Pettoruti. Self-taught in art, he worked mostly with watercolors and tempera, infrequently with oils. Returning to Buenos Aires in 1924, he joined the *Martín Fierro* group and exhibited in the Salón Libre. He showed only some half a dozen times thereafter; yet his reputation increased, and after his death he was given several large retrospective exhibitions, of which the most important was at the Museum of Fine Arts in Buenos Aires (1964). At the third Córdoba Bienal (1966) he was accorded a special *homenaje*, with an excellent introduction by the critic (and member of the jury) Aldo Pellegrini.

Pellegrini considers that Xul Solar's production falls into three main phases or periods. The first, from approximately 1917 to 1930, "is characterized by forms of geometrical tendency that result from the stylization of figures, objects, signs, emblems, which appear to float in an ambiguous space and are like reflections or emanations of what exists. From the pictorial aspect it is characterized by the dynamism of the compositional structure, the richness and subtlety of the color, and the extraordinary fantasy of the imagery."[4] This phase begins with an enchanting, semiabstract, quasiprimitive *Saint Francis* (1917), which shows St. Francis kneeling in prayer on the top of a charmingly rounded mountain in the middle of nowhere. The watercolors of this period are often inhabited by fantastic beings with cylindrical bodies and members (the latter sometimes strewn about the pictorial space), exaggeratedly large oval eyes, and hands with very long fingers. There are numerals, letters, and words, the

[3] As quoted in Svanascini, *Xul Solar* (Buenos Aires, 1962), p. 7.
[4] Aldo Pellegrine, "Xul Solar, homenaje," in *III Bienal Americana de Arte* (Córdoba, 1966).

latter two usually spelling out the "subject" of the picture, as in *Chief of Dragons* (1923). Sometimes the figures are transparent, resulting in double or multiple images (*Double Image* [1932], *Septuplet* [1924]). The serpent reappears frequently (*Man with a Serpent, Figure and Serpent* [both 1923]), always in a highly stylized form. There is an increasing tendency toward abstraction, which reaches its culmination in *Figure and Serpent*, where the "figure" is composed of many small geometrical shapes in a wide spectrum of subdued but intense colors, while the "serpent" provides a dynamic curvilinear accent. The peripheral and background modulations of color are especially noteworthy in this painting.

The second period, from 1930 to 1960, according to Pellegrini, "reveals a tendency toward greater asceticism in color (which at times is even reduced to monochrome) as well as in form. Although retaining its tendency toward geometrical stylization, the work of this period incorporates a frugal modeling of the figures and a sense of perspective approaching the traditional. But what dominates in this phase is the more direct weight of the spiritual and esoteric content." These features can be immediately observed in two of the earliest works of this period: *Forest and Yogi* (1931) and *Palace of Souls* (1932). Architectural and topographical themes (mostly walls and mountains) predominate in this period: *City and Abysms* (1946), *Transparent Mountains with Village* (1948), *Mountains with Nine Towers* (1949), and—with superbly humorous fantasy—*Three Projects for Façades in the Delta* (1954), referring to the houses built on piles over the water in the Paraná Delta near Buenos Aires.

The third and shortest period, beginning around 1960, is marked by the development of "a type of plastic writing in which the figures, signs, and designs represent letters of the alphabet by means of which entire words or phrases are formed. They are legible pictures in the strictest sense of the word. From the pictorial point of view, the artist returns to the enchantment of color, inasmuch as through these images there is projected a very rich fantasy, organized in structures that are nobly decorative and of surprising originality." This phase is closely related to the universal language, which he called *panlengua*, that became Xul

Solar's absorbing interest to the very end of his life, and to a Pan American language, which he called *neocriollo*. An example of the latter is the title of the painting, *Lu diabo muy sabe piu por viejo ke por diabo* (*The Devil Knows More Because He Is Old than Because He Is a Devil* [1962]). A sample of the *panlengua* is *Pax, Worke, Love*, which he painted in four different versions, like variations on a theme. The alphabetical phase is exemplified in *Syllabic Block Letters* (1960); the purely graphic mode in *Graphic Mural* (1960).

All this reminds one of the pictographs of Torres García, while the first period of Xul Solar's production, in particular, recalls the pictorial world of Paul Klee—an artist with whom he has often been compared. The similarity is certainly there, but it is not imitative or derivative. Xul Solar was an original artist, an imaginative mystic, a William Blake of the River Plate. Like Torres García, he aspired to eliminate time and place from the eternal and universal message of art, and he did this in his own way.

Older Figurative Painters

Among the older Argentine figurative painters, the most notable are Miguel Carlos Victorica, Lino Eneas Spilimbergo, and Horacio Butler.

Victorica (1884–1955), born in Buenos Aires, received his early training there before going to Paris in 1911, where he studied with Désiré Lucas. Remaining in Europe until 1917, he traveled in Spain and Italy, but his closest ties were with the French postimpressionists, especially Bonnard and Vuillard. Upon returning to Buenos Aires, he settled in the old port section called La Boca, living for the rest of his life as a semirecluse in a decaying, ramshackle house that also served him as a studio. There he had as neighbor the "painter of La Boca," Benito Quinquela Martín (b. 1890), a specialist in local color, who once remarked that Victorica was "a painter for painters." Although two of the canvases that he sent from Paris were accepted for the National Salon of Buenos Aires and were later acquired by the

National Museum of Fine Arts, Victorica was slow to obtain wide recognition for his work. Introspective, persistent, patient, utterly devoted to his art, never involved in self-promotion, he was as scornful of fashion as he was indifferent to success. Yet fame and recognition came to him, though tardily, and in 1941 he was awarded the Grand National Prize for one of his most celebrated paintings, *Bohemian Kitchen* (1941). He painted many still-lifes and interiors, as well as portraits and figures, especially nudes. In his later years he was widely admired and had many imitators.

Lino Eneas Spilimbergo (1896–1964) was also a native of Buenos Aires, where he studied at the National Academy of Fine Arts before going to Europe in 1925. In Paris he was a pupil of André Lhote and was influenced by cubism, but not, however, deeply or lastingly. More significant was his stay in Italy, where he came under the influence of the painter Massimo Camigli, who in turn had borrowed from Etruscan and Roman art, into which he injected metaphysical overtones. Thus Spilimbergo was drawn toward a type of neoclassicism in which "all is order and equilibrium," building his "beautiful and precise aesthetic structures with the strictness of heraldic standards"—to quote the Argentine writer Manuel Mujica Lainez. His style is architectural and sculpturesque, with firm delineation, strong articulation of figures and objects, and a sense of plastic solidity. Spilimbergo often places his figures within a fanciful architectural and landscape setting that, in spite of the precisely delineated details, manages to convey the illusion of poetry and mystery. One sees this, for example, in the painting titled *Terrace* (1930), with its intricate pattern of tiles and the varied textural and structural elements of the balustrades and walls contrasting with the static quality of the eight female figures, some clothed, some nude, placed in the long perspective of a terrace overlooking the sea.

It would not do, however, to overemphasize the architectural and heraldic aspects of Spilimbergo's work. There is also a deep humanism in his portraits, particularly of women and children, with their classical Mediterranean features, their large, liquid eyes, and their intensity of expression. Spilimbergo's work was widely exhibited in the United States: in Pittsburgh (Carnegie Internnational, 1935), New York, San Francisco, Cleveland; as well as in Paris and Venice. As director of the Instituto Superior de Artes of the National University of Tucumán, in northern Argentina, he contributed to the development of artistic culture in the provinces.

Painter of Buenos Aires

Horacio Butler (b. 1897) is the artist who has most fully and consistently identified himself with Buenos Aires (where he was born) and its environs. He is of Spanish descent and owes his surname to an Irish ancestor who emigrated to Spain at the time of the religious wars. At the age of seventeen he entered the National Academy of Fine Arts, from which he graduated five years later, having meanwhile taken a brief fling at architecture. His first revelation of unsuspected possibilities in painting came to him when he saw the work of the great Uruguayan painter, Pedro Figari, who had an exhibition in Buenos Aires in 1921. The following year he received a grant for foreign study, which took him first to Germany. There he spent some months at the artists' colony of Worpswede and came into contact with the German expressionists, whose visual violence, however, repelled him. Moving on to Paris in 1923, he found himself in the congenial company of several fellow artists from Argentina, among them Spilimbergo, Basaldúa, Berni, Raquel Forner, and the sculptor Bigatti. Like so many other Latin American artists, he went to the atélier of André Lhote, the fashionable cultivator of neocubism, but left in disappointment after two months. He then switched to the atélier of the one-time fauvist painter Othon Friesz, where he remained for the next four years. Later, speaking of Friesz, he said, "I learned from him to seek the unity of the whole in the unity of light and harmony of tone." During these years in Paris, Butler regularly sent his work to be shown at the National Salon in Buenos Aires.

By 1928, Butler had been directly exposed to expressionism, cubism, and fauvism. The first he rejected (save for a few slight traces); from the other two he took what suited him without subjecting himself to either. In the antithesis of cubism and fauvism he saw a means of achieving a synthesis between abstraction and representation—which he equated, respectively, with the classical and romantic tendencies in his own temperament. His purpose, as he later explained, was "to translate plastically the secret behind things, beings, and landscapes." His work was to be representational but never realistic. On the whole, Butler took more from fauvism than from cubism; he never followed the line of analytic cubism, and from synthetic cubism he simply accepted the principle that a painting should be "an objective ordering of the world represented in its essence, and not its appearance." From fauvism, Butler adopted the use of arbitrary colors as a means of transforming the "natural" appearance of the object into an autonomous plastic entity. But he is never as "wild" in his color as the fauves, for he always remained true to his own temperament, which is poetic and meditative rather than extravagant or vehement.

Horacio Butler returned to Buenos Aires in 1932, and has lived there ever since with an occasional trip abroad, including one to the United States in 1940. His work first became known in this country when he exhibited at the Carnegie International of Pittsburgh in 1935. In 1939, the publisher Alfred Knopf commissioned him to illustrate an edition of William H. Hudson's *Green Mansions*. In 1936, he founded, with the painter Aquiles Badi, the Free Studio of Contemporary Art in Buenos Aires. In 1952, he was invited to Milan to design the stage sets at La Scala for the prize-winning Argentine opera by Juan José Castro, *Persephone and the Stranger*. In addition to his oil paintings, watercolors, engravings, and illustrations, Butler in recent years has designed quilted hangings of sewn cloth.

One of the first things that Butler did after his return from Europe was to revisit the suburb of Buenos Aires known as Tigre, located in the delta of the Paraná River, with its numerous canals, floating islands, luxuriant vegetation, and vacation villas. This enchanted world had been his delight in childhood, and when he returned to it in maturity he felt "a strange inward peace which set everything spiritually in its true perspective." This experience helped him to find himself as man and artist, and thereafter the

Tigre became a favorite theme in all his work. Thus, "mixing memory and desire," he became the pictorial poet of the Delta. Among his numerous plastic interpretations of the Tigre, we may mention *Floating Island: Tigre* (1941), *Yellow Landscape* (1950), *Landscape in the Islands* (1953), and *Moonlit Night* (1954).

Yet the city of Buenos Aires itself attracted Butler almost as strongly, and his numerous scenes of the city would form another large collection of his work. This would include, among many others, *Urban Landscape* (1953), *The Square* (1952), *Square in Winter* (1953), and *The Rubber Trees* (1954). In all of these there is a kind of tension between abstract and representational elements, as though the curving limbs and branches of the symmetrical trees were about to undergo a metamorphosis into geometrical configurations, or the high-rise buildings into rectangular masses articulated by vertical and horizontal dominants. Color serves as a unifying element, so that the green of the park grass may reappear in the buildings or in the sky (if green happens to be the dominant tone of the painting, as in *Urban Landscape*). Much of the fascination of Butler's work lies in the unpredictable permutations of color, line, and mass.

Two Contemporaries

Among the contemporaries of Butler, Hector Basaldúa (b. 1895) and Juan del Prete (b. 1897) have achieved a considerable national and international reputation. Basaldúa, like Butler, studied in Paris with Lhote and Friesz. He began to exhibit in the National Salon of Argentina in 1923 and continued every year until 1956, when he was awarded the First National Prize. As official scenographer for the Teatro Colón, the famed opera house of Buenos Aires, from 1932 to 1950 and again from 1955 to 1959, he designed the sets for more than fifty operas and ballets. In 1946, he was invited by the United States government to study stage design and theater techniques in this country. His works have been shown in New York, San Francisco, Pittsburgh, and Dallas.

Basaldúa's earlier works, conventionally figurative, reveal the elegance of style and the formal mastery of a well-schooled painter (for example, the seated portrait of *Señora Mary C. B. de Solá* [1932]). Here he yields to the fascination of a well-poised fan, the rich texture of a sumptuous dress. By the 1950's he had become more austere, more profound, and the portrait of *Doña Cloto* (oil, 1954), divested of all glamor, has for its only decorative element a series of odd-shaped bottles and flasks that might almost be called "homage to Morandi." By the end of that decade he had moved into the sphere of neofiguratism, which was soon to become one of the dominant trends in contemporary Argentine painting. This phase of Basaldúa's work justifies the comment by Mujica Lainez that he is "probing the subconscious is if it were a hothouse of rare and beautiful plants." The painting titled *Abduction* (1959) strikingly exemplifies Basaldúa's neofiguratism, as do also various paintings of the 1960's, such as *Music* and *The Actors*.

Another phase of Basaldúa's late painting remains to be considered: his quasiexpressionistic evocations of local scenes, as in *Carnival*, *The Women*, and *The Carriage* (all shown at the first Córdoba Bienal in 1962). These paintings are very difficult to classify, because they blend various styles in a highly personal manner: the naïve charm of the primitives, the fantasy and freedom of expressionism, the color and composition of post-impressionism. In a way, they recall the "local color" paintings of Figari. They may not be profound but they are certainly delightful.

Juan del Prete is an artist who has been equally at home in the figurative and the nonfigurative realms of expression. A native of Italy, he migrated to Argentina at an early age and became a naturalized citizen in 1929. He sent his first work to the National Salon in 1925, and four years later received a grant to study in Europe. In Paris he exhibited with the group *Abstraction-Creation* at the Galerie Vavin in 1932. The following year he showed nonfigurative works in Argentina for the first time: oils, collages, and montages. In 1951, he had a retrospective show of his abstract work at the Galería Bonino in Buenos Aires. During the 1950's he participated in the biennials of São Paulo, Venice, and Mexico, and in the Brussels International Exposition. In 1959, he had a retrospective show of his figurative work in Buenos Aires.

Del Prete's figurative painting is not, generally speaking, realistic or naturalistic. A good example is the painting titled *Dance*, which depicts a couple executing what is evidently a traditional folk dance, such as the *cueca*—or so we may judge from the use of the handkerchief that is characteristic of this type of dance. But the composition itself is semiabstract, and the figures are expressionistically distorted, delineated with broad, bold brushstrokes that seek the effect of dynamism rather than of realistic description. It might be called "abstract motion with figures."

Del Prete turns to sheer abstract expressionism in such works as *Painting* (1961), and in the three paintings that he exhibited in the first Córdoba Bienal (1962): *Composition in Violet, Sunset,* and *Germinal.*

Raquel Forner: Symbol and Allegory

The first notable Argentine painter to be born after the turn of the century was a woman: Raquel Forner (b. 1902). Unlike most of her fellow artists, she was not of Italian but of Spanish descent: her father from Castile, her mother's family from the Basque provinces. After graduating from the National Academy of Fine Arts in Buenos Aires, she was employed for a time as a teacher of drawing. Then in 1929 she went to Spain with her parents. There she had an artistic revelation that was to be crucial for her own work: the paintings of El Greco. From his coloring, his subtle distortions, his dramatic mysticism, she received an enduring influence. She also visited Italy (where her favorite painters were Giotto and Piero della Francesca), England, France, and Spanish Morocco, where she indulged in local color to her heart's content. Returning to Buenos Aires in 1931, she founded an independent art school (*Cursos Libres de Arte Plástico*) in association with the painter Alfredo Guttero and the sculptor Alfredo Bigatti, whom she married in 1936. Beginning with her first individual show in 1929, she exhibited frequently in Buenos Aires, and from 1930 in Paris, Rome, New York, Pittsburgh, San Francisco, Caracas, São Paulo, and other centers abroad. In 1942, she won the First Prize in the National Salon of Buenos Aires for her painting, *The Drama:* 1942.

In her early years, Raquel Forner painted some conventional still-lifes and picturesque landscapes but, by 1931, she was already concentrating on the female human figure as the central motif in elaborately symbolic and allegorical paintings that eventually became a series of obsessive variations on the theme of war—or rather the suffering and destruction that war brought to mankind. As early as 1931, long before the outbreak of hostilities in Spain or the rest of Europe, her painting titled *Presage* foreshadowed a theme that she was to develop again and again during the ensuing years of destructive violence. The painting depicts an apocalyptic vision of disaster by flood and volcanic eruption, while in the foreground the heads of three women are shown: one covers her ears, another her mouth, the third her eyes. In 1939, in a series inspired by the disasters of the Spanish Civil War, Raquel Forner made this theme more explicit in a painting that she titled *See Not, Hear Not, Speak Not.* And in 1945, after the horrors of World War II, she restated the theme with the same title, but in a more dramatic manner. In this third painting the upper bodies of the three female figures are seen emerging as though from an infernal quagmire, together with bare, twisting, snake-like branches that brush against their faces. It is not the hands now, but these sinister writhing branches, that cover the eyes of one, the mouth of another, the ears of the third woman. The composition is quasisurrealist; but dominated, as always in the war-inspired paintings of this period, by a symbolism that is meant to be powerfully and immediately communicative.

With her first major work, *Women of the World* (1938), Raquel Forner irrevocably committed herself to being an *artiste engagée*, fully involved, emotionally and artistically, in the consequences of mankind's tragic blundering and drive toward self-annihilation. It is characteristic of her sense of universal suffering that this painting, though referring to the Spanish Civil War, was not given a localized title. Although the Spanish struggle touched her deeply because of her personal ties with that unfortunate country, she felt that it was but part of the larger tragedy of violence and suffering that afflicted the whole of mankind. Her

paintings of the 1940's are allegories of death and destruction:
Exodus (1940), The Fall (1941), Desolation (1942), The Drama
(the most complex and powerful of the series [1942]), The
Judgment (1946), Walls of Incomprehension (1947), Figures of
the Farce (1948). Even the Liberation of 1945 is without jubilation,
for the torn and mangled figure of peace emerges from a Dantesque
inferno of desolation and suffering. As for postwar conferences,
in The Conference (1947), the "conferees" are grotesque spectral
shapes facing each other on the shores of a desolate wasteland.

In several of these postwar paintings, such as Walls of Incomprehension, Figures of the Farce, and The Tower of Babel (1947),
Raquel Forner gives prominence to a new textural-symbolic
element, that of rock formations and petrified natural growths.
This element predominates in Potestad (Dominion, 1950), where
the human figures are dwarfed by the huge, hollow structure
that is an allegory of death.

The decade of the 1950's was one of transition for Raquel
Forner. Without abandoning her tragic themes, she introduced
new elements of the grotesque, new animal and vegetable forms
(especially birds and dead branches), and heightened the surrealist
quality in her work. She began to rely less on the naturalistic
human figure, more on expressionist and quasiabstract elements.
For example, in Standards (1951), the four principal figures are
draped in shapeless banners. This theme is repeated in one of
her most strikingly expressionist paintings, Eclipse (1952), in
which the three central figures are little more than spectral
apparitions covered by the banners (the theme of crucifixion is also
clearly implied by the poles and crosspieces of the standards). A
crucial transitional work is Masks (1952), where the only anthropomorphic elements appear as infinitesmal (though not insignificant) figures in the distant background. Forner was on the way
to her neofigurative phase, with strong elements of abstract
expressionism.

In 1958, Forner began a long series of works that she called
Cycle of the Moons, inspired largely by the explorations of outer
space, mixed with age-old mythologies dominated by the symbol
of Taurus (especially the rape of Europa by Jupiter disguised as
a bull). The culmination of the series is The Rape of the Moon

(1962), in five "tempos" (i.e., in five different versions). Each of these "tempos" is dominated by the image of Taurus, presented in quasiabstract form. There are paintings of astronauts, of those who have seen the moon, of *astroseres* (astro-beings), and of all kinds of outer space phenomena. This is, of course, no mere projection of science-fiction lore. The imagery is on the highest level of artistic imagination; each painting stands squarely on its intrinsic aesthetic values; the use of color is extraordinarily personal and subtle. Two paintings in this series, *The Astronaut* and *Those Who Saw the Moon*, obtained the Grand Prize at the first Córdoba Bienal.

After the death of her husband in 1964, Raquel Forner transmuted her personal grief into another remarkable series of paintings, *The Voyage without Return* (1965). The prevailing approach is neofigurative, as in the wonderfully harmonius painting titled *Integration*, or the marvelously rich and complex *Astronaut Labyrinth*. In this series, the theme of the voyage with no return is linked to the theme of the voyage in outer space, so that we have, for example, a strongly expressionist *Astrofaunal Struggle*. There are nine paintings in the series: *The Departure, The Farewell, The Message, Astronaut Labyrinth, Astrofaunal Struggle, Love, Passion, Integration, Memory.*

Other Figurative Painters

Among the predominantly figurative Argentine painters born between 1905 and 1915, Raúl Soldi (b. 1905) is one who chose to remain closest to "reality," in his rural and urban landscapes, and in his portraits of circus performers, of women, and of children. Yet all these subjects are transformed by the lyrical quality of his work, the freedom of the drawing, the expressive use of gesture, his distinctly personal palette. In the words of Mujica Lainez, "His work remains always real, in fact almost documentary, but one which through distorted color and form acquires a dimension of the unreal and evokes the magical quality of poetry." A good example is *The Necklace* (1962), with its two elegantly dressed women seated in rockers, holding necklaces in their hands in the familiar gesture of rewinding yarn. The counter-point of arms and hands is admirable, and the women have a strange, exotic beauty which is obviously not that of the bourgeois milieu to which they belong.

Soldi studied at the Academy of Brera in Italy, and formed part of the group known as *Il Milione* in Milan. After his return to Argentina, he did several stage designs for the Teatro Colón of Buenos Aires, and later received a grant from the National Commission of Culture to study motion picture scenography in the United States for two years. In 1960 he had a personal exhibit of thirty-six works, by special invitation, at the Second Biennal of Mexico. He has illustrated several books, including the *Chansons de Bilitis* of Pierre Louÿs and *Twenty Love Poems* of Pablo Neruda.

Antonio Berni (b. 1905) has been called a painter of "Abstract Realism." Justifying this appellation, the Argentine critic Hugo Parpagnoli wrote, "The people, the local scenes, and the anecdotes that Berni absorbed in the streets were transformed in his studio into plastic images that obey the least gesture of the artist. By their vividness they reflect a time and a place; by their abstractions they belong to universal painting." Berni traveled to Europe on a stipend in 1925, visiting France, Belgium, Holland, Italy, and Spain. In Paris, where he lived until 1931, he studied with Lhote and Friesz. He had already had a one-man show in his native city of Rosario, at the age of sixteen. From 1925, he exhibited regularly in America and Europe, and in 1940 was awarded the first prize at the National Salon in Buenos Aires. In 1937 he obtained the first prize for painting at the International Exposition in Paris. At the Venice Biennale of 1962, he obtained the international prize for drawing and engraving. A one-man retrospective show at the Museum of Contemporary Art in Santiage de Chile (May, 1964), brought together seventy-four paintings, twenty-eight prints, and seven drawings, covering the period from 1922 to 1964.

Berni's early work was entirely figurative, influenced less by his teacher Lhote than by Renoir. He soon began to paint scenes of everyday life, mostly in the poorer quarters of Buenos Aires. From 1959 he began to make frequent use of collage, and from 1961 he worked intensively with prints. In 1959 Berni introduced a boy whom he called *Juanito Laguna, A Boy of Bajo Flores* (a tough section of Buenos Aires), whom he depicted in a series of oil-collages and prints: with his dog, hunting birds, with a catch of fish, bringing lunch to his father (a metallurgical worker), and making his own living. Using both neofigurative and abstract elements, Berni succeeded in making Juanito Laguna both real and symbolic, a local boy of the underprivileged class and an image of universal boyhood. In the print of *Juanito Laguna with Fish* (xilograph-collage), Juanito is shown with the port of Buenos Aires as background, holding a large fish in one hand and an upright fishing-rod in the other, looking like a young Neptune just emerged from the sea. The classical quality of the print reminds us of how deeply Berni was influenced by the Italian masters during his stay in Europe.

Soon afterwards, Berni created another popular character, whom he called Ramona Montiel, whose life and loves he depicted in a series of prints and collages (1961–64) that constitute his most striking and original work to date. Ramona is a girl of the people who has to make her way in the world and is not too particular how she does it. We see Ramona as an adolescent, as a seamstress, as a worker, in the streets ("dressed to kill"), as the friend of various "protectors" (the Colonel, the Count, the Ambassador), at her wedding, and as the protegée of "Señor Pérez y Señora," by whom she is converted to a pious life, ending with her Father Confessor. Ramona in all her finery is a gorgeous and fantastic creature, a combination of odalisque and midinette, of cocotte and *grande dame manquée.* When *Ramona Lives Her Life* (print-collage) she is dressed in an extravagant blend of fashions and textures that never were seen in any one time or place: a montage of discarded furbelows and fripperies of "La Belle Epoque," such as the artist may have found in the Marché aux Puces of Paris. As Michel Ragon observes, Ramona has about her a certain "somewhat old-fashioned Parisian nostalgia." It is in his portraits of some of Ramona's protectors, such as *The Colonel* (print-collage), that Berni comes closest to semiabstraction. The Colonel is an almost mechanistic construction, as though he were all medals and epaulettes and armor plate and machine parts.

Among other artists of this generation whose work combines

figurative and semiabstract elements are Leónidas Gambartes, Luis Seoane, Juan Battle Planas, Raúl Russo, and Leopoldo Presas. Gambartes (b. 1909) is a self-taught artist who has cultivated a quasiprimitive symbolism, with surrealistic overtones, in such paintings as *Mythology* and *Ritual Dance*. Seoane (b. 1910) studied drawing and engraving in Spain and has been very productive in the graphic arts, though he has also done easel paintings and murals. Battle Planas (b. 1911) achieved a considerable reputation as a designer of stage sets (especially for the Teatro Colón), but his oil paintings and temperas are also remarkable for their fantastic and lyrical qualities. In the words of Mujica Lainez.

Juan Battle Planas conjures up a maze of equivocal and subterranean lights. His canvases give a feeling of windows opened onto the unknown, onto a super-reality where this notable artist delves with his spirit into the most Freudian of dreams. Those who are disconcerted by his apparent arbitrariness (and this is a legitimate criticism) should see his drawings, which are limited only to line and color. They will discover in him a surprising sensitivity to chromatic arrangements and elegant contours.[5]

Leopoldo Presas (b. 1915) began to exhibit in Buenos Aires in 1939, as a member of the Orion Group (later disbanded), which had surrealist tendencies. Twenty years later he was awarded the Gran Premio de Honor at the Argentine National Salon. He reveals himself as master of a powerful expressionist style in a painting such as *Descent from the Cross*, shown at the first Córdoba Bienal (1962).

Abstract Trends

The generation of painters born in the 1920's became the leaders of the abstract movement in Argentina, chiefly in the direction of informalism or abstract expressionism. Two artists born in 1920, Sarah Grilo and her husband José Antonio Fernández Muro, are prominently identified with this movement.

[5] Mujica Lainez, *Art in Latin America Today: Argentina*. Pan American Union, 1961, p. 11.

Sarah Grilo lived in Paris and Madrid during 1948–50, and had her first individual show in Madrid in 1949. She participated in the exhibitions *South American Art Today* (Dallas, 1959), *New Departures: Latin America* (Boston, 1961), *Magnet* (New York, 1964), and *The Emergent Decade* (1965–66). In 1962 she came to the United States on a Guggenheim Fellowship.

A self-taught artist, Sarah Grilo painted chiefly in the constructivist tradition during the 1950's, composing with large and small juxtaposed semigeometrical shapes set off by contrasting zones of flat color (an example is *Motif in Blue* [1955]). From the outset she developed a distinctive style, in color and composition, that enabled her to make an important contribution to the constructivist movement without being circumscribed by its tenets. Indeed, during the 1960's she moved toward informalism in such works as *Three Black Zones* and *White and Yellow*. Paintings of this period tend to be dominated by a single color: red, green, gray, yellow, or white. She attained further freedom after coming to New York in 1962, when she began giving prominence to random letterings, numerals, and signs of various sorts—including graffiti—placed on a background of neutral colors. These paintings usually take their titles from some component of the letterings, as in *Charge* and *Inferno* (both 1964).

José Antonio Fernández Muro, who went from his native Spain to Argentina at the age of eighteen, considers New York the most stimulating city in which an artist can live and work, though he deplores its insatiable appetite for novelty. In 1957 and 1958 he traveled in Europe and the United States on a grant from UNESCO to study the organization of museums. In his work prior to 1960, he favored geometrical abstract forms as in the spheres and rectangles of *Red Over Gray* (1959). Since 1960, while maintaining his predilection for circular and rectangular forms, he often embodies these in real objects, such as manhole covers, which he reproduces by the method of *frottage* (rubbings). As he told an interviewer, "When I came to New York I saw manhole covers in the streets and their shape and beauty struck me. I incorporated them in my paintings not for their anecdotal or documentary effect but because they were similar to the forms that I used before in by geometric paintings." One of his most original—and humorous—examples of the use of this central motif is the painting titled *To the Great Argentine Nation* (mixed media, 1964), in which a manhole cover represents the sun in the center of the Argentine flag. At the very bottom of the painting is the word *Salúd!* which, taken together with the title, make up the first line of the Argentine national anthem ("Al gran pueblo argentino, salúd!"). This I take to be a spoof of excessive nationalism and flagwaving patriotism; but of course it is done with absolute artistic integrity and the formal perfection that stamps all of Fernández Muro's work.

Some recent paintings of Fernández Muro reveal that the artist can convey a timely message, become involved in the great social issues of the moment in which he lives, without sacrificing one iota of his stylistic and formal integrity. A case in point is the work titled *Shot in the Back* (mixed media, 1963), which conforms to the abstract geometrical patterns that Fernández Muro prefers and the self-imposed austerity of colors, while projecting the moral condemnation of the dastardly murder of the civil rights worker Medgar Evers in Jackson, Mississippi. The fact that this message is conveyed in the impersonal, objective form of simulated newsprint makes it only the more effective. The use of color is masterly: three fields of very dark and very light gray, with a red circle in the center, where the printed letters stand out accusingly: "SHOT IN THE BACK IN JACKSON" (see Plate 21). Whether evoking a bitter human tragedy or painting a water sewer, Fernández Muro is a master of style, media, form, and color.

Abstract expressionism has had many other adherents in Argentina, among them Miguel Ocampo, Clorindo Testa, Kenneth Kemble, and Mario Pucciarelli. Individually, their styles vary greatly. Ocampo (b. 1922) reveals the purest informal abstraction in such paintings as *Number 168* (1957) and the shimmering immaterialness of *Painting* (1960). Clorindo Testa (b. 1923), architect and painter, likes to borrow his material from architectural shapes and textures, as in *Notes from Machu-Picchu* and *Notes from Herculaneum*, both shown at the second Córdoba Bienal (1964). Kenneth Kemble (b. 1923), who studied with Lhote in Paris for three years, has come to the fore during the 1960's as a master of mixed media (for example, synthetic enamel and paper pasted on canvas) in large paintings that juxtapose apparently disparate elements, such as abstract expressionism, decorative features derived from Art Nouveau, geometrical patterns, and optical designs *à la* Vasarely. His first notable success came with huge mural panels for the International Auto Show in Buenos Aires (1960), done in the bold "action painting" style of Franz Kline. His current synthetic style is actually more personal, because he achieves his own blend of disparate elements.

Pucciarelli (b. 1928) is a self-taught artist who began to paint in 1946. He traveled to England, France, and Italy in 1955, and to the United States in 1960. Since 1961 he has lived in Rome. In 1963 he obtained the International Prize of the Instituto Torcuato Di Tella of Buenos Aires. During the 1950's, Pucciarelli's paintings were essentially abstract-informalist, but in the 1960's he veered toward neofiguratism, as in *Cosmonaut, Nuclear Personage, Teleperson,* and *Radio Person* (all 1963). Yet the abstract element in these paintings remains strong, and in some works of this period it completely predominates (*More than One, Within a Circle, Something Green* [all 1963]). What is always distinctive is Pucciarelli's subtle use of subdued colors, and his mastery of fluid forms.

The group known as *Phases* includes both writers and artists and has for its literary spokesman the poet Julio Llinás, husband of Martha Peluffo, one of the leading painters of the group. Others are Victor Chab and Rogelio Polesello. They share a common attitude toward life rather than a particular style or aesthetic tendency, since the work of each is quite different from the others. Victor Chab (b. 1930), self-taught in painting, has had numerous individual shows since 1952, including one at the Pan American Union in 1964. His most characteristic works of the 1960's are a series of *Untitled Paintings* (oil on canvas, 1963), in which strange semiabstract forms seem to take on the aspect of fantastic insects enlarged as though seen through a telescopic lense. Martha Peluffo (b. 1931) follows the general line of abstract expressionism in such paintings as *The New Era, Deserts of Idleness* (both 1963), and *Blind Island* (1964), but with a style distinctly her own, marked by intense dynamism and an

original use of color. Rogelio Polesello (b. 1939) has adopted some
of the techniques of action painting with a somewhat more auto-
mated approach : he works preferably outdoors, in overalls, with
his canvas spread on the ground (usually the terrace of the old
house where he lives), and uses a spraygun with which he sprays
the metallic meshes and wire screens that are the hallmark of his
paintings. But unlike the older action painters, he does not take
the entire canvas as a field of unified activity; when this
preliminary work is done, he takes the canvas into his studio
and works on it with a precision akin to that of the geometrical
abstractionists, dividing it into large areas delimited by contrasting colors, each with its corresponding forms or objects. These
are generally abstract, but may suggest "real" objects or images.
His paintings are deliberately impersonal and objective, combining
elements of Op, Pop, geometrical, and informal abstract art. The
result has a surprising unity, whose "rightness" is the measure
of Polesello's success. See, for example, *Every Steps, Iota,* and
Kaleidoscope (all 1964)—the last splendidly reproduced (in color)
in *The Emergent Decade* (p. 57).

Neofigurative Painters

A strongly defined neofigurative expressionist movement manifested itself rather explosively in Argentine painting with a
group exhibit at the Galería Bonino of Buenos Aires (October,
1962) consisting of works by Ernesto Deira, Jorge Luis de la Vega,
Rómulo Macció, and Luis Felipe Noé. A fifth painter, Antonio
Segui, though not included in this show, has followed the same
trend and must be counted among the leading neofigurative
expressionist painters of Argentina.

Rómulo Macció (b. 1931) did not have conventional art training.
At the age of fourteen he went to work as an apprentice for an
advertising agency. After doing some graphics and stage sets, he
began to devote himself chiefly to painting; after 1956, he had
many one-man shows in Buenos Aires, New York, Paris, and
other centers. He has shown at the biennials of Paris, Venice,
São Paulo, and Córdoba. In 1961, he received the International

Prize of the Instituto Torcuato Di Tella in Buenos Aires. The Argentine art critic Jorge Romero Brest considers Macció's painting to be very much of our time because of "its neutral spatial dimension," and because "it affirms itself in a present that is antihistorical." In a series titled *To Live* (mixed media, 1963), Macció used circular, octagonal, and square forms to define the limits of his canvases. Each painting has a subtitle that states a different aspect of the main theme, as *To live: without the assurance of living, To live: at all costs, To live: lost time.* The total effect is of horror, anxiety, and futility.

For the catalog of an exhibit of oils titled *Faces* (1964-65), Macció wrote the following comment:

> They derive to some extent from my experience in graphic design and from an image which has been preoccupying me for about the last three years. They are not without a certain "esthétique," they insist on some mechanisms: the brusque interruption of spaces, pure color, formal and procedural contradiction. In them is the human face; they do not pretend to be psychological or social, nor do I think they are subjective, and still less science fiction as someone observed. I would like them to have an element of fiction if this were a poetic science.

Some of the titles are *Enthusiast, Memory, How to Win Friends* (that all-American smile!), *Inside and Outside, Self-Portrait, Two Atmospheres and a Yellow Personage, Emplacement* (Plate 9). In spite of Macció's disclaimer, it is difficult not to read psychological, if not social, implications in these disturbing paintings, in which the human and the inhuman are fiendishly fused.

Social-historical content—though never overtly realistic—is certainly present in the series of paintings by Luis Felipe Noé (b. 1933) dealing with the formative period of Argentine national history (*Federal Series* [1961]). He evokes the "demons" of Federalism and the "agonic image" of a heroic general, the sinister shade of the *caudillo* Facundo Quiroga (immortalized in Sarmiento's masterpiece), the reign of anarchy, and the call to barbarism. This is historical painting with a new dimension, literally a "recreation" of the past in terms of subjective feeling and of a moment that is eternally present in the act of artistic creation. In his more recent work, especially after he went to

New York in 1964, Noé has gone in for assemblages with a marked Pop influence, as in *Lucifer and His Pals Visit Greenwich Village* (oil assemblage, 1964), *Three Doors* (1964), and particularly the large, multipanel assemblage titled *That's Life, Miss* (1965). The oil assemblage titled *Urban Landscape* (1965) is a horrifying phantasmagoria.

In an "open letter" to himself, Noé declares that "chaos" is the only word that is "useful in denominating today's world," and he adds that, "Everything that presupposes a measure of order is incongruent with our most total reality." Beginning in 1960, with "the general romantic atmosphere of a neofigurative work," Noé later tried to "concentrate on the divided painting, with more than one unity and with a multiplicity of atmospheres." Then, in 1964, he began to interpret the problem as one of "a multiplicity of images in greater scale, and of indiscriminate accumulation." To this concept he gave the name *broken vision*. But he doesn't want his "other self" to theorize too much. Noé's parting remark is: "Long live chaos, because it is the only thing which is alive!"[6]

Jorge de la Vega (b. 1930) studied architecture for six years at the University of Buenos Aires, but is self-taught in painting. He began to exhibit in 1946, and had his first one-man show in 1951. Since then he has participated in many international exhibitions, including *New Art of Argentina* (Walker Art Center) and the third Córdoba Bienal (1966), where he was awarded the Special Prize for Argentine Painting. The American art historian and museum director Sam Hunter called him "one of the few powerfully original artists in the Bienal." In the Walker Art Center show, De la Vega exhibited three of his strongly expressionist, semiabstract compositions: *Schizoid Beast, The Memory of an Elephant* (both 1963), and *The Most Illustrious Day* (1964), all in mixed media. But by the third Córdoba Bienal he had switched to a more overtly figurative Pop Art style, based on repetition and distortion of familiar images. For example, the painting titled *Public Relations* projects the grotesquely distorted features of

[6] "Solemn Letter to Myself," in *Catalog of Exhibition No. 17*, Galería Bonino, New York (1966).

the motion picture actor Burt Lancaster. Others are *Police Chronicle*, *Everyday Life*, and *She Never Had a Beau*.

Ernesto Deira (b. 1928) graduated with a degree in law from the University of Buenos Aires, and it was only four years later that he began to study painting. He had his first one-man show in Buenos Aires in 1958. In 1964, he went to the United States, where he was given a one-man show at the Pan American Union in Washington. In that year he also received the Guggenheim International Award of the Solomon R. Guggenheim Museum in New York. In the *New Art of Argentina* exhibition organized by the Walker Art Center he was represented by three paintings in his most extreme expressionist manner of grotesque distortion: *Since Adam and Eve*, Nos. 1, 2, and *The History of the Honorable Bolingbroke* (all 1963). In the works sent to the third Córdoba Bienal (1966), he relied more on very intricate line drawing in segmented figurations that seem to emerge from the subconscious with strong erotic implications, as in *Nine Variations on a Well-stretched Frame*. Deira evades all systems, all methodical approaches to art. He is an interpreter of the irrational.

Antonio Segui, born in Córdoba in 1934, studied painting and sculpture in Argentina and Europe. From 1958 to 1961 he lived in Mexico, and in 1963 he settled in Paris. At the first Córdoba Bienal (1962) he exhibited three paintings in traditional abstract expressionist style, with American indigenist overtones: *For an American Zoology*, *Study of an American Landscape*, and *From Tikal with Sun*. By the time of the second Bienal he had shifted to expressionist neofiguratism with *Portrait of a Friend*, *After that Misfortune*, and *Box with Gentlemen*. The "gentlemen" in the latter painting are grotesque figurines who tumble helter-skelter from a large box painted with orange and yellow stripes: ideas of order contrasted with images of corruption and chaos. Segui continued his neofigurative phase in the four paintings sent to the *New Art of Argentina* exhibition (1964): *My Anatomy Class*, *The Commanders*, *The President of the Academy*, and *The Christ Child* (all 1963). Segui differs from his fellow neoexpressionists in Argentina by his insistence on formal abstract elements in his canvases, a good example being *The Christ Child*, where the entire composition is organized along abstract lines, with large contrasting color areas delineated by rectangular and diagonal forms, the whole serving as a sort of frame for the head in the center, which is that of a Negro child. The theme is spelled out with the kind of block lettering that is used for labelling packing-boxes or crates: "THE CHRIST CHILD—DETA"; the "halo" is simply a circle painted on the crate. Deira's combination of abstract, realistic (vernacular), and figurative elements demonstrates that the artist does not have to make an either/or choice. Whatever its style or component elements, a painting such as *The Christ Child* has an indisputable presence both as a work of art and as a human document.

At the third Córdoba Bienal, Segui showed three works that confirmed his originality and his ability to combine disparate elements into an artistic unity. They were *Love by Remote Control*, *The Electric Waist*, and *Shall We Go to the Sugar Loaf?* (referring to the hill of that name in Rio de Janeiro). Here too there is a combination of abstract and figurative elements, but all is in a realm of fantasy verging on the surrealist, somewhat in the manner of Paul Klee. Some elements of the picture project beyond the frame of the canvas: a large cloud above the Sugar Loaf, a girl in a monokini in *Love by Remote Control*. Here, as Sam Hunter remarks, is genuine wit and invention.

Stefan Strocen (b. 1930) is an artist whose work might be described, for want of a better term, as neofigurative, but he has little in common with the painters we have just discussed. His work is entirely personal and follows no school, no current fashion. Strocen was born in Buenos Aires and graduated from the National School of Fine Arts, where he studied both painting and engraving. A travel grant enabled him to work in Paris from 1959 to 1961, and while in Europe he had one-man shows in Brussels, Madrid, and Paris. In 1962 and 1963 he traveled in Mexico and the United States, exhibiting in both countries, as he did again in 1964 and 1965. In 1957 he was a cofounder of the Buenos Aires Group of young artists.

Strocen's work draws its characteristic features from primitive imagery and ritual. His semiabstract anthropomorphic and animalistic figures are skeletally delineated against a mono-chromatic impasto that provides a harmonious unity, as well as a beautifully rich texture, for each painting, and serves as a stabilizing element for these primitive visions and savage rites. In *Wild Awakening* (1965), *Ritual Image*, *Telluric Divinity*, *Heathen Ritual*, *Primitive Spectre*, and similar paintings, Strocen has given a new dimension to neoprimitivism as well as to neofiguratism. His use of color is exceptionally fine.

Geometrical and Optical Art

In a world entirely apart are the "geometricians" of Argentine painting, exponents of what they call *pintura generativa* (generative painting), who take their point of departure from the so-called "concrete art" of the 1930's (associated with Theo Van Doesburg and Hans Arp). The group consists of Miguel Angel Vidal, Eduardo Mac-Entyre, Ary Brizzi, and Carlos Silva. The term *Arte Generativo*, was proposed by the painter and critic Ignacio Pirovano. In a statement explaining their position, written in 1962, these artists said, "There is no doubt that we have as our starting point the teachings of formalism, and especially of the art called 'concrete.' But we are not concrete artists."[7] The main difference is that generative painting aims at achieving a more dynamic quality. It seeks to convey the illusion of movement. It is interested in the line only as it engenders a figure, and in the figure only as it engenders a geometric form. These forms undergo a series of displacements, either in contrary or in consecutive motion, and they in turn generate a single total form, as well as many other interior subsidiary forms. The whole is conceived as "a series of optical sequences." Thus, generative painting is related to Op Art, but without the latter's propensity to generate actual physical movement.

Generative art is also concerned with the creation of force and energy as aesthetic values derived from the technological age in which we live. Instead of seeking to escape from technology, these painters assert, art should seek new forms of beauty that may be engendered by this technology itself. They believe that their

[7] *Arte generativo*. Museo de Arte Moderno en Río de Janeiro, Junio-Julio, 1962.

art projects another type of life, and that their paintings acquire a new identity in space.

Within the group, Ari Brizzi (b. 1930), who is also a sculptor, is closest to the geometrical abstraction that we associate with Mondrian and Arp. His sculpture is sheer constructivism (*Construction from a Vertical Axis, Kinetic Cube*, etc.). Miguel Angel Vidal (b. 1928) favors dynamically intersecting planes and converging points, with a strong three-dimensional emphasis. Solid forms are contrasted with transparent planes made up of finely drawn, wire-like lines. The titles of his paintings are indicative of the aims of generative art: *Horizontal Displacement of Two Rectangles, Integration with Vibration of the Diagonal, Rectangle Generating Vibration, Radiation and Movement on a Red Background* (all 1965). Carlos Silva (b. 1930) is partial to pointillism with delicately adumbrated abstractions. Eduardo Mac-Entyre (b. 1929) likes to project swirling circular forms, more often mesh-like than solid, which he sometimes intersects with vertical or horizontal lines, as in *Three Openings* (1967).

Deriving from the the geometric Op Art of Victor Vasarely is the Groupe de Recherche d'Art Visuel, founded in Paris in 1960 upon the initiative of several Argentine artists living there, including Julio Le Parc, Hugo R. Demarco, and Gyula Kosice. This group combines constructivism with all sorts of kinetic and optical effects intended to involve the viewer in the work of art. Its members are sculptors rather than painters, yet their work does not strictly belong to either domain: it is an expression of the unclassifiable intermediate art of our time, which tends always to be "something else." Le Parc (b. 1928) went to Paris in 1958 on a grant from the French government and has since made his home there. Early in 1966 he had a one-man show at the Howard Wise Gallery in New York, which a writer for *The New York Times* described as follows: "Kinetic reflectors bounce light patterns on screens. In a glass-topped box, a bevy of ping-pong balls plays madly with a spinning pole. Buttons pressed on a compartmented console cause balls to bobble, spirals to spin, and light to dance." Le Parc, in his campaign to involve the viewer, has invented what he calls "Optacles." In these, "He attaches metal reflectors, strips, and stereoptically-placed plastic discs to eyeglass frames.

They put the wearer in a little Op world of his own." A large traveling exhibition organized by the Groupe in 1964 was extremely successful in Buenos Aires: on a single Sunday it attracted as many as 16,000 visitors to the Museum of Fine Art. Le Parc himself has had his works acquired by many museums in America and Europe. In 1966, he was awarded the First Prize for Painting (*sic*) at the Venice Biennale.

Hugo R. Demarco (b. 1932) studied painting in Buenos Aires, began to exhibit in 1956, and three years later settled in Paris. In *New Art of Argentina* (1964–65) he was represented by a composition titled *Spatial Dynamics* (glass, plexiglass, and metal, 1963), made up of juxtaposed series of small rectangular and circular discs, some of them suspended on vertical metal poles within a box-like frame.

Luis Tomasello (b. 1915) was also trained in Buenos Aires, and in 1957 joined the group of Argentine artists who chose to make their home in Paris. He has participated in many international exhibitions and group shows, both in America and Europe, including the Salon des Réalités Nouvelles in Paris (1959–64). In 1953, he was a founding member of the Salón Arte Nuevo in Buenos Aires. He favors the use of wood in his purely abstract compositions, such as *Reflection # 48* (1960), in which small, prism-shaped pieces of wood are affixed to the surface in asymmetrical patterns.

Marcelo Bonevardi (b. 1929) also works with wood, but in entirely different types of constructions, which are architectural in concept—in fact, Bonevardi was trained as an architect before taking up his special kind of "painting." His works might be described as painting-constructions, since he uses oil on canvas together with shaped pieces of wood that are built into the painting, in either concave or convex forms, usually the former. Bonevardi has lived in New York since 1958, when he obtained a Guggenheim Fellowship. His work has been widely recognized for its originality, its inventiveness, its inalterable identity, its formal and textural interest, and its cool objectivity. Representative painting-constructions are *Reliquary, Oracle, Moon Shine, Sacred Enclosure, The Sky Watcher,* and *Sun Wheel* (Plate 22). As may be noted from these titles—and from the imagery of the works themselves—Bonevardi's constructivism is not strictly formalist but, on the contrary, is imbued with metaphysical implications. The key to this duality is perhaps contained in a passage from his note-book,

> If my dreams had the obsessive persistence of time, if in meditation I could contemplate the mystery of my own skeleton and ascend the Rainbow until I reached the Great Silence, and then dared to venture in my boat through the Labyrinth of a mystic geography, perhaps one day I could construct that object—of which I once caught a glimpse in a small wood box with a dead scarab....[8]

César Paternosto (b. 1931) cultivates a strictly abstract style that has been called "chromatic geometry." Its distinctive feature, which distinguishes it from other types of geometric abstraction that we have discussed, is that the artist shapes his canvas to correspond with the outline of his forms, which are both rectilinear and curvilinear. Strictly speaking, there is no "picture," no composition within a frame, since the artist deliberately sets out to destroy the concept of a rectangular space for the canvas. Moreover, his compositions are divided into two segments, spatially separated, which further breaks down the concept of a unified field of vision. And even though the two parts would symmetrically mesh or interlock (in their linear configurations) if brought together, the fact that they are separated gives them a special kind of dynamism. The rhythm is at once flowing and interrupted, and its dynamism is reinforced by the bold and effective use of contrasting color areas. Paternosto won a well-deserved first prize at the third Córdoba Bienal in 1966, where he exhibited four works, among them *Solitude* (reproduced in *Art in America*, March–April, 1967) and *Duino*.

Pop Art

Delia Cancela (b. 1940) belongs to the generation that came of age in the heyday of Pop Art, and she immediately stepped into it with both feet. Two of her Pop Art assemblages, *Girls*

[8] *Catalog of Exhibition No. 15*, Galería Bonino, New York (1965).

Don't Go Out Alone and *The Temptations of Mr. X*, were shown in the exhibit, *New Art of Argentina* (Walker Art Center, 1964–65). They are in the Rauschenberg manner. Since 1964, Delia Cancela has been working in collaboration with the painter Pablo Mesejeán (b. 1937). They exhibited four works in the third Córdoba Bienal (1966), including *Bob Dylan and Cloud, Rita Tushingham and Cloud*, and *Saint-Laurent Model and Landscape*— all in a straightforward cartoon style resembling that of Roy Lichtenstein. The most that can be said for these artists at present is that they have brought classical Pop Art into the Argentine spectrum with a certain spontaneous naïveté and youthful freshness.

The same might be said of Marta Minujín (b. 1941), who lived in Paris from 1961 to 1964 and who has been up front with the avant-garde ever since she began exhibiting in 1957. She early abandoned two-dimensional painting for constructions or "combines" using all kinds of materials and found objects, as in *The Plight of the Pillow* (painted pillows and cardboard, 1961), and *Mattress* (painted fabric, 1964), definitely an *hommage à Rauschenberg*. In view of this trend toward working in three dimensions, it is not surprising that Marta Minujín has turned to sculpture, and it was in this category that she obtained, in 1967, a grant from the Guggenheim Foundation. She has also been active in promoting "happenings" in Buenos Aires, including a large one staged at the Instituto Torcuato Di Tella, on the fashionable Calle Florida, in October, 1966. On this occasion she displayed one of her recent works, *El Batacazo* (*The Violent Contusion*), described as "a construction of plastic and neon lights containing live rabbits and flies."

Sculpture

The tradition of naturalistic and monumental sculpture is represented in Argentina by Rogelio Yrurtia (1879–1950), José Fioravante (b. 1896), and Alfredo Bigatti (1898–1964). Yrurtia was responsible for the admirable equestrian statue of Colonel Dorrego and for the tomb of President Rivadavia in Buenos Aires.

Fioravanti's monuments in the same city include those of Nicolas Avellaneda, Roque Sáenz Peña, Bolívar, and Franklin D. Roosevelt. He also made an excellent bronze bust of Bolívar. Bigatti and Fioravanti both worked on the immense monument to the national banner, designed by the architect Angel Guido, in the port city of Rosario, on the Paraná River. Of the sculptors who have chosen to continue the naturalistic tradition, the most notable is José Alonso (b. 1911).

Pablo Curatela Manes (1891–1962), a pupil of Bourdelle in Paris, began to work in the naturalistic manner, but very soon found new paths and became the first great innovator in Argentine sculpture. He developed his own style in Paris during the years 1920–26, working largely with bronze, and pioneered in the use of open structures (*The Acrobats, Icarius*). In 1926, he was appointed councillor of the Argentine Embassy in Paris, which made heavy demands on his time but enabled him to continue living in France. After becoming accustomed to his new situation, he resumed work in 1930 with such important bronzes as *The Three Graces, The Annunciation I, The Gaucho and His Horse, Head of an Apostle, Feminine Torso, Torso with Two Planes, Triangular Torso,* and *Maternity* (some of these were not completed until ten years later). His work of this period culminated in his bas-reliefs for the Paris International Exposition of 1937.

Curatela Manes remained in France during World War II, and the anguish of these years is reflected in many sculptures, including *War*. He returned to Buenos Aires in 1950, and in 1958 was appointed Argentine Commissioner to the Brussels' World Fair. In spite of his official appointments, he never enjoyed the financial rewards and the creative freedom that his achievements merited. Not until 1961 did he have an adequate studio of his own. And a year later he died, still in full creative activity. From his early massive figures to the fantastic inventiveness of his last works, Curatela Manes revealed both mastery of his material and an unceasing imaginative vitality. His last works were indeed the most iconoclastic and original of his entire production.

Of the newer generation, two women have especially distinguished themselves in Argentine sculpture: Noemi Gerstein and Alicia Peñalba. Noemi Gerstein (b. 1910) studied with Alfredo

Bigatti in Buenos Aires and with Ossip Zadkine in Paris (1950–51). After *The Cyclist* (1951) she ceased to be directly influenced by Zadkine and moved nearer to the world of Henry Moore, as reflected in *Mother and Child* (bronze, 1952). She was, however, moving beyond this phase to a completely open and entirely abstract form, as in the *Model for the Unknown Political Prisoner* (bronze and steel, 1953–54), *Orpheus* (black bronze, 1954), and *Maternity* (iron, bronze, and brass, 1954). The use of iron was especially significant, for it led to a new development in which slender, delicately shaped, variform iron components were employed in freestanding vertical structures (*Scherzo* and *Homage to the Sun* [both 1958]),or within a large rectangular metal frame, as in the *Palier Grate* (1959). These were followed by other vertical structures in iron: *Personage* (1958), *Cactus* (1958–59), using larger, more solid components, grouped asymmetrically around a central axis. As the artist herself said in an interview given in 1961, "I have always been attracted by all kinds of metallic constructions, and I have doubtless also been influenced by having lived for the past few years near a factory where I daily observe the functioning of many varied types of machinery. This circumstance enabled me to have access to soldering equipment which I began to use about four years ago, and which is now my principal working tool."

Thus from the world of machinery and industrial design, Noemi Gerstein developed the materials, the forms, and the techniques that, since 1959, she has applied to her most characteristic creations: structures made by soldering together small tubes of metal, in both round and quadrangular forms. The material consists of iron, bronze, brass, or tin. In the words of the artist: "These materials permit me to create with great freedom, for if sometimes I use them according to a pre-established plan, as a rule I begin by taking small components, without a basic scheme, and as I solder these together they suggest an image that I then use and transform." In this manner were created such works as *The Girl* (brass and silver, 1959–60), *Warlike Image* (iron, 1960), *The Lovers* (brass and silver, 1961), *Homage to Van Gogh* (iron, 1961), and *Goliath* (iron, 1962). These are essentially vertical structures, though in *Warlike Image* lateral tubular projections are used to give an impression of guns or cannons, in keeping with the theme, and in *Homage to Van Gogh* the small sections of metal tube are arranged in a free horseshoe shape, an inverted arch that is used again, with greater freedom and complexity, in an important work titled *The Origin* (iron, 1962). In these works, as also in *From the Depths* (iron, 1960–61), the principle of verticality is abandoned in favor of free, asymmetrical spatial projections that give an expressive, dynamic quality to the creations of this period. The culmination of this tendency is found in the extraordinary work titled *Scorpion* (brass and silver, 1962, Instituto Di Tella Acquisition Prize). In the apt phrase of Osvaldo Svanascini, this work "is organized like a poem that has been petrified in full flight." It forms a large ascending curve punctuated by eight nuclei from which radiate, like the rays of a metallic star, clusters of tubes of varied length. It soars into space explosively, but repudiates the sleek functionalism of a rocket or nuclear spaceship. It brings the stars down to earth while proclaiming man's imaginative freedom.

These star-like clusters, boldly and beautifully equilibrated in space, reappear in some of Noemi Gerstein's most remarkable works of the 1960's, notably *Constellation* (1963), *Mandragora II* (1963–64), and *Tritónico* (1964), all in bronze and silver. At the same time, she continued to use the small tubular segments with increasing spontaneity and formal freedom, as in *The Small Dragon* (brass and silver, 1962), *Atolon* (bronze and silver, 1961), *The Great Bear* (bronze and silver, 1962), and *Looping* (bronze and silver, 1964), perhaps her most daring venture in the conquest of space. An exceptionally interesting work of this period is *The Blaze* (silverplated bronze, 1961), which combines tubular clusters with curvilinear metal plates that suggest the upward twisting of flames. To this period also belong such successful fantasies as *Don Quixote and Sancho* (iron, stainless steel, bronze, and silver) and *The Big Bad Wolf* (iron), both executed in 1964.

Alicia Peñalba (b. 1918) also studied with Zadkine in Paris, but his influence was less important to her early work than that of Arp and Brancusi. She has lived in Paris since 1948, and it was there, in 1957, that she had her first individual show, at the Galerie du Dragon. In 1960, she had two important personal shows, one at the Galerie Claude Bernard in Paris, the other at the Otto Gerson Gallery in New York. The following year she was awarded the International Sculpture Prize at the sixth Bienal of São Paulo. A selection of her work from the years 1960–65 was shown at the Galería Bonino, New York, in April– May, 1966. Meanwhile, she had participated in many international exhibitions, in Antwerp, Tokyo, Kassel, Vienna, Pittsburgh, Paris, and elsewhere.

In her earlier work, Peñalba drew upon primitive sources of inspiration and created a number of totem-like structures, such as *Magic Forest*, which appeared to have phallic connotations. Regarding the works of this period, the artist has said,

> Too much has been said about vegetal forms with respect to my early sculptures. That period of my work, which has been called "totémique," was motivated by a need to spiritualize the symbols of eroticism, which is the source of all creation and the purest and most sacred state in the life of man. The whole embodiment of the mystery of procreation was lifted toward the sky in solid, entwined forms, protecting the delicate fruit placed inside and suggesting as much the idealization of the flesh as its birth. This world of forms did not come from leaves or branches, nor even from a direct reference to nature. Moreover, it is not the imitation of forms of nature which makes the finished work, but the placing in order of these forms, made rhythmic by the individual. Through the need for poetical expression of one's deepest consciousness the most unknown part of man is revealed. This first period (from 1952 to 1957) exhausted an interior necessity. Thus exorcised, my sculpture took other roads, which are answerable to a more civilized and more complex epoch, to the search for a perfection of sculptural means. It was in this way that my sculptures began to be more aerial, transpierced with light, and seeking balance of form in all dimensions.[9]

The Belgian art critic Roger van Gindertael speaks of "the sublimated sensuality" in Peñalba's more recent sculpture. Here she reveals her predilection for clay, "the only truly plastic sub-stance." One can find, if one wishes, vestiges of totemic structure and of eroticism in a work such as *Great Double* (1962); but her characteristic works of this period consist rather of soaring,

[9] As quoted in Roger van Gindertael, Preface to *Catalog of Exhibition No. 20*, Galería Bonino, New York (1966).

asymmetrical compositions, "more aerial," suggesting motion in space, an impression of wings, of flight, as in *Absent* (1961), *Alada* (1963), *Annonciatrice* (1963), and the small *Winged Object* (1965 [Plate 23]). The imagery of wings is also seen in some of Peñalba's reliefs, such as *Scorcery on the Wall* (1960) and the large *Orolirio* (1962), and in some of her large group compositions, such as *Winged Field*, installed on the grounds of the St. Gall University in Switzerland (1963), and *Trilogy* (begun in 1958, completed in 1965). Another striking group composition is the polyester relief installed on the park wall of the Kroller-Muller Museum, Holland (1960); here the forms projecting from the wall in balanced groups seem partly to suggest wings and partly the marine forms (fins, sleek porpoise-like bodies) of the sculpture titled *Sea Fruit* (1962). One may persist in finding traces of animal forms in the splendid *Trophy* of 1962; but there is certainly no thought of "naturalism" in any of Peñalba's work. She is a creative artist in the truest sense of the term. By "seeking balance of form in all dimensions," she has created an enduring world in which matter is shaped by aspiration, imagination, and creative skill.

Gyula Kosice (b. 1924), of Czech origin, was brought to Buenos Aires as a child and has lived there ever since. He studied both drawing and sculpture and has been very active as an aesthetic theorist, as the organizer of artistic groups, and as a poet. He founded the movement known as Arte Madí, which issued its manifesto in 1946, and which published a review that appeared in eight issues (1947). He was a pioneer of abstract constructivism in Latin America, and he has been called (by Michel Seuphor) an "artist-inventor." His inventive vein led Kosice to create what he calls "hydraulic sculpture," first exhibited at the Galerie Denise René of Paris in April, 1960. In a manifesto titled *The Architecture of Water in Sculpture*, Kosice pointed to the importance of water as a mobile element and declared that in spite of this, "water has not been utilized up to the present as a possible aesthetic material and outlet." He undertook to remedy such neglect. In order to accomplish this it was necessary to enclose the water within a transparent sculpture and "to utilize its tendency to dispersion, inherent in its fluidity, bestowing upon it a capacity for circulation by means of the displacement of air in all controllable directions." This was, in principle, the point of departure for "hydraulic sculpture." (Kosice recognizes the absurdity of using the term "sculpture" in such a context, but he pleads the impossibility of finding a satisfactory substitute.) He writes:

> *It will be necessary to investigate progressively the possibilities and the behavior offered by cubic measurement, the liquid volume; to permute its poetic conduct and its exact inward nature, changeful and mobile; its pulsation at each change of position and its approximations of level and of refraction. It will be necessary to determine its precise limits in order that its spatial-temporal orbit may function within a compositional order, not only to resolve the antinomy of content and container but also to go beyond it. It will be necessary, above all, to understand that the arts of our time (and not only the visual arts) are in continual revolution, and that every style is, in the final analysis, a crystallization of forms that are both valuable and usable.*[10]

For his hydraulic sculpture, Kosice chose the medium of plexiglass because it is both transparent and flexible. At the international exhibition of sculpture organized in 1962 by the Instituto Torcuato Di Tella—at which Kosice received the National Prize for Argentina—he showed his *Giratory Hydraulic Semisphere* (plexiglass and water, 1961), *Alternation of Form with the Word* (aluminum, plexiglass, and water, 1960–62), and a tryptich, *Mobile Hydraulic Relief* (plexiglass, water, and light, 1960–62). Michel Seuphor summed up Kosice's waterworks as a new statement of an old problem (with which he himself was much concerned around 1925): that of the *perpetuum mobile* within the *perpetuum stabile*.

As early as 1946, Kosice made the model of a *Project for a suspended hydraulic habitat*, consisting largely of circular and hemispheric forms, which is so far-out that it might conceivably prefigure the Space City of the future. In an important exhibit at the Galería Bonino, New York, in May 1967, Kosice experimented further with the interplay of water, light, and movement, in such works as *Theoretical island of a half world* (plexiglass and water), *Mobile hydromural* (plexiglass, water, and light),

---

[10] As quoted in *Premio Internacional de Escultura Instituto Torcuato Di Tella,* Catalog (Buenos Aires), 1962), p. 41.

Reflection and linear movement of water (plexiglass and water), and *Diyi all the time* (idem; see Plate 20).

Many other Argentine sculptors are involved in various kinds of abstract creation. Naun Knop (b. 1917), working chiefly in marble or metal, shows a predilection for massive, truncated stylizations of the human body (*Figure* [1959], *Torso* [1960], *Reminiscence* [1960)]. Aldo Paparella (born in Italy, 1920), who has lived in Argentina since 1950, works mostly with aluminum, which he uses in asymmetrical, crumpled, multi-faceted conglomerations that give the impression of having been conceived with complete spontaneity. He calls these sculptures *Suggestions,* and identifies them merely by number and date. In the work of Eduardo Sabelli (b. 1925), who is a member of the Madí Group, we find a pure type of constructivism in metal. The titles are indicative : *Structure According to Two Spaces* (iron, 1961), *Verticality* (bluish bronze, 1961), *Space in Flight* (iron, 1961). Sabelli describes his sculpture as based on the ordering of tensions, equilibrium through equivalency, and harmonious relations between open and solid forms. Alberto Wells (b. 1939) studied drawing, engraving, and illustrating, as well as sculpture. He works with wood, employing both tubular and rectangular components in juxtaposition, and in a quasisurrealistic vein of allusion and illusion : *The Domestic Phantom, Topography of the Night, Walkyrie, Elevator for the Scaffold* (all from the early 1960's).

Returning to the question of the polarity of artistic expression in Argentina and Mexico, we can now observe that Argentina has been essentially modern since about 1920, while Mexico was somewhat archaic for several decades longer. In other words, Argentine painting, in particular, was strictly contemporary in the full meaning of the term—"with the present time"—while Mexican painting was anachronistic, behind the times. In Argentina, the emphasis has been on art for art's sake; in Mexico, on art for the sake of social and ideological values. In Argentina, the private art of the easel predominated, while in Mexico the public art of the mural held the center of the stage. National and ethnic factors were strong in Mexican painting, negligible in Argentine painting. Mexican art was controversial and polemical, its leading representatives often involved in private and public scandals.

Argentine art has been unsensational, controversial only within the context of aesthetics, and far removed from the arena of revolutionary politics. With the founding in the early 1960's of the American Art Biennials in Córdoba and the Division of Visual Arts of the Instituto Torcuato Di Tella in Buenos Aires—the latter under the dynamic direction of Jorge Romero Brest—Argentina immediately assumed an important and influential role in the international art scene. With the general decline of nationalism and the rapidly growing acceptance of cosmopolitan currents in contemporary art, the new art of Argentina, particularly in painting, sculpture, and mixed media, quickly acquired greater international prestige. Virtually all currents of contemporary art are well represented in Argentina and some of them—the kinetic-optical art of Julio Le Parc and the abstract sculpture of Alicia Peñabla, for example—have been universally acclaimed. It may be objected that the art of Peñalba and Le Parc is not Argentine but completely international. But that is precisely the point.

URUGUAY

Uruguay owes its importance in the history of Latin American art above all to two artists, Pedro Figari and Joaquín Torres García, who were not only remarkably fine and original painters but also remarkable men in all respects: in their intellectual capacities, their moral strength, and their many-sided talents.

Figari (1861–1938) was born in Montevideo, where he studied law and obtained his degree in 1886. He also studied painting with an Italian artist named Godofredo Somavilla, but he did not at this early stage take up painting seriously. Instead, he embarked on a highly successful public career in law (becoming widely known as a defense counsel), as publisher and journalist (he founded the newspaper *El Diario*), and as a writer on many subjects, from jurisprudence to poetry, including education and aesthetics. He also entered politics and was elected to a seat in the Chamber of Deputies. In 1915, he was appointed Director of the Escuela de Artes y Oficios, a national vocational school, where he instituted reforms in industrial training. But art proved to have the strongest hold upon his allegiance. Moving to Buenos Aires in 1921, he devoted himself intensively to painting during the next four years. He then settled in Paris where, during a long stay of nearly nine years, he fully realized himself as an artist within the postimpressionist manner of Bonnard and Vuillard but with an authentic individuality of style. Figari became a master of what Maurice Denis called "subjective distortion"—the quality that brings into play the artist's own perception within the framework of "a purely aesthetic and decorative concept." He concentrated on landscapes of the River Plate region (the pampa), on provincial domestic scenes—especially the *tertulias* or social gatherings that he depicted with such charm and character—and on scenes of everyday life.

In 1933, Figari returned to Montevideo, where he spent his last years. There is probably no other South American painter of his time whose work is more highly prized today. Many of his paintings are in private collections in Argentina and Uruguay; others are in the Museo Histórico Nacional of Montevideo.

Torres García and "Constructive Universalism"

Although Joaquín Torres García (1874–1949) spent over forty years of his life away from the country of his birth, his influence on the artistic and intellectual climate of Uruguay, and to a certain extent of Argentina also, was strong and deep. His father, a small merchant from Catalonia who had migrated to Uruguay as a youth, decided to return to his homeland with his family in 1891, when Joaquín was seventeen. Soon afterwards young Torres García enrolled in the Academy of Fine Arts in Barcelona, and later at the Academia Baixa. But a reaction against academicism threw him into the Bohemian circles of Barcelona, where he found congenial fellowship among painters, writers, and musicians who met at a cabaret called The Four Cats. Rejecting the fashionable mode of impressionism, Torres García, like his companions Picasso and Sunyer, adhered to the example of Toulouse-Lautrec.

The influence of Puvis de Chavannes revealed to Torres García a classical ideal of art, to which he was strongly attracted. This in turn led him to the study of the Italian primitive painters, and beyond them to the art of Greek antiquity. These classical sources were to retain their lasting effect on his aesthetic thought, for he was eventually to equate the terms classicism, humanism, and universalism. In the meantime, he painted some frescoes for two churches in Barcelona and began to work for an artist who showed him quite a different world from that of Puvis de Chavannes, the architect Antonio Gaudí, whose exuberant neobaroque forms still fill us with amazement. Under Gaudí's guidance he worked on the stained-glass windows of the Cathedral of Palma de Mallorca. In 1910, he painted two panels for the Uruguayan Pavilion at the World's Fair in Brussels. Returning to Barcelona, he was commissioned to paint a series of murals for the great hall of the *Diputació* (Provincial Government), through the patronage of Prat de la Riba, the eminent champion of Catalan nationalism. Upon the latter's death in 1917, the work was discontinued because of factional rivalries. Discouraged and disgusted, Torres García resolved to quit Spain in 1920. Receiving no encouragement from Uruguay, he thought first of going to Mexico, but then decided in favor of New York. By this time he had a wife and children to support, he was little known outside of Barcelona, and the enterprise was altogether hazardous.

First impressions of New York were enthusiastic: "This is civilization! And the heart leaps with joy. Why didn't we come here before?" But enthusiasm dwindled with depleted funds—and with the cold, blustery weather that Torres García detested. There was the discouraging search for work, an uncongenial commercial job, uncertain patronage, and the pinch of poverty. Withal, he went on painting, as he had done in Barcelona—scenes of the city, its people, its streets, its traffic, its waterfront. The paintings of this period he described as a synthesis of expressionist and geometric elements, with free rhythms, "but already with vertical and horizontal dominants that later were to be the foundation for another style of painting" (i.e., his own brand of "constructivist" painting). Eventually he gave up the struggle for existence in New York, and in 1922 returned to Europe with his family, going first to Italy and then to Paris (1926). In Paris he managed to gain a foothold in the art world and for a time enjoyed relative prosperity, exhibiting and selling his work in some of the leading galleries.

In 1928, after Torres García and several of his friends had their paintings refused by the Salon d'Automne, they organized a group show called *Cinq Refusés*, which attracted considerable attention. As a result, Torres García began to meet and associate with some of the leading proponents of abstract art: Theo Van Doesburg, Vantongerloo, Mondrian (the founders of neoplasticism), and the art critic Michel Seuphor, with whom he founded a review and a group called *Cercle et Carré* (Circle and Square). The group organized an important exhibition of abstract art, in which more than eighty painters participated. In spite of his association with the leaders of neoplasticism, Torres García did not altogether abandon figurative painting. He was always seeking a synthesis of the abstract and the figurative, and in 1928 he made a definitive breakthrough in this direction. In the words of Dario Suro, "The assimilation of cubism, the violent brush strokes of the fauvists, and the rectangular forms of the neoplasticists led Torres García to realize or to divine a painting of rectangular divisions; but the rectangular forms do not stand in space, in nothingness; the pure constructive aspect has been exchanged for symbolic constructions, a new humanism, a mystical humanism."[11]

In his autobiography, where he always wrote of himself in the third person, Torres García explains the change that occurred in his painting in 1928.

The difficulty is that if a painting is composed with abstract forms only—geometric or irregular—what will the painter do with something that he also wishes to express and which has to do with concrete things? For if he tries to ally the two things (as he has done a hundred times), naturalism loses, and so does the plastic construction. But one day the thought comes to him: to every abstraction there must always correspond, as the idea of a thing, something that is also abstract. What can this be? In order to be depicted graphically, it must be either the written name of the thing, or a schematic image, resembling

[11] Catalog of *Fifteenth Memorial Exhibition*, Rose Fried Gallery, New York (1964).

the apparent reality as little as possible: like a sign. And this is what he does. He places, in the compartmentalized construction, designed like a stone fence, and in each compartment, the design of a particular thing. And there it is! By pure chance . . . or obeying unconsciously an inner vision, he placed in that first work, and in their respective niches, a House (like those that children draw), a Ship, an Anchor, the letter B, a man, a Fish. . . .[12]

Such, in essence, was the genesis, at once empirical and mystical, of the aesthetic principle that Torres García eventually elaborated, in his voluminous writings and lectures, under the name of "Constructive Universalism."

The years from 1925 to 1932 were very productive for Torres García; he produced some fifteen hundred works during this period. And, most important, he found his own path as a creative artist. Yet after 1929 his material situation in Paris became increasingly difficult (as did the situations of many other artists). In 1929, he sold only one canvas—to the American collector Katherine S. Dreier. At the end of 1932, he decided to try his luck in Madrid; but this proved to be an unfortunate move. A year later he was casting about for another haven. By this time his friends in Uruguay had succeeded in preparing the climate for his return. In April, 1934, Torres García and his family embarked for Montevideo. There, in the city of his birth and of his adolescence, he was to spend the rest of his days, a prophet at long last honored in his own land.

Torres García in Montevideo

In Montevideo, Torres García continued for a time the publication, in Spanish, of the review *Circle and Square*, making it primarily a vehicle for his theories and for the art school that he founded. He also established the Association of Constructivist Art, which sponsored courses on art, archaeology, and aesthetics, as well as several publications by Torres García, including his *Metafísica de la prehistoria indoamericana* (1939)—his major statement on the aesthetic theory of Indoamerican art. Torres García

[12] *Historia de mi Vida*, p. 268.

believed that the pre-Columbian past—its myths, its artifacts, its prehistoric retentions—could provide a key to creative culture in Latin America. He maintained that the pre-Incaic cultures of South America were worthy of being incorporated into what he called "The Great Human Tradition," chiefly by virtue of their "representative symbolism," to which he ascribed a human universality. He gave special importance to the most archaic types of ceramic design and decoration, from which he developed many elements of his own pictographic painting. He believed in the possibility of an authentic and autonomous American art, radically different from that of the Old World, the product of a new civilization, "symbol and image of the man of the New World." And he held that such an art must necessarily be metaphysical. In his own work, he believed that he had created a paradigm with his *Cosmic Monument* (1938) erected in the Parque Rodó of Montevideo.

This monument, in the words of Paul F. Damaz,

> *embodies the whole philosophy of his "humanistic constructivism": universal man represented through abstraction, geometry, rhythm, proportion, lines, plants and idealization of objects. It also reflects his aspiration toward "a decorative monumental art, with a sense generally human, religiously laic, and related to craftsmanship." The monument is basically a pink granite stele divided by a series of vertical and horizontal lines into rectangular spaces, in which the artist has represented by single lines symbols and objects that are part of the collective life of man.*[13]

The symbol is the message.

The objects, figures, signs, and symbols used by Torres García were not chosen at random or merely for a decorative or pictorial purpose. In a book titled *Estructura* (1935), he explained in detail the meaning of these elements and their significance in his philosophy of universal-humanist constructivism. Beginning with the most basic elements, the vertical line represents Man, the horizontal, Nature; their intersection represents the relation of the one to the other. The rectilinear and curvilinear represent the

---

[13] *Art in Latin American Architecture*, p. 205.

dual principle of life, the positive and negative poles, as in the two sexes. The numeral one (1) represents Reason, the Idea, "since the one is the sum and beginning of all; that which was before creation, and is therefore at its base. . . . In this unity everything is in potential." In its latent or potential state, as possibility, this prime unity is represented by the number one; in its active manifestation, by the number two (2) (the will to existence, being); and in its organization or materialization, by the figure three (3). The result is a perfect triangle:

This triangle also corresponds to the three dimensions of man's existence: reason, abstraction, in the first dimension; emotion, will, desire or nondesire (i.e., duality), in the second dimension; and three dimensions for the "reality" of the objective world.

According to Torres García, "These components—the abstract, emotional, and material—make up the aggregate of each human being. But they do not exist in all in equal proportion. In some, reason dominates, in others the material part, in others the soul." This leads to the artist's schematic representation of the human figure, in rectlinear outlines, with each main segment varying in size according to the proportion of the basic components. Each component also has its symbol:

An extrapolation of the triangle concept produces a further schematization, by means of three triangles that correspond to the intellectual, moral, and physical spheres:

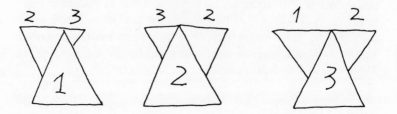

This in turn leads to a diagrammatic representation of the three "proportions" (Torres García calls these diagrams *psicogramas*):

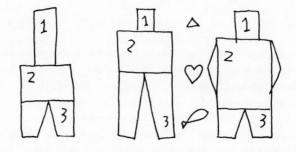

For the rest, Torres García's basic symbols are related to the various geological and biological ages of the earth: primitive, primary, secondary, tertiary, quaternary; and to the earliest artifacts and figurative representations of mankind. From these he is led to the primitive or preliterate cultures that have survived in the modern world. His aim is to represent *all* the phases of man's existence: past, present, and eternal (timeless). Hence in a single painting, we may find a juxtaposition of figures or symbols ranging from the paleolithic to the industrial era. Prehistoric designs, cosmic symbols, forms of animal and plant life, stand beside the clock, the steamship, the steam engine. Their simultaneous presentation through spatial juxtaposition achieves the unity of time, space, and culture that is the aim of universal constructivism. It is in this sense that the work of Torres García becomes truly modern, contemporary with the electronic age of the twentieth century and beyond. Several analysts of contemporary culture have remarked that modern electronic technology, which succeeded the "chirographic-typographic" era of the alphabet and the printing press, is in a way (through its emphasis on the visual image: motion pictures, television, photography) a throwback to the earlier primitive cultures of mankind. By his visual projection of simultaneity in space and time, Torres García spans the gap between preliterate and electronic cultures. As Father Walter J. Ong writes, "All cultures are present within us today simultaneously—if they are not, we are to that extent today unrealized human beings."[14] Similarly, all cultures were simultaneously present within the artistic-humanistic vision of Joaquín Torres García, one of the most fully realized human beings who ever lived; and by a long and persistent search he found both the means to express this vision graphically and the power to formulate its principles conceptually. Seldom has there been a closer cohesion between an artistic theory and its plastic realization. (See Plate 16.)

In the foregoing sketch we have attempted merely to indicate some of the basic concepts and procedures used by Torres García in developing his theory and practice of constructive universalism. A complete explanation lies outside the scope of a general survey such as this. But the indications here given, however incomplete and inadequate, will at least give the reader a clue to the meaning of many symbols and figures that appear in the "constructivist" paintings of Torres García, as well as in his *Cosmic Monument*. Even though his method can be described in general terms as a division of the canvas into (roughly) rectilinear compartments, in each of which is located a symbol, an image, or a figure, this description is far too mechanical to convey the infinite variety, the sense of spontaneous creativity, the interplay of the spiritual and the material, of the complex and the primitive, the stylistic metamorphoses of the basic elements, the varying degrees of

[14] *In the Human Grain: Further Explorations of Contemporary Culture* (New York, 1967).

density and openness in the graphic configuration, the constantly varied visual rhythms, the dialectic confrontation of abstract and figurative elements, the subtle and poetic use of color, the dynamic contrast of rectilinear and curvilinear forms—in short, the unceasing fascination of a pictorial universe that achieves the maximum potential of unity in variety, and in which all symbolic, humanistic, and cosmic concepts are conveyed through strictly plastic values. I am in complete agreement with Jean Cassou's statement that Torres García "is one of the greatest and finest figures among the artists of our time."

The presence of Torres García in Montevideo gave impetus to the development of artistic cosmopolitanism in that capital, which furthermore was traditionally in close cultural contact with Buenos Aires. Hence it is not surprising to find that many contemporary tendencies are represented in the art world of Montevideo.

Other Painters and Graphic Artists

The majority of Uruguayan painters have favored abstract expressionism. The list includes Oscar García Reino, José Cuneo Perinetti, Vicente Martín, Norberto Berdia (who has also done figurative murals in the manner of the Mexican muralists), Andrés R. Montani (who manifests a strong affinity with the Spanish school), Jorge Páez (an abstract indigenist), and Nelson Ramos (especially notable for his dynamic drawings).

Vicente Martín (b. 1914) and Jorge Páez (b. 1922) have made the transition to neofigurative painting, which has recently won several other adherents in Uruguay. Notable among these are Luis Solari (b. 1918), with his expressionistic allegories and angels and Hermenegildo Sabat (b. 1933), whose grotesque distorted portraits push expressionism to the edge of caricature (*Marilyn, Torre Nilsson, Victoria Regina, Professor Ego*). In his more recent work, such as the paintings shown at the third Córdoba Bienal (1966), Jorge Páez has tended toward a tentative Pop approach, exemplified in the canvas titled *Miniskirts, Monokinis and Bikinis for Solo Eye*. Solari specializes in collages.

The two most prominent geometric abstractionists are Lincoln

Presno (b. 1917) and Antonio Llorens (b. 1928). Presno studied wth Torres García and Guillermo Laborde and has specialized in mural painting. He has also worked in oil, tempera, and watercolor. Llorens became a member of the Grupo Madí in Buenos Aires and experimented with "active space," a kind of kinetic art capable of undergoing transformation by the addition or substraction of movable parts.

Among the painters whom it is difficult to place within any group or movement, mention should be made of Juan Ventayol (b. 1915), whose work has elements of both abstract expressionism and neofiguratism. Winner of many national and international prizes, he was awarded the prize for best Latin American painter at the VI Bienal of São Paulo in 1961.

Of the younger Uruguayan painters, the one who appears to be closest to the spirit—though certainly not the letter—of Torres García's example and precept is José Gamarra (b. 1934). Since Gamarra began his studies in art after the death of Torres García, there can be no question of personal influence; nor do we find any similarity of structure or style in the work of the younger painter. The affinity resides simply in the fact that although most Uruguayan painters have embraced abstract expressionism, Gamarra has chosen to take signs and symbols as the basis of his paintings. These signs and symbols, however, are not systematically structured but appear as free forms asymmetrically distributed over the space of the canvas. The figures are sometimes presented in embossed relief and sometimes are incised in a heavy impasto. Whereas Torres García wished to achieve a time-space continuum representing all the ages of man's existence, the canvases of Gamarra appear to concentrate on the prehistoric and primitive aspects of man's culture. Since he gives no descriptive titles to his paintings (he calls each simply *Painting*, often with an identifying number), and is not given to verbal explanations, his symbolism remains enigmatic to the uninitiated. The sun is a recurrent symbol, and there are also animal and human configurations. But the subjective imagination of the artist is also at work in creating signs and forms that proliferate from the given elements. In the paintings shown at the second Córdoba Bienal in 1964 there is a more symmetrical vertical-horizontal ordering of the signs and symbols, and one gets the impression of a kind of invented calligraphy that may be read in all directions without ever being deciphered but also without exhausting either its mysterious power or its pictorial attraction.

Gamarra spent two years (1959–61) in Brazil studying with Iberê Camargo and Friedlander. In 1963, he won a fellowship award at the III Biennale des Jeunes in Paris, where he then settled.

Carlos Páez Vilaró (b. 1923) has been very active as muralist, ceramist, easel painter, graphic artist, sculptor, and author. In 1956, he founded the Museum of Modern Art in Montevideo, of which he became director. He has executed large murals in a semiabstract style for many public and private buildings in Uruguay, and in 1960 he completed what is said to be the longest mural in the world, for the tunnel connecting the two buildings of the Pan American Union in Washington (525 feet long, painted in oil). The theme of this mural is "The Roots of Peace." In January, 1961, he showed ten oils at the Pan American Union, collectively titled *Rodoviarios* (*Personages on Wheels*). These are semiabstract inventions done with considerable humor, that might be called "freewheeling fantasies." Since 1960, Páez Vilaró has concentrated mainly on ceramics and sculpture, in which he also displays fantasy, invention, and humor.

5

Modern Art in the Tropics: Brazil

THE International Art Biennial of São Paulo, inaugurated in 1951 and vying with the famous Venice Biennale in scope and prestige, has placed Brazil in the forefront of contemporary activity in the plastic arts. This enormous exhibition, attracting artists from all over the world, has been both a stimulus and a challenge to Brazilian artists. From it they have felt the direct, immediate impact of contemporary styles and trends, from French and Spanish informalism to the "new realism" of the North Americans. At the same time, the artistic climate that made possible the establishment and success of the Bienal of São Paulo was created over the years by the Brazilian artists themselves, supported and encouraged on the one hand by the writers and intellectuals, such as Mário de Andrade and Gilberto Freyre, and on the other hand by the wealthy patrons of art, such as Francisco Matarazzo Sobrino and Assis Chateaubriand, who in Brazil have had a more preponderant role in the arts than elsewhere in Latin America. Nor have the arts in Brazil lacked government support—federal, state, and municipal—in the form of commissions, subsidies, stipends, grants, and general propaganda. The Brazilian Ministry of Foreign Affairs is extremely active in promoting the arts of Brazil. Besides organizing hundreds of art exhibits abroad, it maintains permanent art galleries in Paris, Rome, and other foreign capitals for the express purpose of introducing the work of Brazilian artists. It provides for the participation of Brazilian artists in major international exhibitions, furnishing them with funds for travel and for the transportation of their works. The Ministry also provides the $10,000 in cash to be offered as first prize at the São Paulo Bienal, which serves as a strong incentive for wide international participation. The Ministry spends the equivalent of some $300,000 yearly for the promotion of Brazilian art.

Modern art, of course, encountered opposition in Brazil, as it does everywhere: there was the customary reaction of the outraged bourgeoisie, of the scandalized academics, and of the critics hostile to innovation. But since 1920, there has always been an active spearhead of the avant-garde, bringing together poets, novelists, writers in many fields, and plastic artists—from the notorious Semana de Arte Moderna of 1922 to the concretists of the Grupo Invenção in the 1960's.[1] The fact that both of these last two manifestations, as well as the Bienal, originated in São Paulo, would appear to indicate that this city has had a role of particular significance in the modern art movement of Brazil. This is certainly true; but it is also true that Brazilian culture has never been dominated by a single city, unlike most Latin American countries. São Paulo, the dynamic modern city, has long provided a foil to the attraction and influence of Rio de Janeiro, the former national capital. Surely it will not be long before the new capital, Brasilia, inaugurated in 1960, provides another focal point for the arts of Brazil as it has already done in architecture. Meanwhile other regional centers, such as Recife in the state of Pernambuco, Salvador in Bahia, and Belo Horizonte in Minas Gerais, have their flourishing art movements through which regionalism has become a factor to reckon with in Brazilian art. Modernism, nationalism, regionalism, internationalism—all have contributed to the dynamic development of the contemporary arts in Brazil, strengthening their vitality, variety and creative vigor.

[1] See *Invenção: Revista de Arte de Vanguarda*, São Paulo, 1962–63.

Beginnings of Modern Art

Two women painters, Anita Malfatti and Tarsila do Amaral, both from São Paulo, were among the pioneers of modern art in Brazil. Others were the sculptor Victor Brecheret (another *paulista*), the painters Emiliano Di Cavalcanti (Rio de Janeiro) and Lasar Segall, who was born in Lithuania and settled in São Paulo; and Flávio Rezende de Carvalho (São Paulo), who has been active as architect, designer, painter, engraver, writer, and aesthetic gadfly.

Anita Malfatti (1896–1964) went to Europe at an early age and there, at an art exhibit in Germany, received an overwhelming impression from the expressionist paintings of Lovis Corinth— chiefly because of the strong, boldly juxtaposed colors. Within a week she had arranged to take lessons with him—a move that brought her at once into a mainstream of contemporary European painting and graphic art. From Europe, Malfatti went to the United States where she worked with Homer Boss of the Fifteen Group in New York, made the acquaintance of Marcel Duchamp, and became interested in cubism. Returning to Brazil, Malfatti organized an exhibit of her work at São Paulo in December, 1916—the first exhibit of modern art ever to be held in Brazil, and one of the first in the whole of Latin America. It created a scandal. Indicative of the general reaction was an article by the critic Monteiro Lobato titled "Humbug or Paranoia?" In 1922, Malfatti took part in the famous "Week of Modern Art" in São Paulo, which some writers—doubtless with considerable exaggeration—have publicized as an epocal moment in the development of modern art in Brazil. It was at least symptomatic, and as such merits more than passing mention.

The Week of Modern Art was an act of defiance, "a war cry, a signal for mobilization," against the Establishment. Its two leading spirits were the novelist, poet, and polemicist Oswald de Andrade and the poet, essayist, novelist, critic, and musicologist Mário de Andrade, both of whom were *paulistas* and rebels. Oswald de Andrade had founded, in 1911, a humorous and mili-- tant weekly called O *Pirralho* (*The Brat*); and in 1920 he launched another journal, *Papel e Tinta* (*Paper and Ink*). Both were vehicles for the "corrosive violence" of his attacks on accepted values and conventional standards in art and literature. He met Mário de Andrade in 1920, found in him a kindred spirit, brought him before the public, and planned with him some kind of manifestation in favor of the new art. In this enterprise they were joined by the poet Guilherme de Almeida and the painter Emiliano Di Cavalcanti, who illustrated the catalog of the exhibit for the Week. Held in the Municipal Theatre of São Paulo, during February, 1922, the Week included concerts of new music and recitals of poetry and lectures as well as art exhibits. Music by Heitor Villa-Lobos was performed amid public protests. In fact, the whole Week was received with hostility, by both press and public; we are told of a gentleman who attacked one of the paintings with his walking stick. A São Paulo newspaper announced, "The free columns of this paper are at the disposal of those who wish to attack the Week of Modern Art and defend our artistic heritage." The basic tactics were elementary: provocation and reaction, attack and counterattack. But there was no manifesto, no doctrinal program. Insofar as the organizers had a program, it centered on adoption of the advanced techniques of artistic expression and the use of Brazilian themes for a national art. Mário de Andrade himself was also much interested in the social function of art. But the movement was entirely free of the rigid dogmatism that characterized the contemporary post-Revolutionary movement in Mexico. As one of the São Paulo group declared, "Rebellion is our aesthetic." Freedom of expression was their aim.

Anita Malfatti was represented in the Week of Modern Art with some of her expressionist portraits. These probably shocked viewers by their arbitrary use of color: *The Man of Seven Colors* (pastel, 1917), *The Woman with Green Hair* (oil, 1916), *The Yellow Man* (oil, 1918). Tarsila do Amaral showed her striking portraits of Mário de Andrade and Oswald de Andrade (oils, 1922). Lasar Segall revealed his obsessive concern with human suffering in *Sick Family* (oil, 1920). Di Cavalcanti displayed his sophisticated postimpressionist manner in *Bohemians* (pastel on paper), while a more conventional type of nativism was represented by the work of Vicente do Rego Monteiro, *Brazilian*

Legend and *Negro Heads*—the latter perhaps significant for its emphasis on the theme of the Negro, which was to become so prominent in Brazilian painting. There was actually nothing very "extreme" about the exhibit, judged by the standards of the most "advanced" European art of the early 1920's. But the fact that it was considered scandalously subversive in São Paulo indicates what a long and rough road there was to travel before this city could become a world capital of contemporary art. Incidentally, the Museum of Modern Art of São Paulo, in 1952— thirty years after the event—gave a *Commemorative Exhibition of the Week of Modern Art* with works by most of the original participants. So, whatever may have been the immediate impact of the Week, its historical significance has not been forgotten.

Meanwhile Anita Malfatti continued to paint in a figurative style, except for some early cubist works. In some cases—particularly her religious paintings, like *The Resurrection of Lazarus* (oil, 1930)—she adhered to the Italian Renaissance tradition. At the VII São Paulo Bienal (1963) she was given a retrospective show covering the period 1916 to 1962, with thirty-nine paintings and seven drawings. In some of her later work she fell into a kind of neoprivitivism which, though it may have been entirely personal, went along with a fairly widespread trend in Brazilian painting in the 1940's and 1950's.

The second woman painter represented in the Week of Modern Art, Tarsila do Amaral (b. 1897), was actually in Paris during that scandalous time. She had gone to Paris in 1920, had studied first at the Académie Julien with Emile Renard and then, in search of a more modern orientation, switched to the teaching of Fernand Léger, André Lhote, and Albert Gleizes, who introduced her to cubism. Her studio soon became a meeting place for modern-minded Brazilians and Europeans. Oswald de Andrade, Sérgio Millet, Villa-Lobos, Di Cavalcanti, Anita Malfatti, Victor Brecheret (among the Brazilians) went there, as did such Parisian celebrities as Cocteau, Satie, Valéry-Larbaud, and Blaise Cendrars (the poet, novelist and world traveler who was soon to visit Brazil). When Tarsila (as she is always called) returned to her native country in 1924, she had discovered modern art; now she needed to discover Brazil.

But Brazil is a huge country with many different aspects: how was she to discover *her* Brazil, the aspect that she needed as an artist? This happened when, in the company of Blaise Cendrars, she visited the former Captaincy General (now the State) of Minas Gerais where, in a mountainous panorama, they explored the old towns—Ouro Preto, Mariana, Sabará, Congonhas do Campo and others—that remained almost unchanged since the eighteenth century, when the local mines were exhausted. She was captivated by the combination of archaic simplicity and baroque exuberance: in the houses, in the numerous churches, in the statuary, in the decorations. In Minas Gerais she found the colors that she had "adored" as a child. She conquered her nostalgia for the past by transferring these colors to her canvases: pure blue, violet rose, bright yellow, vivid green (*verde cantante*), "all with more or less strong gradations, according to the mixture of white." As regards form, she aimed at "clear outlines, giving a perfect impression of the distance that separates one object from another." This was the type of painting—a synthesis of the old and new, of the international and the local—that Tarsila presented at her first individual exhibit in Paris, in 1926.

By that time, the kind of painting that Tarsila was doing had been given a name and converted into a "movement" by the irrepressible Oswald de Andrade, who was now in Europe engaged in high-voltage propaganda for a native Brazilian art: he called it *Páu-Brasil*, on the principle that nothing could be more Brazilian than the kind of wood from which the country had taken its name (brazilwood). Tarsila's *Landscape* (1925) is a colorful, vivid example of her "Páu-Brasil" phase; but its tropical exuberance does not exclude the influence of the Paris School, especially that of Léger, whose geometrical forms reappear in both the natural and the man-made objects of this rural São Paulo landscape with figures. But Tarsila was not disposed to remain on a single track, nor was Andrade loath to invent another movement. This he did with the founding of the *Revista de Antropofagia* in 1927, launching the movement known as *Antropófago* (*Anthropophagous*). This was the Brazilian version of indigenism, based on the image of the Indian as cannibal: a sort of aesthetic cannibalism.

Doubtless Tarsila had no intention of starting another artistic movement when, in 1928, she made a pen and ink drawing titled *O Abaporu* (*The Indian Cannibal*). But the ferment of the times called for the launching of movements and manifestos, so Oswald de Andrade picked up this image and framed it conceptually in a manifesto that presented the Indian as the primitive "master of the land, for whom happiness was the only aim." The *abaporu* was depicted as a kind of pathetic and contemplative monstrosity, with a very tiny head and a huge body, terminating in enormous feet. The figure suggested to Andrade "the fatalistic creature, bound to the earth by its huge and heavy feet." And as Luiz de Almeida Cunha points out, Portinari may have been influenced by this idea when he enlarged the feet of the figures in his murals for the Ministry of Education and the Library of Congress.

In 1929, Tarsila had her first one-man show in São Paulo—a rather tardy recognition of her importance. As she had experimented with cubism in the 1920's, so in the 1930's she had her phase of social realism, as may be seen in her canvas titled *Workers* (1933). What remained constant in her work, however, was her twofold preoccupation with the Brazilian scene and its plastic reality. Landscapes predominate in her later paintings. Tarsila do Amaral was given two large retrospective exhibitions, the first at the Museum of Modern Art in São Paulo in 1950, the second at the VII Bienal of São Paulo in 1963. While it cannot be claimed that she is an important international artist, her place in the history of Brazilian art is indisputable.

Two Expressionists

Lasar Segall (1891–1957) was actually the first modern painter to exhibit in Brazil, with two shows in 1913, at São Paulo and nearby Campinas. They did not make much of a stir, but they attracted the attention of the avant-garde intellectuals and resulted in the inclusion of Segall's work in the Week of Modern Art. Two years later, in 1924, Segall became a permanent resident (and eventually a citizen) of Brazil. From 1930 he was also active as a sculptor, chiefly in bronze. Segall, a native of Vilna, in

Lithuania, studied painting and engraving in Berlin and Dresden, and identified himself with the German expressionists, particularly those who were influenced by the movement known as *Die Brücke*. The sufferings of the Jews in Europe never left his memory: again and again he returned to this theme, as in *Exodus* (1947), an oil painting acquired by the Jewish Museum of New York, *Pogrom*, *Immigrant Ship* (1939–41), *Concentration Camp*, and *The Condemned*. The Brazilian environment also made its impact upon his work, in various landscapes, including the series titled *Forests*. In some of these paintings (for example, *Landscape* [1925]), Segall combined expressionistic coloring with neocubist forms and geometrical construction, presenting the figurative elements in a semiabstract manner while emphasizing the bidimensional quality of the composition. Since his death, Segall has been increasingly recognized as one of the important artists of the contemporary expressionist movement.

Of the native-born Brazilian painters, the one most closely identified with expressionism is Flávio de Rezende Carvalho (b. 1899). He is described by Clarival Valladares as "an eminently revolutionary spirit, who was at the head of innumerable avantgarde movements that manifested themselves in Brazilian arts and letters after 1930." Le Corbusier called him "le Révolutionnaire Romantique." In 1932 he founded the *Experimental Theatre*, with which he produced his *Ballet of the Death of God*, which caused a sensation. After studies in Brazil, he went to France and England, attending the University of Durham. In 1932, together with Di Cavalcanti and others, he founded the Club of Modern Artists in São Paulo. His one-man show in 1934 was closed by order of the police, whereupon he brought suit against the Government—and won. In a set of drawings titled *Tragic Series* (acquired by the Museum of Contemporary Art of São Paulo) he depicted the varying facial expressions of his mother on her deathbed. He also executed several stage sets, especially for ballet, and a number of sculptures, including a *Psychological Self-Portrait* (1930). But he is best known for his numerous portraits, mostly of celebrated persons in the artistic world, such as Pablo Neruda, Nicolás Guillén, Camargo Guarnieri, Roberto Burle-Marx, Oswald de Andrade, the Russian composer Katchaturian, the conductor Eleazar de Carvalho, and the novelist José Lins do Rego. The last-mentioned portrait (1948) appears in a full-page color reproduction in the volume *The Emergent Decade*, and gives an excellent idea of Carvalho's semiabstract expressionist style, with its bold coloring (in this case dominated by yellow and orange tones) and dynamic composition. There is probably no more striking example of Brazilian expressionist painting than Carvalho's *Yellow Reclining Nude* (1932), which carries both figurative distortion and color dissonance to their extreme limits within the framework of this essentially lyrical and representational style.

Carvalho's adventures have not all been aesthetic or experimental. In 1958, he joined an expedition that made contact with completely savage Indian tribes in the upper Amazon basin (from the Rio Negro to the River Camanau), gathering more material for his incessant explorations into all aspects of Brazilian life. Most of his explorations lead to experiments that in turn have explosive effects. At the ninth São Paulo Bienal (1967), Carvalho was awarded First Prize among Brazilian artists. The award, coming as a surprise, demonstrated that on occasion the Establishment will honor its most notorious rebels.

Painters of Brazilian Life

Emiliano Di Cavalcanti (b. 1897), although he participated prominently in the Week of Modern Art in São Paulo, is essentially a *carioco*, much attached to the city of his birth, Rio de Janeiro. For a time he studied law, but the success of his first show, held in 1916, when he was only nineteen, set him on the road to a career in art. In 1923, he went to Europe where he discovered Picasso, whose work deeply impressed him though it did not overwhelm him. It was the neoclassical phase of Picasso that attracted him, especially the exuberant "Mediterranean" nudes of this period. In the words of Luis Martins, "That intrinsically Brazilian—or, perhaps more precisely, *carioca*—quality in Di Cavalcanti, led him to a personal reinterpretation, a sort of 'translation to the mulatto,' of the classical and somewhat

Olympian women of Picasso, giving them a vibrancy (*frêmito*), a malice, and an indolence not found in the original models." If Picasso was Mediterranean, Di Cavalcanti is tropical. The *Nude Woman Seated* of 1927 is neo-Picassian, if you will, but scarcely neoclassical—certainly not Olympian. A later and more striking example is *Woman with Fan* (1937), a sort of Brazilian-mulatto odalisque, whom the artist depicts with compassion (there is despair in the eyes of this prostitute) as well as with the sensuous and decorative qualities of a richly resourceful palette. Di Cavalcanti has painted or drawn women all his life, but he prefers them in a state of seminudity—chorus girls, society women with low-cut gowns, or else the provocative *déshabillé* of a sensual mulatress, as in the straw-hatted half-clad *Seated Figure* (oil, 1947), whose striped dress provides a touch of the vivid color that this painter likes. Di Cavalcanti, like Toulouse-Lautrec, can sum up an entire period and milieu in his paintings of women, as in *Woman with Lorgnette* (1927), which Walter Zanini sees as "assimilating influences of German expressionism and of Picasso into the climate of his own personal poetry"—a poetry, let it be said, that is never sentimental, with a touch of caricature tempered by compassion.

In a sense Di Cavalcanti is a "social painter," because he looks with an analytical eye at men and women in society—both high and low and in between. No American painter has more acutely caught the spirit of Paris in the late 1920's and 1930's. At the same time, no painter has more fully or faithfully depicted the scenes and types of Brazilian life (only Portinari can compare with him in this respect), and at least one critic has called him "the most Brazilian" of all painters. Luis Martins believes that "he achieves a lyrical valorization of what is deep and permanent in the Brazilian soul," while Flávio de Aquino finds that his various influences "were filtered and translated first into human terms, secondly into Brazilian terms." The same critic stresses Di Cavalcanti's empathy for "the poor, the workers, the fishermen . . . the forsaken people who at every moment cross our vision." The painter said of his canvas, *Fishermen* (1942), "It is sincere because I grew up among fishermen by the sea."

At the second São Paulo Bienal (1953) Di Cavalcanti shared

with Volpi the Prize for the Best National Painter. At the seventh Bienal (1963) he was given a retrospective exhibit consisting of fifty-three works covering the period from 1920 to 1963. He has been called "the most consistent of modern Brazilian painters," and saluted as "uma glória nacional."

Alberto da Veiga Guignard and Alfredo Volpi, painters of the same generation as Di Cavalcanti, were also much concerned with the Brazilian scene, each in an entirely different manner. Guignard (1896–1962) was born in the State of Rio de Janeiro, but at an early age went to Europe with his mother and his stepfather, a German Baron whom Guignard intensely disliked and who forced him to study agronomy. But since he spent all his time drawing, his parents finally allowed him to enroll at the Royal Academy of Fine Arts in Munich. In 1929, he returned briefly to Rio de Janeiro and began to exhibit in the National Salons and to do some teaching. But he lived mostly in Europe, gaining a considerable reputation in Paris, until 1944, when he returned to Brazil for good. Juscelino Kubitschek, at that time mayor of Belo Horizonte, invited him to go there and establish a School of Fine Arts. Guignard accepted the offer and settled permanently in Belo Horizonte, transforming its artistic life through his excellent teaching and his own fine example. He became enamored of the old towns of Minas Gerais, especially Ouro Preto, which he called *"cidade amor-inspiração,"* and these remained among his favorite subjects. His former students and admirers in Belo Horizonte established the Guignard Foundation to preserve and promote his work, and to guarantee his financial security. One of his students described him as "very generous, extremely simple and disinterested in material things, and quite shy."

Guignard was a well-trained painter, a skilled draftsman and a master of color, who deliberately kept his work on a level of apparent simplicity, capturing the charm of the *naïf* without any of its stylistic awkwardness or technical inadequacy. Though he painted landscapes and townscapes, portraits and scenes of everyday life, he was not a realist but a poet. His paintings of Ouro Preto (there is one in the New York Museum of Modern Art, painted in 1942 [Plate 4]) and of the other old towns of Minas Gerais are never documentary or achitectural in their emphasis. He likes their archaic quality for its quaintness and colorfulness, but into this he blends his own fantasies from childhood memories, such as the large gas balloons that float through his pictures—a recollection of the traditional celebration of St. John's Day, when the merrymaking includes the release of flaming gas balloons at night. Guignard looked for color—including human pigmentation—and found it not only in the houses of Ouro Preto and other old towns, but also in the life about him, in street scenes, interiors, and people. In such paintings he preferred the posed scene rather than the fugitive moment of the "candid camera." Typical of his approach is the painting titled *Family in the Square*, which depicts a Negro family—mother, father, and four children—dressed in their best finery in a public square, and all posed as though facing the camera for one of those family portraits taken by street photographers. Again, in the very colorful and beautifully composed painting titled *The Newlyweds* (oil on wood, 1927), the bridal couple are deliberately posing for their picture, she seated with a bouquet of flowers in her lap, he standing beside her in his red-jacketed military uniform. On the balcony waves a Brazilian flag, on the wall is a conventional painting of Christ. It is a sort of tropical Matisse with a touch of the Douanier Rousseau. The bride and groom have chocolate-colored skin.

Alfredo Volpi was born in Lucca, Italy, in 1896, but was brought to Brazil as an infant. His family settled in São Paulo, and there he taught himself to paint, commencing his artistic career by decorating the walls of houses at the age of twenty. From 1922, he began to exhibit in group shows, and after 1944 he had many one-man shows, chiefly in São Paulo and Rio de Janeiro. In 1952, he obtained First Prize at the National Salon of Modern Art, and an acquisition prize at the Venice Biennale. By the time of his first retrospective exhibition, in 1956, he had made the transition from overtly figurative landscape painting to a semiabstract stylization of architectural forms on a flat surface, done with tempera. In the words of Clarival Valladares,

His themes are based on the early architecture of Colonial Brazil, medieval in spirit, which even today is manifested in the humble houses

of the suburbs and hamlets, in the human landscape of Brazil (such
as the streamers of the street festivals), and in the primitive Catholic
iconography.... For several critics, Alfredo Volpi represents the most
significant level of Brazilian painting, in consideration of the aesthetic
intent of his invention.[2]

A representative example of Volpi's mature manner may be
seen in the oil painting *Houses by the Sea* (1953), in which the
usual landscape features are present, including the boats in the
distance, but there is no illusion of depth, no attempt at perspective.
The façades of the houses are superimposed in horizontal tiers,
with the sea and the sky at the top. The streets are horizontal
bands separating the various sections of the canvas, and the
vertical patterns of doors and windows are like abstract compositional elements. During the 1950's, Volpi began to give many
of his paintings abstract titles (*Composition in Green, Composition
in Rectangles, Composition in Triangles*), thus emphasizing the
semiabstract bidimensional ideal toward which his work had increasingly tended. From around 1946, nearly all his painting was
done in tempera. Having passed through various figurative phases,
including neoimpressionism and a modified social realism, Volpi
eventually found his personal plastic vision in the cool objectivity
of his bidimensional architectural compositions, through which he
is both artist and artisan, experiencing equally the joy of the
craftsman and of the creative spirit.

The Primitive Painters

While painters like Guignard and Volpi may have flirted with
primitivism—or, more accurately, with the deliberately ingenu-
ous—Brazil also has its authentic primitives, among whom two
of the best known are Heitor Dos Prazeres and Djanira. Heitor
Dos Prazeres (1898–1966) was a composer of popular music as
well as a painter. With only a primary education, entirely self-
taught in art, he began to paint in 1937 just "to decorate the
walls." In 1951, he received a prize at the first Bienal of São

[2] *Quem É Quem Nas Artes e Nas Letras do Brasil*, p. 105.

Paulo, and thereafter exhibited frequently both in Brazil and abroad. He participated in the exhibition *Eight Primitive Brazilian Painters* at the Galerie Massol of Paris in 1965, and in the Festival of Negro Arts at Dakar in 1966. He painted scenes of his native city, Rio de Janeiro, especially of the hillside tenements, the popular festivals, and the various occupations. A painting such as *Samba on the Hillside* (1943) is much more than a projection of local color: it has what Carlos Cavalcanti calls "the plastic translation of pure rhythms of vitality." The grouping of the musicians and dancers and the harmony of colors convey a poetic effect, a feeling at once sad and intense, which the Brazilians call *saudade*.

The artist who calls herself Djanira (b. 1914; her family name is Mota e Silva), was born in the State of São Paulo and is largely self-taught. She had her first individual show in 1943, and in that same year received a prize at the National Salon of Fine Arts. Djanira lived in New York from 1945 to 1947, and also visited the United States again in 1964. In 1966 she was scheduled to have major exhibitions of her work in New York and Washington, but her visa was cancelled on orders from the State Department. "If I can't go, my paintings don't go," she said at a news conference. And she added, "It's a big world, in which the United States isn't everything, but I did want to go very much because I have very warm memories of New York and the American people."

Almost every aspect of Brazilian daily life and its folkways and popular scenes have been depicted by Djanira, from urban amusements to a *Tea Plantation in Itacolomi* (1958). She has also done considerable religious painting, inspired chiefly by the popular statues of saints—for example, *Saint Peter* and *Station of the Cross* (both 1943). Her painting titled *Dream* (1946) has a surrealist quality, and there are elements of abstract stylization in a painting such as *Tea Plantation*. As summed up by Clarival Valladares, "The most notable quality in the work of Djanira is its thematic coherence, consistent and fully defined from her very first drawings. The folkloric aspect, though quite apparent and even dominant, remains nevertheless secondary in value to the plastic and aesthetic attributes."

If one takes the term in its literal sense, then the most authentically "primitive" of contemporary Brazilian artists would be Francisco Domingos da Silva (b. 1910), who is of Indian stock. He was discovered by the French painter Jean-Pierre Chabloz, with whom he studied and who brought him to public attention with an article in *Cahiers d'Art* (1952) titled "A Brazilian Indian Reinvents Painting." Meanwhile, he had been exhibiting in various European cities, always with increasing success, culminating in an honorable mention at the Venice Biennale in 1966. Presenting themes drawn from Indian mythology mixed with fantasy, and depicting the flora and fauna of the Amazon basin, Francisco Domingos da Silva gave to Europeans the exotic and primitive image of Brazil that they wished to see.

José Antônio da Silva (b. 1909) is a self-taught painter from the State of São Paulo who did not begin to paint until he was thirty-seven. He then concentrated on scenes and anecdotes of his native state, especially those relating to rural life. He is considered by Clarival Valladares to be "one of the most expressive painters among the authentic Brazilian primitives." He achieved national and international recognition at the biennials of São Paulo and Venice, and his autobiography was published by the São Paulo Museum of Modern Art.

Brazil also has its equivalent of Grandma Moses in the person of Grauben Monte Lima (b. 1889), who took up painting after her retirement from the civil service in 1960. Following a period of study with Ivan Serpa at the Museum of Modern Art in Rio, she quickly won recognition through exhibits at the São Paulo Bienal (1963 and 1965), the Córdoba Bienal of 1964, and the Galerie Massol in Paris (*Eight Primitive Brazilian Painters* [1965]). A truly naïve painter, her favorite subjects are taken from nature—especially birds and flowers—depicted with the intricate detail of embroidery.

The Brazilian primitives or *peintres naïfs* constitute one of the most distinctive and successful groups in contemporary South American painting.

In the 1930's, Brazil was a country with many fine painters representing a wide diversity of artistic styles and regional cultures. But there was none who could represent the nation as a whole, and who could command recognition abroad as well as admiration at home on a scale commensurate with the greatness of Brazil. In the words of Flávio de Aquino, "We lacked someone capable of dramatic heroism, imbued with the desire to express himself violently through the exploitation of our social themes." Cândido Portinari was to be that someone.

Cândido Portinari and Nationalism

Cândido Portinari (1903–1962) was born in Brodowsky (or Brodosqui, in the local spelling), State of São Paulo. The son of poor Italian immigrants who worked as harvesters of coffee and cotton on the nearby plantations, Portinari grew up amid poverty, in daily contact with the ill-paid field hands and laborers. These conditions he never forgot; they were to influence not only his painting but also his political beliefs. His artistic vocation was awakened when a professional painter, commissioned to restore the local church, allowed him to assist in the task. At fifteen he set off for Rio de Janeiro and enrolled as a student in the National School of Fine Arts. In 1928, he obtained a travel award at the National Salon that enabled him to study and travel in Europe for the next two years. When he returned to Brazil he "joined the group of young intellectuals who, like those in other countries of the hemisphere, were concerned with social problems and with the realities of life for contemporary man in the Americas." Through his forceful personality and energy he gathered a following and influenced many of the younger painters. His first important international recognition came in 1935 when his canvas of that year titled *Coffee* was awarded honorable mention at the Carnegie International in Pittsburgh.

Shortly afterwards, Portinari was commissioned to depict "the epic of Brazil" in a series of murals for the new Ministry of Education building in Rio de Janeiro, portraying the principal regions, products, occupations, and ethnic types of the country. This he accomplished by depicting the cultivation of sugar cane, tobacco, cotton, coffee, and rubber, as well as cattle raising and prospecting for gold. In 1939, when he painted three murals in tempera for the Brazilian pavilion at the New York World's Fair, he concentrated on the four principal regions of Brazil, using local themes decoratively rather than dramatically. Two years later he completed four murals in tempera commissioned for the Hispanic Foundation in the Library of Congress, which were intended to represent "the epic of Hispanic America"—its discovery, colonization, and the development of human and natural resources. All this had to be done within a very limited space. Portinari decided to develop four basic themes: (1) Discovery of the Land, (2) The Entry into the Forest, (3) The Teaching of the Indians, (4) The Mining of Gold. According to the authoritative account of Dr. Robert C. Smith, "Portinari originally conceived the subject of the Discovery in purely decorative, almost heraldic terms, as a view of many caravels seen from high above sailing through the wooded islands of a tropical coast. This he discarded almost immediately because it offered no opportunity to show the men who made the discovery. To do this he decided to represent a scene aboard a ship and developed the idea in a gouache sketch. . . ."

The change is significant, because it shows where Portinari's real strength lay: in his power of empathy, in his ultimate rejection of the decorative and the conventionally heroic in favor of the specific human situation, the individual either dominating, or struggling with, or being overcome by his environment. The panel of "The Discovery" is dominated by the strongly dynamic figures of two sailors vigorously hauling on the rigging ropes, while other sailors raise their arms in joy at the sight of land. Again, in the panel on gold mining, Portinari "abandoned the first idea of many boats floating on a winding river, to concentrate on a single boat with a single group of figures." He chose the closeup rather than the panorama. He depicts the moment when the prospectors actually find the gold, their joy and excitement manifested in their gestures and facial expressions (Plate 18). The same qualities are evident in the murals that he executed for the headquarters of the United Nations in New York entitled *War and Peace* (1953–55). In 1949, Portinari executed an important historical series of mural panels (tempera on canvas) on *Tiradentes* (Joaquim José da Silva Xavier), the leader of a conspiracy in Ouro Preto, who was hanged and quartered in 1792 "for the hideous crime of rebellion and high treason," and yet became a popular hero.

In 1939, Mário de Andrade, in one of the earliest and best essays on Portinari, defined his work in terms of four qualities: traditionalism, lyricism, realism, and nationalism. And he added that Portinari was most traditional in his portraits, "which take us back to the great Renaissance tradition of portraiture." Incidentally, one of Portinari's best portraits is that of Andrade himself. Others are *Portrait of the Artist's Mother* (1938) and *Self-Portrait* (1939). He painted a great many portraits, some of celebrated or fashionable persons, others of the anonymous "common people" of his native land, including the various ethnic types—Negro, mulatto, Indian, mestizo—whom he portrayed with the accuracy of an ethnologist as well as the insight of an artist. He covered the entire human and social spectrum of Brazil. A few characteristic examples are *The Old-Fashioned Ice Cream Vendor* (1934), *Immigrant Woman* (tempera, 1935), *Baiana with Children* (oil, 1935), and *Coffee Carriers* (oil, 1938).

Portinari was a many-sided artist, both in his themes and in his styles. He took what he needed from cubism, from surrealism, from expressionism, assimilating the lessons of Braque and Picasso as well as of Diego Rivera in his murals. His social realism is counterbalanced by the lyrical freedom and imaginative fantasy of such paintings as *Women with Flowers and Child, Figures with a Child,* or *Three Women* (all 1939). The formal perfection and planned symmetry of such a work as *Coffee Carriers* is in marked contrast to the deliberately naïf quality of many of his typical scenes, such as *Wedding at Brodowski* (watercolor, 1933) or *Rural Wedding* (oil, 1940). At other times he injects a note of surrealism into his typical scenes, as in *Scarecrow Under the Stars* and *Harassing Judas* (both 1940). His expressionism achieves its culmination in the series of paintings inspired by the terrible drought that afflicted the northeastern region of Ceará in 1945: *The Dead Child, Refugees, Burial in the Net.* Here all the horror of the medieval "Dance of Death" is reinforced by the emphasis of distortion and of expressionistic violence. Even the living are scarcely more than ill-clad skeletons; Death has the visage of starvation; hideous tears fall in globules from the eye sockets of the mourners; all is dissolution and despair. This is, if you will, "social surrealism," since it goes beyond realism to express the hopeless misery and suffering of a social reality in terms of intense compassion. This sense of compassion, manifested in so many of Portinari's paintings, along with his "enormous technical richness and expressive variety" (Mário de Andrade), goes far to explain why Portinari is considered by some critics to be the greatest Brazilian painter of his time.

Nevertheless, Mário de Andrade, with his customary perception, was right when he called Portinari "o mas moderno dos antigos." He was not so much the first of the moderns as the last of the traditionalists. Even such a typically Brazilian subject as *Migrants* (1936), a group of women and children, is composed in the manner of the Italian Renaissance painters. Portinari represented the "heroic age" of Brazilian painting; he made history even while he passed into history himself. Before his death he was already a part of the past. A prodigious worker, he left thousands of paintings that constitute a pictorial record of Brazil, its people, its history, and its land, unmatched in scope and variety, in depth and grandeur, in humanism and sincerity.

The nationalism of Portinari was largely a synthesis of regional factors. He painted the cattlemen of Rio Grande do Sul, the Negro women of Bahia, the hillside slum dwellers of Rio de Janeiro, the sugar cane workers of the northeast, the laborers of the São Paulo coffee plantations, the historic scenes of Minas Gerais, and many others. But he did not identify himself with any single region. He was interested in the local scene only as a part of the general epic, the total panorama. Yet regionalism has been a force in Brazilian culture, and in the visual arts no less than in literature.

Gilberto Freyre and Regionalism

Gilberto Freyre, the famous and influential sociologist, whose interpretation of Brazil's cultural evolution has had a world-wide impact, is the chief spokesman and champion of Brazilian regionalism in the arts. Born in Pernambuco, he has been particularly active in fomenting the artistic activity of that region, and persuasive in describing its peculiar fascination. "There is probably no other tropical landscape like that of the Northeast of Brazil," he writes, "so rich in suggestions for the painter; animated by so many greens, so many vermilions, so many reds, so many yellows." Then he goes into detail, describing the local flora whose very names are strangely evocative: *ibirapitanga, mandacaru, quipás, mamoeiros, maracujás, coroas-de-frade.* The name of this last flower—literally, "friar's crowns"—leads him by association to evoke the past,

> *Friar's crowns which, in the silence of mid-day in the churches of the countryside and of the wilderness, seem to remind us of the martyred friars and the heroic padres whom the Northeast gave to Brazil. It is as though the landscape possessed at the same time something that was historical, and ecclesiastical, and civic; and which participated in the traditions of the region, associating itself through its forms of vegetation with human events: with the sacrifices and the heroism of the men who gave it an essentially Brazilian and Catholic character.*[3]

The Pernambucan painter Lula Cardoso Ayres (b. 1909) tells us that Gilberto Freyre "aroused the interest of Brazilian painters in the plastic values of the Negro, the Mulatto, and the Indian." In the case of this painter, Freyre's influence was absolutely decisive. Cardoso Ayres had studied in Paris in 1925 and had imbibed there a superficial modernism. As the son of wealthy parents, he lived what he calls "a futile and empty life" in Rio de Janeiro, painting superficially and without conviction. Then one day a visit to the studio of a fellow-artist from Pernambuco changed the entire course of his life and work. He went to visit Cícero Dias, who had just arrived from Recife, and saw on the walls of his studio sugar mills, plantation houses, Negroes, mulattoes, oxen, horses, sheep, sugar cane, cane-fields—all that Gilberto

[3] "Algums Notas sobre a Pintura no Nordeste do Brasil," in Freyre's collected essays, *Vida, Form e Côr* (Rio de Janeiro, 1962). Other quotations from Freyre are from the same source. Also included are essays on Cícero Dias, Lula Cardoso Ayres, Francisco Brennand, and on "Uma Estética da Miscigenação." The reader interested in Freyre's role in the arts of Brazil should also consult the collective work titled *Gilberto Freyre: Sua Ciencia, Sua Filosofia, Sua Arte* (Rio de Janeiro, 1962).

Freyre since 1923 had been urging Brazilian painters to feel and to paint. He felt irresistibly drawn back to Recife, to its old houses, its popular festivals, its folklore.

Cardoso Ayres was among the artists who took part in the First Afro-Brazilian Congress organized by Gilberto Freyre at Recife in 1933—an event that had important repercussions, for it brought the Afro-Brazilian artifacts of the Northeast to the attention of many Brazilian artists. In 1938, Cardoso Ayres went to live on his father's sugar mill in the interior of Pernambuco, and set about the task of interpreting that region in his painting. To supplement his own sketches and observations, he made an enormous collection of photographs. Above all, he began, in his own words, "to paint what I saw, what I felt, and what I heard told around me : stories of the plantations, of the hinterland, of apparitions, of slaves. With Gilberto Freyre I learned to see the beauty—plastic yet at the same time fantastic—of the *bumba-meu-boi*. The Negroes of the *Maracatú* came to have a decisive significance in my painting. The land, the region, the province, began to exist intensely for me."

The *bumba-meu-boi* is a traditional pantomime that is found almost everywhere in Brazil; but each region has its distinctive manner of performance. The *boi* is an ox, but in this case not a real one : it is a crude imitation made by hanging a cloth over a frame of wood slats, the most realistic feature being the head, which consists of the decorated skull of an ox or a cow. A man gets inside of this contraption and carries it around, performing the necessary motions for the pantomime. This consists principally of "sacrificing" the ox, then "resurrecting" it, and finally "eating" it. The "meat" of the animal is distributed among the participants in the festival. Many other simulated animals—some fantastic, like the seahorse—also take part in the pantomime. When Cardoso Ayres painted his first *bumba-meu-boi* series in 1943, he stressed its fantastic aspects with surrealist intentions. Later, when he had turned to abstraction, he declared, "All the abstract forms of my present painting have their point of departure chiefly in the figures of the *bumba-meu-boi*."

Before turning to abstraction, however, Cardoso Ayres painted a series of murals depicting the development of the Northeast.

But these are not, Freyre reminds us "the conventionally heroic epic, because they depict the daily struggle of the Brazilian against the obstacles to his progress; because they evoke the brotherhood of men and women of different races and colors; and because of their aesthetic valorization of the forms and colors of Recife. . . ."

The cycle of departure and return, of alienation and reintegration, that characterized Cardoso Ayres' relation to his region is also apparent in the case of Cícero Dias (b. 1908), although the "return" in his case was less enduring. From Pernambuco he went to Rio de Janeiro for study at the School of Fine Arts, then to Paris (1930), where he has since lived most of the time. He belonged to the group called *Espace*, of which André Bloc was the guiding spirit, and became an adherent of non-objective painting. He prefers not to use the term "abstract" because "it conveys the idea of an art divorced from Nature, when in reality this art does not tend to separate itself from Nature; on the contrary, it tends to penetrate it more and more, gathering what is most essential, in its deep and intimate truth." As if to emphasize this link with Nature, Cícero (as he is generally called) often gives to his paintings an evocative title, as in *Landscape* (1952), with its quasigeometrical yet lyrical suggestion of the colors of the tropics. Freyre sees "the green of Pernambuco" in the nonobjective paintings of Cícero: "Alone the colors of his painting, in themselves, are an expression of that Brazil which the French poet Eluard found to be as unmistakably present in Cícero as Spain is in Picasso."

Early in his career, when he was still painting figuratively, Cícero did return to his native region and threw himself with zest into exploring its traditions, its legends, its folk arts, and its people. Himself a member of the upper class, he tried to identify himself with the predominantly negroid population as well as with the aristocratic tradition of the large plantations and their mansions. It was he who illustrated Gilberto Freyre's great work on the sociocultural history of the Northeast, *Casa Grande e Senzala*. At this time Cícero espoused social realism, as evidenced in such canvases as *A Family in Mourning* and *Judgment of the Factory Workers*. But in 1948 he painted an "abstract" mural in Recife, which is said to be the first of its kind done in South America.

In 1965 he was given a special retrospective show at the VIII Bienal of São Paulo.

Francisco Brennand (b. 1927)—painter, sculptor, ceramist—studied for several years in Europe, but on the whole has preferred to live in his native city of Recife. He has been especially attracted by the local ceramic crafts and by the popular *santos* (images of saints) of the Northeast. His art is both complex and deeply personal, rooted in childhood memories and extremely sensitive to the culture of his native region, with its animistic cults, its tutelary spirits, its vivid vegetation. Freyre calls his art "autobiographical," in the sense that "it has evolved as a continuous development of his own personality in relation to his country and his time." He sees Brennand not simply as a regional artist, but also as "a new interpreter of the tropics."

Aloísio Magalhães (b. 1927), painter and print-maker, is hardly a regional artist in the usual meaning of the term. But then, the distinctive character of Brazilian regionalism is precisely in its aesthetic freedom, its lack of stylistic restraints or dogmatic formulas. To be regional is to identify one's self in some way with the region—but the manner of so doing, whether in one's life or one's art, is a matter of individual choice and temperament. Gilberto Freyre insists on "the touch of the humid tropics that characterizes the abstract compositions of Magalhães." The titles that the artist has given to some of his paintings—*Palm Tree by the Sea, In the Form of a Palm Tree, In the Form of a Verandah*—as well as the prevalence of "tropical" colors—green, yellow, blue, vermilion—might tend to support Freyre's thesis. The artist himself, in an interview with the poet Ariano Suassuna, in 1958, expressed his views on the relation of art to "reality."

Asked if he thought art should have a "profound communication with the real," Magalhães replied that he preferred "an art that aspires to create with more freedom, without concerning itself too much with what exists." He admitted that "nature perhaps furnishes certain elements of this art," but maintained that the aim of the artist should be to achieve "unlimited and fascinating combinations and inventions." Explaining his method of work, he said, "As a rule my paintings, when they are successful, are conceived while they are being painted. For me, there exists no hiatus between the conception of the painting and its realization. Nevertheless, this does not prevent me from experiencing a certain satisfaction when combinations and inventions born in my paintings coincide with natural forms. In this way, they receive a kind of authority, of legitimacy." In conclusion, Magalhães said: "I am enormously fascinated by this world of combinations and inventions in which lines, colors, and spaces have a life of their own. ... The admission of forms as possible— and not as real—increases, in my case, the joy of creation, the sense of adventure that should preside at the birth of every work of art."[4]

In the 1962 exhibit *New Art of Brazil*, organized by the Walker Art Center of Minneapolis, Magalhães was represented by a series of paintings titled *Images* (oil on wood, 1961), each designated simply by a number, except for one subtitled "Orange Blossoms" In his notes for the catalog, Martin L. Friedman stressed the importance of the artist's native environment, "the tropical countryside of Pernambuco," which inspired "subjective interpretations of that area's luxuriant growth." Technically, the artist "intensifies their color by using a printer's extender and never uses an opaque white to light a tone. Thus, the highly glazed, luminous surfaces of his pictures express the violent contrast of light, humidity, and exuberant vegetation of the sugar plantation."

The Brazilian critic Almeida Cunha points out that Magalhães "has been painting with typographic dyes, worked over the paper with a spatula, obtaining in this manner the most surprising and fortunate plastic and chromatic effects."

Regionalism: Bahia

Thirteen degrees south of the Equator, on the coast of Brazil, is the picturesque seaport of Salvador, capital of the large State of Bahia and former capital of Brazil (during the colonial period). The city's official name was São Salvador da Bahia de Todos os

---

[4] Diálogo com Aloísio Magalhães sobre a natureza de sua pintura," in the catalog of an exhibition at the Museum of Modern Art, Rio de Janeiro (September, 1958).

Santos; now it is called Salvador, though often referred to as Bahia. Its striking topography, numerous churches, rich folklore, typical cuisine, seductive women (baíanas), and African cult survivals have made it a center of attraction for Brazilians and foreigners alike. The coast of Bahia is a land of fishing villages, of white beaches, of lagoons and palm trees.

While many artists have been attracted by Salvador and the region of Bahia, none has been more so than José Gianini Pancetti (1903–1959)—although he was actually born in Campinas, State of São Paulo. After holding various odd jobs, he enlisted in the Navy at the age of nineteen. He remained in the service until 1946 while continuing to paint and to exhibit at the National Salon, obtaining a Gold Medal in 1948. The sea made such a deep impression on him that when he became a painter he devoted himself chiefly to marine landscapes. In 1947 he obtained an award at the National Salon that enabled him to travel and paint in various parts of Brazil. Then, a victim of tuberculosis, he went to a sanatorium in the mountains in 1948, and soon afterwards settled in Salvador, with which he identified himself completely. He loved to live and work among the fishermen of Bahia. In the words of Almeida Cunha, "His spirit and his work are forever linked to the dark lagoon of Itapoã, encircled by white sand." Furthermore, "Pancetti's colors are bright and of a purity rare in Brazilian painting—as if he had washed them in the white of zinc. He is also very careful in the use of hues and simplifies them to a minimum. His brush strokes slide horizontally over the basic surfaces and are then cut by the schematic drawing of the several planes."[5] Though best known for his land- and seascapes, Pancetti also painted excellent portraits (including a series of self-portraits) and still-lifes. The title "citizen of the City of Salvador" was officially bestowed upon him by the Municipality of Salvador.

Pancetti's landscapes combine elements of impressionism and expressionism, as in the canvas titled *Campos de Jordão* (1949), with its flame-like autumnal trees, their branches writhing upwards against a dark-green background of shaded trees—the whole somewhat reminiscent of Van Gogh. Pancetti loved to paint the

[5] *Art in Latin America Today: Brazil*. Pan American Union, 1960, p. 17.

broad curving sweep of the shoreline in counterpoint with the curvilinear forms of the dunes and hillocks of the Brazilian coast—as in *Dunes in Cabo Frio* (1947) or *Headland of Monteserrate* (1951), with its view of the Bay of Todos os Santos (Bahia). One of his best seascapes is *Itanhaem* (1945), which displays Pancetti's tendency toward abstraction in the composition of the topographical features (beach, headland, sea, sky) and in the schematic representation of figures (fishermen) and objects (boats). This tendency toward abstraction is even more pronounced in such later canvases as *Pituba* (1951), *Seascape at Saquarema* (1955), and *Washerwomen of Abaeté* (1956), in which, as Clarival Valladares remarks, the human figures are integrated in the plastic composition, together with the rectangular cloths spread out to dry on the sand. Concerning *Pituba*, Valladares perceptively observes, "This seascape is almost entirely constructed on planes and horizontal lines, amid contrasts and harmonies [of color]. There is a perfect balance in the order of the compositional elements. . . . Pancetti's painting is firm in its abstract values."

The rightness of his plastic concepts and of his compositional forms, combined with a remarkable feeling for color, give to Pancetti's work a depth and solidarity that transcend the merely superficial attraction of the picturesque. He may be an interpreter of the tropics, but he is first and foremost *a painter*, a master of his medium in spite of being selftaught.

The artist known as Carybé (b. 1911), whose real name is Hector Bernabo, was born in Argentina but settled in Brazil in 1950 and made his home in Bahia. His favorite themes are the animals, the children, the fishermen, the women of Bahia, and the Afro-Brazilian divinities (*Orixás*) of the *candomblés* (popular religious cults, syncretizing African and Catholic elements). In addition to oils and gouaches, he has executed murals in mosaic and is also a notable print-maker. In 1957, he won first prize for Best National Engraver at the III Bienal of São Paulo.

The modern art movement of Bahia is characterized by a variety of forms and media within a regional context. Particularly interesting are the tapestry designs of Genaro de Carvalho (b. 1926), a pupil of André Lhote in Paris. Although he has been active as painter and engraver, since 1955 he has concentrated on tapestry designing. The idea of making tapestries occurred to him one day, after his return from Europe, when he visited the market in Salvador and noticed that the nets for sale there were woven in a manner similar to that of tapestries in the Middle Ages, before the invention of the loom. He forthwith hired some local net-makers and established a workshop with thirty-six women workers. Using local methods and manual skills, Carvalho developed a distinctive and aesthetically valid type of regional art that has been received with acclaim in numerous exhibitions both in Brazil and abroad. In 1965, he represented Brazil in the Biennale Internationale de la Tapisserie at Lausanne, Switzerland.

One of the artists most closely identified with the regional folk art of Bahia—not literally, but in transferring its spirit to his own personal artistic expression—was Raimundo de Oliveira (1930–1966), born in the town of Feira de Santana, State of Bahia. He moved to Salvador in 1950, and in 1958 to São Paulo. He participated in the VII and VIII Bienal de São Paulo, in the Salón Comparaison, Paris, in 1965, and in the exhibition *The Emergent Decade* (1965–66). Although he was included in the exhibit *Eight Primitive Brazilian Painters* at the Galerie Massol, Paris, in 1965, he was not really a primitive painter—he simply chose to appear as one superficially, for anyone who looked at his work with discrimination would see that it was the product of a trained artist with a full command of design and composition.

Raimundo de Oliveira devoted himself to religious painting, in the spirit of the popular *santeros* of the Northeast, whose trade it is to recount episodes from the Bible in pictures. The critic Geraldo Ferraz called him "a great *imaginário*" (maker of popular religious images). But, though he worked in the spirit of the *santeros*, he drew also on other sources for his style, notably that of Byzantine art. In the words of Ferraz, "The greater part of these inventions owes its existence to the extordinary disposition of figures, angels, soldiers, people, as a processional composition surrounding the events narrated in the picture. . . . This vast iconography, illustrating the lives of the saints and the stories of the Scriptures . . . is imbued with a kind of rapture, in which Nature, the flowers and boughs, are summoned to lend their hommage to the Divinity."[6] These are certainly not orthodox religious paintings : they have a touch of caricature that, curiously, enhances the religious sentiment and gives the familiar episodes a freshness and vitality that more conventional methods might fail to evoke. Consistent with his deliberately naïf approach, the figures that surround the central episode in a painting by Oliveiros (like the attendants in *Solomon and the Queen of Sheba*) may be shown standing on their heads at the bottom of the canvas, or standing horizontally on either side, as in *The Flagellation of Christ* (1964). The latter painting, reproduced in color in the volume *The Emergent Decade,* is an excellent example of Oliveiros' style, especially of the way he frames the central episode with intricate and subtly varied configurations (in this case columns and human figures) that have their own dynamism and yet always draw the viewer's attention to the main theme. The use of color, never naturalistic, is also very personal and immensely effective in its calculated dissonances and multiple modulations.

At the age of thirty-six, and at the height of his fame, Raimundo de Oliveiros committed suicide. What appears inexplicable becomes easier to understand as we learn more of his character. He was one of the nine artists from Latin America about whom Cornell Capa did "profiles" for *The Emergent Decade,* with photographs showing the artist at work and in the daily round of his life in São Paulo. In the accompanying commentary, we learn that, "His devout mother wanted him to become a priest, and would let him read only the Bible and his school books. His father . . . wanted his only son to become a respectable merchant, like himself." There was surely the beginning of a painful dichotomy. Furthermore, "Twice he felt ready to enter a monastery, but his Catholicism was considered too unorthodox." He became friendly with the Dominican fathers, and took communion with them. For me, Capa's most moving and symbolic photograph is the one that shows the artist sitting on a bench under two large trees, conversing with a Dominican. Was he trying to find a cure for his incurable unhappiness, his sense of unbearable solitude?

[6] From the catalog of an exhibition at the Galería Bonino, Buenos Aires (September, 1964).

Nonobjective Tendencies

We have already encountered abstract tendencies in the work of such painters as Alfredo Volpi, Flávio de Rezende Carvalho, Cícero Dias, and Aloísio Magalhães, and it will be our task now to explore further the development of nonobjective painting in Brazil. Iberê Camargo, who was born in Rio Grande do Sul in 1914, is equally important as engraver and as painter. After a brief period of study at the National School of Fine Arts, Camargo became a pupil of Guignard. In 1947, he obtained a foreign travel award at the National Salon and went to Europe for further study, with Lhote in France and with Di Chirico in Italy. Di Chirico's influence, incidentally, made itself quite widely felt in Brazil during the 1940's. Camargo participated in the Bienal of São Paulo in 1951, 1959, 1961 (Best National Painter), and 1963 (special exhibit), in the Venice Biennale of 1962, and in *The New Art of Brazil* (Walker Art Center, 1962). He began as a landscape painter, but eventually evolved toward autonomous forms that explore dynamic and spatial relations, as in *Dynamic Structure* (1961), *Structure in Tension* (1962), *Space and Movement* (1963), or the series of *Wheels* that he showed at the Walker Art Center in 1962: *Space with Wheels, Dynamo with Wheels, String of Wheels*. He uses a thick impasto, and his method resembles that of action painting. As described by Mário Pedrosa, "Through successive layers of impasto, now with short and nervous brushstrokes, the painter jumbles and mixes everything, even to soiling with white the ground of his material; now, on the contrary, with violent jabs of the spatula, on the surface, he establishes and builds up layers that mark, in luminous and pulsating borders, the rhythm, or rather, the cadence of the artist's own movements as he works."[7] Martin Friedman speaks of "these especially sombre, richly painted, dark abstractions that repeat an austere vocabulary of forms," and likens their "passive intensity" to that of the Spanish school.[8]

While many Brazilian artists, as we have seen, looked to Paris for training and stimulus, none has achieved a closer identification

[7] Catalog of VI Bienal de São Paulo (1963), p. 112.
[8] Catalog, *New Art of Brazil*, Walker Art Center, Minneapolis (1962).

with the *Jeune Ecole de Paris* (the second Paris School that arose after World War II) than Antonio Bandeira (1922–1967). A native of Fortaleza in the State of Ceará in the Northeast, Bandeira took an active part in founding the Sociedade de Artes Plasticas, and its annual Salon, in that city. After going to Rio de Janeiro in 1945, he was awarded a grant by the French Government for study in Paris. There he specialized in engraving and gravitated toward Saint-Germain-des-Prés, forming a three-man group with the informalist painters Camille Bryen and Wols (Otto Battman, who died in 1951). They called themselves BRANRYOLS. From 1951 to 1953 he was in Rio de Janeiro, but then won another travel award that enabled him to return to Europe, where he remained until 1959. The following year he participated in the Venice Biennale and was given a one-man show in the Museum of Modern Art in Rio de Janeiro. He exhibited in the São Paulo Bienal four times, and in many other international exhibitions, including the Salon des Réalités Nouvelles in Paris.

The painters in Paris with whom Bandeira was associated were in revolt against geometric abstraction and constructivism. They wanted their painting to be informal, lyrical, perhaps metaphysical, creatively spontaneous, seeking poetic values rather than relying upon architectural forms and geometrical abstractions. To this type of informalism, Bandeira gave his allegiance, both in his oils and his gouaches. His paintings have the poetic, evocative, or literary titles to which many of the informalists were partial (*Night Over the City*, "*Lointain . . . très Lointain*," "*Les Bateaux Ivres*"); but this does not affect their strictly "painterly" quality as abstract compositions, taking their point of departure from the reality of the visible world. It is through color, above all, that he seeks "a new reality."

Danilo Di Prete (b. Pisa, Italy, 1911) is another painter very close to the lyrical abstraction of the informalists. Self-taught, he exhibited in Italy during the 1930's, and during World War II he belonged to a group called Italian Artists in Arms, documenting episodes of the war. In 1946, he emigrated to Brazil and for the next four years worked only on books and posters. Beginning in 1951, he participated in all the Biennials of São Paulo, winning prizes for the Best National Painter in 1951 and 1965. He also participated in the Venice Biennale in 1952 and 1960, and sent seven paintings to *New Art of Brazil* in 1962. Martin Friedman said of his work, "He floats forms raised in high relief across his canvas, and the result is a highly subjective form of nature painting." Most of his canvases have only functional designations (*Painting No. V*, and so forth), but some have titles that reflect his penchant for "cosmic landscapes" (*Cosmic Gesture, Southern Cross* [both 1960]). At the seventh São Paulo Bienal he exhibited a whole series of canvases under the generic title *Cosmic Landscape*. He belongs to the group of Brazilian painters who have been more influenced by the informalism of the Spanish school (Tapies and others) than by that of Paris.

Other Abstract Expressionists

A leading exponent of abstract expressionism is the Japanese-born painter Manabu Mabe (b. 1924), who emigrated to Brazil and settled in São Paulo. Self-taught in art, he had to take many odd jobs to make a living before becoming known as a painter (at one time he painted abstract designs for neckties). Beginning in 1953, he participated in several of the São Paulo Biennials, winning First Prize for Best National Painter in 1961 and enjoying a special exhibit of twenty paintings in 1963. The metaphysical overtones of lyrical abstraction are present in many of his canvases (*The Infinite, Voice of the Earth, Voice of the Heaven, Dream of the Prophet*), together with a personal and highly effective sense of color as a compositional element, with marked partiality for blues.

Although Frans Krajcberg (b. Poland, 1921) also paints within the general realm of abstract expressionism with metaphysical overtones, he has given his work a particular distinction through the use of mixed media that provide a three-dimensional quality to his compositions, and that have caused them to be described as "sculpture-painting." In the words of Martin Friedman, "Their rich, convoluted surfaces are built up of painted Japanese paper adhered to a support and modeled in relief. In these perforated, creviced vistas, Krajcberg creates elementary microcosms that suggest volcanic eruptions and constant metamorphoses of terrestrial surfaces."[9] The titles of his paintings indicate Krajcberg's cosmic preoccupations: *Scorched Planet, Small Cosmogony, Stratus, Moon Shadows, Geology* (all mixed media, 1961). At the VII São Paulo Bienal (1963), Krajcberg was given an important retrospective show consisting of fifty-seven works covering the period 1952 to 1962.

The Brazilian art critic Luiz de Almeida Cunha, writing in 1959, placed Ivan Serpa (b. 1923) in the center of "the concrete movement which, influenced by the doctrines of Max Bill and Maldonado, developed several years ago in Rio and São Paulo among the national painters who were anxious to find a form of expression better suited to the schematic lines of Brazilian architecture."[10] But during the 1960's he cultivated a sort of abstract informalism, represented by the seven canvases (in tempera) that he sent to the *New Art of Brazil* exhibition in 1962. As described by Martin Friedman, "Like finely sliced tree root sections, their images are complex. The lean surfaces of his canvases are achieved more by staining than brushing, and there is a controlled use of small incidental paint effects in these highly rarefied works." In the works, such as *Birds* (1963) and *Figures* (1964), selected for the exhibition *The Emergent Decade*, we find Serpa deeply involved in expressionistic neofiguratism. At the third Bienal of Córdoba (1966), he combined Pop and Op elements with geometrical configurations akin to the hard-edge style. A retrospective show of Serpa's work at the Museum of Modern Art, Rio de Janeiro, in 1965, was like a display of contemporary art trends in Brazil.

Arcangello Ianelli (b. São Paulo, 1922) is a painter who thus far has preferred to remain within the abstract tendencies of the New School of Paris, with a particular affinity to the work of De Staël, exposing large, loosely-defined geometrical forms within a context of rather austere color tones. He has exhibited extensively in Brazil, and in 1965 participated in the Salon Comparaison, Paris. In 1966 he had one-man shows in Rome and Munich.

[9] *Ibid.*
[10] *Art in Latin America Today: Brazil*, p. 27.

Also an adherent of abstract expressionism is Yolanda Mohalyi (b. Hungary, 1909), who has lived in Brazil since 1931 and had her first one-man show in 1946. At the VII Bienal of São Paulo she was awarded a prize for Best National Painter (1963), and in 1965 she was given a large individual show at the Museum of Modern Art in Rio. Both she and Ianelli were included in *The Emergent Decade* exhibition.

In 1959, Almeida Cunha gave first place to Milton Dacosta (b. 1915) among the "rationalists" of Brazilian painting—meaning the adherents of geometrical abstraction. But Dacosta, like Ivan Serpa, is a painter who has gone through many phases. He studied for a time with Portinari, won a travel award at the National Salon in 1944, and spent the next two years in Paris. In 1955 he received the Prize for Best National Painter at the III São Paulo Bienal. In July, 1959, the Museum of Modern Art in Rio gave him a large retrospective show, covering his work since 1939.

Dacosta's early work was figurative, though with marked cubist elements. By 1952 he had assimilated what was of use to him in cubism, and in such a work as *Two Figures* (oil, 1952) he achieved a personal synthesis of cubist and lyrical elements. The canvas titled *Over the Horizontal* (1954) is a geometrically stylized still-life, including the consecrated bowl of fruit. From this it was but a step to completely abstract compositions, such as *Construction on a Black Background* (1957), in which vertical geometrical structures, built of small rectangular components, rise from and through horizontal demarcations; and *In Red* (1958), where the vertical components are reduced to four asymmetrical white rectangles enclosed in the bottom of the canvas by a single horizontal line. At the same time, Dacosta was painting quasi-geometrical figurations like *Figure with Hat* (1955, with many later variants, 1956-58), combining rectilinear and curvilinear forms. In his more recent works Dacosta has discarded all geometrical forms in favor of free configurations to which he imparts a certain baroque dynamism.

Wesley Duke Lee (b. 1931), painter and engraver, is an artist too volatile to categorize and too talented to ignore. His studies include a stint at Parson's School of Design in New York, at

Friedlaender's atelier in Paris, and the Académie de la Grande Chaumière. In Paris, where he had a one-man show in 1963, he belonged to the group called Phases. In 1965 he won the International Prize for Painting at the Tokyo Biennial. He participated in the thirty-third Biennale of Venice and in *The Emergent Decade*. In connection with the latter, Thomas Messer characterized him as "a young eclectic in the linear tradition of Toulouse-Lautrec, Art Noveau, Klimt, and Schiele." Three examples of Lee's work are included in the volume *The Emergent Decade*: *Valneria, Assistant to Marcadium* (1960), a monstrous neofigurative nude; *A Zone: I-Ching* (1964), Chinese calligraphy combined with elements of art nouveau and Pop Art (the reference is to the ancient Chinese Book of Changes); and *View of the Doorway and the Forest* (1960), an abstract work juxtaposing areas of informalism and constructivism. "Creation by incongruity" might be Lee's motto. The culmination of this method is found in *Porta Factum* (oil, 1965), in which each of the rectangular segments or compartments into which the canvas is divided represents a different style of painting: geometric, hard-edge figurative, neofigurative, surrealist, expressionist, lyrical abstract, and so forth. So far the method has worked, in that each of his canvases or drawings exerts a visual fascination for the viewer. Wesley Duke Lee remains uncommitted to any *ism*, even while he has flirted with many.

Graphic Arts

The contemporary graphic arts of Brazil are widely recognized as standing among the most important of this century. This prestige is due in large measure to the work, the example, and the influence of Oswaldo Goeldi (1895–1961), generally acknowledged to be the greatest engraver Brazil has produced. At the age of six his family took him to Switzerland, where he lived until his return to Brazil in 1919. He had his first one-man show in Bern in 1917. During these formative years he came under the spell of expressionism, which remained a powerful influence for the rest of his life. He was also deeply impressed by the work of Van Gogh and Edvard Munch. The strongest and most direct influence, however, came from the Austrian artist Alfred Kubin, through whom—as Goeldi himself acknowledged—he was enabled to find his own creative path. From 1927 he corresponded and exchanged drawings and prints with Kubin, whom he visited in 1930.

Goeldi had a one-man show in Rio de Janeiro in 1921, and in 1930 and 1931 he had other shows in Switzerland and Germany. But it was many years before he obtained sufficient recognition to live independently as an artist. Meanwhile he illustrated books and taught xylography for a time at the National School of Fine Arts. His existence was solitary and hampered by poverty; yet he never wavered in his artistic convictions. In 1949, he could truthfully say, "Never did I sacrifice to any passing fashion my own personal view—a difficult path but the only one for me, and worth every sort of deprivation." He had the tragic sense of life, tempered by his romantic bent. As António Bento observes, "In common with the Romantics, Goeldi was in love with the mystery of the night, with humble streets, with old houses, with unhappy lovers, and with the tragedy of death." His sense of compassion, of empathy with sad and lonely people, is evident in much of his work. We may cite as an example the woodcut printed in color titled *Old Age*. Here there is a characteristic contrast between the expressionistic human figure—an old man looking over a wall toward the horizon—and the impersonal, quasigeometrical compositional structure with its thrust of planes, masses, and angles.

At the first Bienal of São Paulo, in 1951, Goeldi was awarded the prize for Best National Engraver, and thereafter his fame rapidly increased. He won the First Prize for Engraving at the second Interamerican Bienal of Mexico, in 1960. In 1961, the year of his death, he was given two important retrospective exhibitions, one at the Bienal of São Paulo and one at the Museum of Modern Art in Rio de Janeiro, consisting of engravings, drawings, and watercolors. The catalog of this exhibit reads like an inventory of romantic themes: *Promise, Blue Afternoon, Lagoon, Parting, Calm Sea, Tropical Night*. But this is a romanticism that has been transposed to a modern mode by the power of expressionism. There is sentiment but no sentimentality in the many scenes of life among the poor and forsaken—the vagabonds, the beggars, the humble toilers of the city and the countryside. And in the three series of drawings on World War II Goeldi bears witness to the tragedy of his time. He was a complete artist in the fullest sense of the term: deeply dedicated to his craft and at the same time greatly involved in the drama of humanity.

Lívio Abramo (b. 1903), began under the double expressionist influence of Goeldi and Segall, but gradually evolved toward a distinctive style of his own in which expressionism played a subordinate role. He was a pioneer in wood engraving (xylography), in which medium most of his work has been done. Beginning to exhibit collectively in 1935, he had his first one-man show at São Paulo in 1942. In 1950, he obtained the foreign travel award in the National Salon, enabling him to travel widely in Europe during the next two years. He participated in the Venice Biennale in 1950, 1952, and 1954; in 1953, at the second Bienal of São Paulo, he was awarded the prize for Best Engraver. Meanwhile, he earned his living as a newspaper artist, making drawings for various journals of São Paulo. In 1948 he illustrated, with woodcuts, the book *Pelo Sertão* (*Through the Backlands*), a collection of realistic stories by Afonso Arinos. After 1955 he had many individual shows in Europe and America, and also participated in important international shows such as *Latin American Art Since Independence*. For several years he lived in Asunción, as a member of the Brazilian Cultural Mission to Paraguay. His residence there is reflected in some of the wood engravings, e.g. the *Variations on a Paraguayan Theme* (1963) that he showed at the VI São Paulo Bienal.

Although he has done line engravings, drawings, gouaches, and watercolors, Abramo's major accomplishment has been in the medium of wood engravings (xylographs), which he was the first to cultivate intensively in Brazil. His work of the 1930's, essentially naturalistic though with touches of expressionism—as in *Worker* (1935)—already reveal a firm technical mastery but no particular distinction of style. This he was to achieve after 1940—it is fully evident in the São Paulo exhibit of 1942—culminating in the illustrations for the 1948 de luxe edition of *Pelo Sertão*. During the 1950's, Abramo moved toward greater abstraction, though without abandoning the figure completely. The most representative work of this period is the series entitled *Rio* (1951–54), in which elements of the urban landscape are atomized and rearranged with a dazzling virtuosity of form and texture.

During this period Abramo was also doing a series of drawings, gouaches, and xylographs on the *Macumba*, which is the name given to the Afro-Brazilian religious cults in the region of Rio de Janeiro. Abramo's work has greatly enriched the repertory of Brazilian themes and of that "tropical civilization" which Gilberto Freyre sees as the essence of Brazilian culture. All this he has reinterpreted in terms of an exacting artistry that shuns compromise of any kind, and that transmutes the human environment into visual poetry. There is every reason for regarding Lívio Abramo as "one of the most significant plastic artists of Brazil."

Among graphic artists of the next generation, Marcelo Grassmann (b. 1925) is probably closest to the expressionism of Goeldi, though he has concentrated on the fantastic and grotesque, which was only one aspect of Goeldi's work. Self-taught in art, he began to exhibit in 1946, and in 1952 obtained a travel award at the National Salon of Modern Art that took him to Europe for two years. At the third São Paulo Bienal (1955) he won the prize for Best National Engraver, and at the fifth Bienal (1959) the prize for drawing. In 1958 he received a special sprize for sacred art at the Venice Biennale; in 1965 he had a one-man show in Mexico City that was highly acclaimed. In the Walker Art Center's *New Art of Brazil* (1962) he was represented by eight watercolors in the series titled *The Knight and Other Themes* (1961) that reveal his penchant for the macabre and the grotesque. His work shows kinship with the monstrous images of Hieronymus Bosch and the nightmarish fantasies of Goya. Grassmann's *Untitled* (ink on paper, 1961), included in the exhibit *Latin American Art Since Independence*, shows his obsession with the hideous semi-human monstrosities that people his imagination, characterized by one commentator as "monster-like fusions of men and animals."

Aldemir Martins (b. 1922) began his career as a painter, but since 1950 he has devoted himself entirely to drawing and engraving. At the third São Paulo Bienal (1955) he won the prize for Best National Draftsman; in 1956 he was awarded the Grand International Prize for Drawing at the Venice Biennale; in 1959 he obtained the foreign travel award at the National Salon of Modern Art in Rio de Janeiro, which award he used chiefly for a sojourn in Rome. He was given a special exhibit at the VI Bienal of São Paulo (1961), and he participated in *Latin American Art Since Independence* with a lithograph titled *Woman* (1961). Although this and a few other recent works remain figurative, much of Martins' production since his return from Europe tends to be nonfigurative. He often deals in a semiabstract manner with the popular types, folkways, and typical scenes of Brazil, having familiarized himself with the land and its people through a "See Brazil" travel grant awarded to him at the seventh São Paulo Salon of Modern Art. His best-known series, drawn from Brazilian folkways, is *Cangaceiros e Rendeiras* (*Ruffians and Lacemakers,* 1951–53). Martins has also executed murals and designs for industry.

Arthur Luiz Piza (b. 1928) has achieved international distinction above all for the unusual textures of his prints. After studies in São Paulo he had further training with Friedlaender in Paris, where his first one-man show took place in 1957. This consisted of acquatints, revealing the influence of Klee and Kandinsky. After 1959 he no longer worked with acid, but used instead the burin and the rounded gouge for his engravings on copper, such as *Cosmogony* (1959), *Great Light* (1960), and *Great Cosmic* (1961). He aspired to give a primordial and universal significance to his works of this period through the use of cosmic imagery, as in *The Three Elements* (1963). He also did a series of purely abstract engravings identified simply as numbered *Compositions* (1961). Five of these were included in the Walker Art Center's *New Art of Brazil.* Piza has also done a number of embossed collages, in which small pieces of light cardboard, previously painted with watercolor or oil, cut in rectangular shapes, are glued to the canvas in overlapping patterns, like roof tiles. According to the critic Bernard Gheerbrant, the artist does not start from a previous design, but works intuitively, "Either the form is born from the ends of his fingers, or it fails completely." There is no margin for error.

Piza, who lives in Paris, won a prize at the Venice Biennale of 1966. This is but one among many awards that confirm his stature as the foremost Brazilian graphic artist of his generation.

Roberto De Lamonica, described in the catalog of *Latin American Art Since Independence* as "one of the master contemporary engravers of the Western Hemisphere," was born in the State of Mato Grosso in 1933. He studied with a number of teachers, among them Friedlaender, and had his first one-man show in 1953. In 1957, at the "Salon for Everyone," he won a prize for engraving which consisted of a trip to China and the Soviet Union. He also traveled in Western Europe, and after his return to Brazil continued his studies in Rio. He gave courses in engraving in Lima in 1961 and in Chicago in 1964. The following year he was awarded a Guggenheim Foundation Fellowship, and in 1966 he had one-man shows in Rome and Milan. He participated in *New Art of Brazil* (Walker Art Center) and in the seventh and eighth Biennials of São Paulo (1963 and 1965), receiving a prize for Best National Engraver in 1963 and having a *sala especial* in 1965.

De Lamonica adheres strictly to metal engraving in purely abstract modes characterized by superb technical mastery, impressive formal composition, and imaginative inventiveness. His works are equally fascinating for their variety of texture and beauty of detail, as for their dynamic yet perfectly balanced contrasts and juxtapositions. As Martin Friedman writes, "His vital compositions are inventive and complex, yet all formal elements are strongly controlled and nothing left to chance."

Five Women Engravers

Several women have distinguished themselves in the graphic arts of Brazil. Among them are three foreign-born artists: Isabel Pons (Spain), Fayga Ostrower (Poland), and Maria Bonomi (Italy); and two who were born in Brazil: Edith Behring and Anna Letycia (Quadros). The last two have been influential through their classes in engraving at the Museum of Modern Art in Rio.

Isabel Pons (b. 1912) studied metal engraving with Friedlaender and began to exhibit in 1943. Up to the time that she settled in Brazil (1956) she had been doing both painting and engraving, but she soon began to concentrate exclusively on engraving. She quickly obtained recognition when she was awarded the prize for Best National Engraver at the São Paulo Bienal of 1961. Working with metal engraving in figurative and abstract modes, she uses superimposed colors in many of her recent works, among them the eight etchings that she exhibited at São Paulo in 1967.

Edith Behring (b. 1916) studied with Portinari in Rio and with Friedlaender in Paris. From 1957 she participated in international shows, winning the Grand Prize at the Bienal Americana de Gravura in Santiage de Chile, 1963. Two years later she was awarded First Prize for Engraving at the second National Salon of Brazilian Art, held in Brasilia. Her first individual show was at the Museum of Modern Art in Rio, in 1959. Her metal engravings, displaying a strong sense of form, are abstract, and are identified simply by number and date.

Fayga Ostrower (b. 1920) went to Brazil in 1934, and from 1946 studied graphic arts at the Fundação Getúlio Vargas in Rio. She then received a Fulbright grant for further study in the United States. In 1957, at the fourth São Paulo Bienal, she obtained the prize for Best National Engraver, and in 1958 the International Prize for Engraving at the Venice Biennale. Ostrower works in both metal and wood engraving, with entirely abstract forms, technically brilliant and inventive. At São Paulo in 1967 she showed eight abstract woodcuts in color on rice paper.

Maria Bonomi was a pupil of Yolanda Mohalyi and began her career as a painter. In 1955 she studied engraving with Lívio Abramo, whose influence proved to be decisive. Following her first individual show in 1956 she studied for a year in the United States with Shapero and Seong Moy. She participated in the Venice Biennale of 1964 and in the São Paulo Bienal of 1965, where she obtained the prize for Best National Engraver. Her large abstract woodcuts have descriptive or evocative titles, such as as *Pour la Paix* (*For Peace*) and *All the Tombs of the World*.

Anna Letycia (Quadros), who was born in 1929, also began as a painter, but from 1954 devoted herself to metal engraving, studying with Iberê Camargo and Goeldi. She exhibited in Paris in 1963 and 1965, as well as in London, Vienna, and Madrid.

Her engravings are abstract, identified only by number and date. She has also won international recognition for her stageset designs.

Several of the younger Brazilian artists, born since 1940, have distinguished themselves and won international recognition in the graphic arts. Among them are Roberto Magalhães, Rubens Gerchman, and Antônio Dias. Magalhães (b. 1940), who studied engraving with Adir Botelho, has specialized in drawing and wood engraving. Gerchman (b. 1942) also studied with Botelho at the National School of Fine Arts, and has worked in both wood engraving and drawing (neofigurative). He has the added distinction of having promoted the first "happenings" in Rio de Janeiro (1966). Dias (b. 1944) is a self-taught artist who has been successful in both painting and drawing. In 1965 he participated in the Salon de la Jeune Peinture in Paris. In that same year, together with Gerchman and Wesley Duke Lee, he made a tour of universities in the United States to accompany a collective traveling exhibition of their drawings.

Sculpture

Victor Brecheret (1894–1956), previously mentioned in connection with the Week of Modern Art, was the pioneer of modern sculpture in Brazil. While still very young, he had a one-man show in the city of his birth, São Paulo, after which he participated in the 1925 International Exhibition in Rome. Going to Paris, he became one of the founders of the *Salon des Tuileries*. There he also studied with Mestrovic, who influenced his early work. After his return to Brazil, Brecheret joined forces with those artists and intellectuals who wanted to combine modernism with the expression of Brazilian culture. He traveled through the interior, studied the folklore and ethnography of Brazil, and from these indigenous sources drew the inspiration for a series that he called *Stones*. Although some of his work tended toward semi-abstraction, his most important achievements were in figurative sculpture, notably the huge *Monument to the Flags*, consisting

of about forty gigantic figures—some nearly twenty feet high—
erected in São Paulo to commemorate the epic of the *bandeirantes*:
the pioneers and frontiersmen of the region of São Paulo who
explored and settled the Brazilian hinterland in the seventeenth
and eighteenth centuries. In 1951, at the first Bienal of São Paulo,
Brecheret was awarded the prize for the Best National Sculptor;
and at the fourth Bienal, in 1957, he was given a posthumous
retrospective exhibit.

Bruno Giorgi (b. 1905), another *paulista*, is generally regarded
as the most important contemporary sculptor of Brazil. He studied
first in Rome with Lessa and then in Paris with Maillol, also
attending the Académie de la Grande Chaumière (1936-39). After
his return he settled in São Paulo, but later moved to Rio de
Janeiro. He was awarded the prize for the Best National Sculptor
at the second São Paulo Bienal in 1953. Ten years later he traveled
through Europe and exhibited in the principal capitals of the
continent (1962-63).

Bruno Giorgi's work has ranged from the realistic to the semiabstract. In the former category are his statues and portraits of
famous figures of Brazil and the world, such as that of the
Portuguese poet Camões. For a time, his massive recumbent figures
resembled somewhat those of Henry Moore. Eventually he arrived
at his most personal and characteristic style, consisting of
elongated, semiabstract anthropomorphic figures, reduced to the
utmost simplicity of line and mass, with the vertical dimension
strongly accented. A celebrated example of this style is the bronze
group (two figures) titled *Two Warriors* (1961), which stands in
the Plaza of the Three Powers in Brasília. Actually, this sculpture
is meant to symbolize the men of the hinterland who helped in
the building of the new capital. Another famous sculpture by
Georgi, *Meteor*, of Carrara marble, stands at the entrance of the
new Ministry of Foreign Affairs in Brasília (see Chapter 6).

Another sculptor whose work is represented in Brasília is Maria
Martins (b. 1900), who executed the striking abstract sculpture
in bronze that faces the rear façade of the President's Palace.
Born in Campanha, Minas Gerais, Maria Martins began to
sculpt when she was twenty-six, but it was only in 1939, when
she became a pupil of Oscar Jespers in Brussels, that she devoted

herself professionally to her work. She had her first individual show in Washington in 1941 and rapidly achieved prominence thereafter. Identifying herself with the surrealist movement, she took part in the Surrealist Exhibition at Paris in 1947. Her work won praise from one of the leading critics of contemporary art, Michel Seuphor, who compared her work to that of Germaine Richier.

Alfredo Ceschiatti (b. 1918) first came into prominence when he did the bas-reliefs for the modernistic Church of St. Francis in Pampulha, designed by Oscar Niemeyer (1942). In Rio de Janeiro he was responsible for the *Three Figures of the Armed Forces* in the *Monument to the Dead of the Second World War* (1960), located in a park near the Museum of Modern Art, on Guanabara Bay. For Brasília, he executed two important works: the bronze group titled *The Bathers*, and a heroic statue of Justice. Although not unaware of contemporary trends, Ceschiatti remains essentially an academic sculptor in the monumental tradition.

Lygia Clark (b. 1921) began her career as a painter, having studied with Burle-Marx in Rio and later in Paris with Dobrinsky, Arpad Szennes, and Fernand Léger. In 1952, after a one-man show in Paris, she returned to Brazil and continued to paint in the style of geometric abstraction. In 1959 she was a cofounder of the Brazilian Neoconcretist Association, which proved to be short-lived. By this time she was already becoming dissatisfied with the static quality of constructivist painting. As early as 1957 she had written in her notebook, "The work of art should demand a direct participation from the spectator, and the latter should be immediately involved with it." She was evidently moving toward a kinetic art, and in pursuit of this aim she turned to articulated sculptures—simple but very original and effective geometrical constructions gyrating around a central axis, with interacting rectangles, triangles, circles, and other geometric shapes that acquire a wide diversity of changing forms as they are manipulated by the spectator. For some reason—probably a fancied organic analogy suggested by some of their mobile conformations—these articulated sculptures came to be called *Bichos. Bicho* means any unspecified animal, and is usually applied to insects. But the *Bichos* of Lygia Clark are essentially abstract-constructivist inventions, even when they have associative titles: *Object from an Outer World, Endless Screw, Project for a Planet, Space Bird, Fantastic Carriage.* In the word of Mário Pedrosa, "They are fabulous architectonic entities that design themselves in space."

After she turned to sculpture, Lygia Clark's success was quickly assured. In 1960 she had her first individual exhibition; a year later, at the fourth Bienal of São Paulo, she won the prize for Best National Sculptor. At the next Bienal (1963) she was given a special exhibit consisting of *Bichos*, abstract reliefs, and "fantastic" architectural projects (freely invented abstract forms). There was even a model for a *Casa-Bicho*. Lygia Clark represented Brazil at the Venice Biennale in 1960 and 1962, and in 1965 she was given a fifteen-year retrospective show of some sixty works at the London Signals Exposition. She has had exhibits in Paris, Rome, New York, Washington, São Paulo, and other art centers.

Two sculptors closely identified with Bahia are Mário Cravo (b. 1923) and Agnaldo Manoel dos Santos (1926–1962), both born in Salvador. Dos Santos has been called "the most important Negro sculptor of Brazil" by Clarival Valladares. Agnaldo, as he was generally called, worked within the Afro-Brazilian tradition that has persisted so strongly in Bahia. Working mostly in wood, less often in metal, he identified himself not only with the popular inconography of Bahia, with its syncretism of African and Catholic elements, but also with traditional African sculpture, which he studied through photographs. He began to work as an assistant to Mário Cravo and later traveled to the Rio São Francisco to seek out Francisco Biquiba Guarani, an indigenous sculptor who specialized in carving figureheads (*carrancas*) for the craft that plied this river. From this native craftsman he learned much that was useful in his own art. Agnaldo aimed to fuse the traditional and the contemporary, the primitive and the modern. His first one-man show, held in Rio de Janeiro in 1957, was very successful. In the same year he participated in the fourth Bienal of São Paulo, and in 1961 in the National Salon of Modern Art. His work was chosen to represent Brazil at the Festival of Negro Art at Dakar in 1966, where it obtained first prize for sculpture.

Mário Cravo is another artist who has tried to bridge the gap between folk art and modern expression. Symbolically, his first teacher was *um santeiro bahiano* (a popular sculptor of saints from Bahia) and his last the sculptor Mestrovic, with whom he studied in the United States in 1949. He won prizes at the São Paulo Bienal in 1951 and 1953, and was awarded First Prize for Sculpture at the Salão Paulista de Arte Moderna in 1955. During 1963 and 1964 he traveled and exhibited in Europe. He taught engraving at the University of Bahia and later was appointed Director of the Museums of Modern Art and of Folk Art (*Arte Popular*) in Salvador. His figurative sculptures, deriving from the Brazilian baroque tradition of religious imagery and iconography, are expressionist in style, but he has also experimented with nonfigurative forms. In a statement on his artistic convictions made on the occasion of a one-man show at the Museum of Modern Art, Rio de Janeiro, in 1959, Mário Cravo said, "I do not accept international formulas in art." He has gone his own way, deriving strength from his native environment, from contemporary techniques, and from his inner struggle to achieve a synthesis of these elements.

Brazil is clearly one of the three leading nations of Latin America—along with Argentina and Mexico—in the contemporary arts. With the inauguration of the São Paulo Bienal in 1951, Brazil assumed an unprecedented international importance in contemporary painting, sculpture, and graphic arts. In the latter field its artists have achieved an indisputable pre-eminence, winning high awards and critical acclaim throughout the world. The same is true of architecture, particularly the work of Oscar Niemeyer in Brasília. If painting and sculpture have not attained to quite the same heights of international recognition as architecture and graphic arts, they are nevertheless represented by a large body of varied, dynamic, and often fascinating work, with no lack of individual talent or of distinctive national character. In the person of Cândido Portinari, Brazil produced the only Latin American painter outside of Mexico who succeeded in creating a national pictorial epic in the manner of an heroic age that may never return. The talent of the new generation, born since 1940, already has made its presence felt on the international scene, and promises an unbroken continuity for Brazil's many-sided achievements in modern art.

6

Architecture
and
Integration
of the Arts

I N keeping with the character of this book, architecture will be treated primarily as a form of artistic expression rather than in its important social and economic aspects. Yet these aspects are always present as conditioning factors. The emergence of the middle class, belated and limited industrial development, the relentless population explosion, the unequal distribution of wealth, growing concern for the welfare of the underprivileged, the role of government patronage, the thrust of national pride—all exert their influence in varying degrees on both private and public construction, on urban planning and development, on the growth of low-cost housing projects, on the building of schools and hospitals, and on such major achievements as Brazil's new capital, Brasília, and the University Cities of Mexico and Caracas. These boldly conceived and magnificently executed projects have captured the attention and stirred the admiration of the entire world, highlighting the extraordinary accomplishments of Latin American architects during the last twenty years or so.

The rise of a significant modern architecture in Latin America occurred in the 1930's, although there were incipient steps in that direction during the previous decade—such as Warchavchik's "Functionalist Manifesto" published in 1925, followed two years later by his construction of the first "modernist house" in Brazil, and the functionalist movement launched about the same time in Mexico by Villagrán García and Juan O'Gorman. But there was a heavy weight of tradition to overcome. The French Beaux Arts influence had entrenched itself in the nineteenth century, shaping the ornate and ostentatious character of many public and private buildings from Mexico City to Rio de Janeiro and Buenos Aires. The palatial private houses became a means by which the oligarchy and the newly rich could display conspicuous consumption. Municipal pride was nourished by the construction of such large and lavish showcases as the splendidly massive Teatro Colón in Buenos Aires and the impressively ornate Palacio de Bellas Artes in Mexico City—the latter revealing the art nouveau influence that was pervasive around the turn of the century. The situation was summed up by the Mexican art historian Justino Fernández, "By the end of the nineteenth century, the 'romantic attitude' was rampant; residences were built in any style, including the Chinese, and office buildings might be designed after operatic decorations. There were efforts to revive the old baroque, and nationalism bethought itself of dressing its façades with pre-Cortesian Indian sculpture."[1] He was thinking of Mexico but, allowing for local differences—it would be most unlikely to encounter pre-Hispanic Indian sculpture on a house in Buenos Aires or Montevideo—the essentials of the picture apply to most of Latin America: indiscriminate eclecticism, rampant romanticism, superficial revivalism (including the neocolonial and the pseudo-baroque), misguided nationalism, and, in general, reliance on the past rather than awareness of the present. Most architects looked toward the example of history and to consecrated styles instead of toward the dynamism of the twentieth century and the resources of modern technology.

But Latin American architecture could not remain immune to the advances of technology or to the impact of international styles and concepts emanating from the minds of such creative personalities as Le Corbusier, Gropius, and Mies van der Rohe. (Strange to say, the influence of Frank Lloyd Wright was never

[1] In Esther Born, The New Architecture in Mexico. William Morrow and Co., 1937, p. 14.

important in Latin America.) This was particularly true of those countries—notably Mexico and Brazil—that were propelled toward the modern age by strong national currents of social reform and economic expansion. In Mexico, it was the architects who made modernism a vital force while the muralist painters were applying archaic pictorial concepts for the ends of political propaganda. In Brazil, architects were in the vanguard of the modernist movement that had its first explosive outburst in the Week of Modern Art of São Paulo in 1922.

Rise of Functionalism

Functionalism was the swing of the pendulum away from historicism, eclecticism, nationalism and romanticism in Latin American architecture. In Mexico, functionalism was in the paradoxical situation of going counter to the prevailing nationalist spirit while at the same time, through its economy of means and ends, providing a workable and much-needed solution for many of the urgent construction requirements of the post-Revolutionary era. The movement was started by José Villagrán García (b. 1901), who had received his degree in architecture in 1923 from the Academy of San Carlos, which at that time undertook to teach all the arts without satisfying the essential needs of any in the modern world. Villagrán García, assigned to teach a course on "Composition and Theory of Architecture" at the Academy, advocated a strictly functional, practical, technological, and socially-oriented approach to the problems of contemporary building in Mexico. The architect should study the needs of the nation and build accordingly, with intelligent application of advanced techniques and new materials. Appointed Architect of the Department of Public Health in 1925, Villagrán García designed the Institute of Hygiene and the Sanatorium of Huipulco along functional lines. By this time a group of young architects (among them Juan O'Gorman, Enrique del Moral, Francisco Arece, and Carlos Vergara) had been converted to functionalism, and they collaborated with Villagrán García in constructing the Sanitary Farm in Tucuba, completed in 1926—the first group of buildings in Mexico to be designed entirely on functional principles. When Villagrán García was appointed Director of the newly-created National School of Architecture in 1932, he became even more influential in stressing the functional approach to architecture that he has continued to apply, with certain modifications, in all his subsequent works, including sanatoria, schools, office buildings, markets, and the slaughterhouse of Mexico City (1955).

In those early years, Juan O'Gorman (b. 1905)—architect, painter, sculptor—was one of the most militant advocates of functionalism. He broke completely with traditional aesthetic criteria, insisting that architecture was strictly utilitarian and should be based exclusively on science and technology. His basic formula was the maximum return from the minimum expenditure. This formula proved attractive to the government, which commissioned O'Gorman to design and build twenty elementary schools and a technical school; they were built quickly, economically, and efficiently. He applied the same principles to a group of private houses in Mexico City—including one for Diego Rivera—which became celebrated as the first "functional" houses to be built in Mexico (1927–29). It should be observed that the austerity of O'Gorman's functionalism was broken by the use of bright exterior colors: blue, rose, red-brown, Venetian red, with steel work painted in orange vermilion.

O'Gorman helped to organize the so-called "School of Construction," together with Engineer José L. Cuevas (1932–35), where architecture was taught solely as a branch of engineering, as a problem in building construction. Also on the staff was a gifted young architect named Juan Legarreta, whose chief interest was in low-cost housing for workers. Among other adherents of functionalism at that time were Enrique de la Mora and Enrique Yáñez, both destined for billiant careers. This is how Yáñez summed up the accomplishments of Mexican functionalism, "The functionalists as a group destroyed the old academicism and with systematic analysis and almost puritanical logic cleansed construction to a nearly prearchitectural level. At the same time their investigations established the important principle of a

Mexican architecture related to the peculiarities of our varied climate and social customs."[2]

Functionalism, however, came under attack from two quarters: (1) the adherents of nationalism who wanted Mexican architecture to reflect national traits in an overt manner; and (2) the architects who felt that functionalism stifled personal invention and creative imagination and that it failed to satisfy man's spiritual aspirations. As we shall see, O'Gorman himself eventually repudiated his allegiance to functionalism—swinging, in fact, to the opposite extreme.

In Brazil, as we have noted, the theory and practice of functionalism were introduced by Gregori Warchavchik (b. 1896), a Russian-born architect who studied in Rome and who in 1923 went to Brazil under contract to a construction company in Santos. On November 1, 1925, he published in the newspaper *Correio de Manhã* of Rio de Janeiro a "manifesto" advocating the adoption of modern architectural methods and principles in Brazil. In 1927 he designed and built in São Paulo the first "modernist" house to be constructed in Brazil; in 1930 he organized the *Exhibition of a Modernist House* in Rio de Janeiro. Meanwhile, Le Corbusier, on his first visit to Brazil in 1929, was so impressed by Warchavchik's work that he proposed him as the Brazilian delegate to the International Congress of Modern Architecture. In 1932 Warchavchik formed an architectural and construction firm in partnership with Lúcio Costa, and the following year they promoted the *First Exposition of Tropical Architecture* in Rio de Janeiro.

Thus, in Brazil as in Mexico, modern architecture began with functionalism; but in neither case was this to prove the ultimate solution. Functionalism swept aside much traditional debris and cleared the ground for new concepts. But it left unsatisfied an innate predilection for the baroque—a touch of the extravagant and the irrational—that characterizes both of these countries. And it provided no outlet for the emotional lyricism of the Brazilian temperament or the cultural atavism of the Mexicans. So strict

[2] As quoted in Irving E. Myers, *Mexico's Modern Architecture.* Foreword by Enrique Yáñez. Architectural Book Publishing Co., 1952.

functionalism, having served as a catalyst, declined and virtually disappeared from the scene except as a vestige of past change.

MEXICO

With the establishment of the National School of Architecture as part of the National University of Mexico, supplemented by some training abroad; with abundant native talent assimilating the best international influences; with remarkable balance between individualism and group activity; with strong government support and private patronage; with a generally effective synthesis of modern methods and ancient traditions derived from pre-Hispanic cultures—architecture in Mexico has flourished during the past twenty years and has to its credit some of the finest contemporary achievements of Latin America. The most celebrated of these is doubtless the University City of the National University of Mexico, on the outskirts of the federal capital, covering an area of 1,500 acres.

Construction of the University City was begun in 1950 under the general direction of Carlos Lazo, with Mario Pani and Enrique del Moral as the chief architects. Actually, more than a hundred architects participated in the project, with a consequent strain on the unity and integrity of the "master plan." In spite of this and other defects—such as the incongruity of certain murals and the enormous distances to be traversed in getting around the campus—it remains one of the three outstanding achievements of contemporary Latin American architecture (with the University City of Caracas and Brasília). The most impressive building in it is doubtless the famous Central Library, designed by Juan O'Gorman, Gustavo Saavedra, and Juan Martínez de Velasco. Thanks to the stone mosaics designed by O'Gorman it is also the most successful example of integration of the arts in the University City, and probably in all of Mexico, at least on such a large scale. The mosaics cover all four sides of the huge rectangular block—190 feet long, 45 feet wide, 116 feet high—that constitutes the main portion (stacks) of the library (it is almost entirely "blind"—i.e., without exterior openings). This oblong block rises above a wider and more open structure, of which the most interesting feature is the lava-stone wall enclosing the garden courtyard, with stone reliefs by O'Gorman based on ancient Mexican motifs. As Max Cetto informs us, "The materials used on the building, such as lava, sandstone, onyx, and the multicolored stones of the mosaics, were collected from every Mexican state."[3] Historically, this principle of inclusiveness is carried out in the themes of the main wall mosaics. The two largest walls are devoted to symbolic representations of the pre-Cortesian and the Colonial periods, respectively, while the other two walls depict the modern culture of Mexico.

While a building-by-building description of the University City is not feasible here, several structures merit special mention. One of these is the Olympic Stadium (architects: Augusto Pérez Palacios, Raúl Salinas, and Jorge Bravo), one of the largest in the world with a normal seating capacity of 80,000 and a maximum capacity (with standing room) of up to 110,000. Instead of stairs, access and egress is by means of forty-eight sloping tunnels. Cantilevered bleachers, projecting thirty feet, provide protection from sun and rain for about 20,000 spectators. Over the main entrance is a polychrome stone relief by Diego Rivera, probably his most successful architectural composition. The most original structural feature of the stadium is that it is made almost entirely by scooping out and piling up earth, which was then covered with stones for the exterior walls, high and sloping at either side but curving gracefully downward at either end. This natural, telluric design gives the stadium a unique harmony and unity, justifying Max Cetto's dictum that it is "the most notable structure in University City."

On the other hand, Diego Rivera is quoted as having said that the only really "Mexican" structures in the University City are the *frontones* (handball courts), "because their pyramidal shapes imitate in simplified form the Aztec pyramids." Certainly they are one of the most striking architectural manifestations of that cultural continuity with the pre-Hispanic past to which modern Mexico has attributed such importance. Designed by Alberto T. Arai, the courts (of varying sizes and for various types of games) are surrounded on three sides by smooth-surfaced perpendicular

[3] *Modern Architecture in Mexico.* Frederick A. Praeger, 1961, p. 70.

concrete playing walls, but these are backed on the outside by sloping stone walls so that the total effect is that of the truncated pyramids in the ancient Mexican style to which Rivera referred.

Apart from the colored mosaics of the Central Library and the stone reliefs of the Olympic Stadium, most of the art work in University City consists of murals that are not always entirely successful. This is due chiefly to the aesthetic discrepancy between the outmoded social realism of the painters and the functional modernism of the architects. The Central Administration Building (Rectoría), for example, designed by Mario Pani, Enrique del Moral, and Salvador Ortega Flores, is a handsome though rather conventional high-rise office building standing on pilotis, with wide horizontal bands. A variety of materials, ranging from glass bricks to onyx and concrete, provide textural interest. Protruding from one façade is a three-sided mural by Siqueiros that Paul Damaz rather cruelly likens to "colored bubble gum sticking out of the mouth of a mechanical monster." Adjoining the main tower is a three-story structure used for student activities, one entire wall of which is occupied by a monumental Siqueiros mural in his most blatant public style. According to Max Cetto, "Siqueiros believes that one can appreciate it even while driving past at 60 m.p.h." That may be, in fact, the best way to appreciate this mural.

Other ambitious murals are the three by José Chávez Morado on the exterior wall of the School of Sciences, two of which are glass mosaics, the third painted in hydrochloric vinylite. The dominant theme is "The Conquest of Energy." A glass mosaic by Francisco Eppens, on the theme of "Fire, Earth, Air and Water, Life and Death," occupies a huge exterior wall of the Medical School. It is based on Mayan and Aztec mythology and, as explained by the artist, "The whole composition is surrounded by a huge snake biting its tail (the symbol of eternity)."

Museums of Anthropology and of Modern Art

If the University City represents Mexico's confrontation with the modern age, the new National Museum of Anthropology

(1960–62), represents its confrontation with the past—the outward and visible symbol of an ancient and magnificent cultural heritage, going back thousands of years, in which the Mexicans of today take great pride and to which they ascribe the highest didactic as well as aesthetic values. For these reasons, the Museum of Anthropology and Archaeology becomes a kind of secular national shrine where children are taught to know and reverence the grandeur that was Mexico before the coming of the Spaniards and from which millions of people will carry away a lasting memory of past glories and present accomplishments. To fulfill this combination of spiritual, aesthetic, didactic, and scientific functions the project was planned with the utmost thoroughness and precision. The functional plans were drawn up by a large body of experts whose recommendations and specifications filled nearly 3,000 pages. The main structural requirement was for twenty-five large halls or galleries for the permanent exhibitions. The architect chosen to carry out this project was Pedro Ramírez Vázquez, designer of many notable buildings (mostly in collaboration with other architects), such as the Mexican Pavilion at the Brussels World's Fair (1958, with Rafael Mijares) and the Market at Coyoacán (1956, with Mijares and Candela). The site chosen for the new Museum was in the Bosque de Chapultepec.

The principal architectural criterion was to convey a massive and monumental effect in keeping with the form and character of ancient Middle American architecture and sculpture. The building had to be inviting as well as imposing, designed for the convenience and pleasure of the public as well as for the technical and scientific needs of the museum.

One of the paramount aims . . . was to preserve those values of pre-Hispanic architecture that have continued influentially alive down to contemporary times. These include the concept of great open spaces; a deft, clean use of materials that show off to advantage their natural colors and textures; and an audacity of construction in relation to the known techniques of an era. For example, without repeating ancient solutions or copying past forms, the museum's patio preserves the proportions and aesthetics of Mayan architecture; its façades revert to the simplicity and severity of Teotihuacán; while the entrance hall, in its use of carved woods, echoes a latter-day baroque.[4]

The general plan is that of a central distributing area, in the form of a large patio, giving independent access to each exhibition hall. This patio is partly covered by a huge "umbrella" supported by a central sculptured column decorated with bronze reliefs by José and Tomás Chávez Morado symbolizing the indigenous and Hispanic elements that have gone into the making of Mexico. The basic theme of *mestizaje* is symbolized by the double-headed image of an Indian and a Spaniard. The whole is surmounted by the circle of a mariner's compass symbolizing the extension of Mexican culture in all directions.

The massive stone walls are lightened by apertures for windows and balconies, as well as by the bright and spacious entrance area, which is decorated with murals and abstract reliefs in geometric patterns. Extensive use has been made of locally produced materials: black and rose pavingstones from Querétaro, marble from Santo Tomás de Puebla, black marble from Tepeaca, tropical woods (for the interior walls). The famous Stone of the Sun, popularly called the Aztec Calendar, is displayed in splendid isolation above a three-stepped platform backed by a large rectangular slab. And near the entrance stands an impressive Tláloc monolith, showing how effectively an archaeological piece has been used as a form of exterior architectural sculpture.

Pedro Ramírez Vázquez also designed the splendid Museum of Modern Art, in collaboration with Rafael Mijares. Inaugurated in September, 1964, the Museum is also located in the Bosque de Chapultepec and its extensive gardens are an integral part of the environment. This relation between exterior and interior space is emphasized by the large glass areas of the Museum's gallery walls. The architect's purpose was to provide a constantly attractive outlook so that visitors would be induced to prolong their stay in the galleries. The interior itself is spacious and attractive, with a large amount of natural light (controlled by

---

[4] As quoted in *Artes de México*, 12 (1965), 66–67. This magnificent issue (221 pp.) was devoted entirely to the new Museum, with summaries of the text in English, French, and German.

movable plastic curtains and by solar green and solar gray filter glass).

The building, irregular in form, is characterized by simplicity and elegance combined with utility. The basic structure is steel, with generous use of aluminum and glass. There are four main exhibition halls, located on two levels. The central monumental staircase is surmounted by a dome that appears to be of alabaster but is actually made of fiberglass and polyester resin, applied in layers until the specified thickness is attained. There are four other similar domes, smaller in size, over the exhibition halls.

Along with such distinctively Mexican conceptions as the Central is intended for temporary exhibits and also provides the principal storage space for the Museum. The surrounding gardens are used to exhibit the work of Mexican sculptors who have participated in the Mexican Sculpture Biennials.

Along with such distinctively Mexican conceptions as the Central Library and Olympic Stadium of the University City, and the Museum of Anthropology, Mexican architecture displays a wide variety of buildings of all kinds, both in private and public construction, designed along contemporary international lines. If this were a strictly architectural study, closer attention would have to be given to such accomplishments as the low-cost housing development "Presidente Juárez" in Mexico City (1952), designed with such distinction by Mario Pani and Salvador Ortega Flores; the immense housing development known as "Balbuena Gardens" (1956), designed to house 50,000 persons, with its own schools, churches, shopping areas, clinics, parks, playgrounds, and sports and cultural centers, for which Félix Sánchez was the chief architect; the Medical Center built under the direction of Enrique Yáñez (1960–61); the many notable schools, office buildings, hotels, and markets, such as the fine "Mercado La Merced" in Mexico City (1957) designed by Enrique del Moral or the even more remarkable Market at Coyoacán (1956) designed by Pedro Ramírez Vázquez and Rafael Mijares with construction by Félix Candela. All of these, and many others, constitute the solid, workaday accomplishments that have led to Mexico's recognition as one of the three leading nations in contemporary architecture in Latin America. But in a brief survey emphasizing artistic expression a place must be found for those manifestations that are primarily aesthetic and emotional in their intent, that are freely imaginative creations striving to transcend the limitations of a single medium.

Irrational and Emotional Architecture

As already noted, Juan O'Gorman was one of the first to turn against the "puritanism" of functional architecture, to which he opposed an antithetical concept that he called "Organic Architecture." This he applied in designing and building his own house (1956) in the section on the outskirts of Mexico City known as the Pedregal of San Angel, an immense lava field. As he said,

> I set out to make a house that would fit esthetically, harmoniously, into the landscape of the lava formation of the Pedregal, and to express the tradition of the ancient architecture of Mexico, as distinct from the Spanish and other Colonial styles imported from Europe.... Organic Architecture produces edifices which, on account of their form and color—as works of art—achieve harmony between man and the part of the world in which he lives, between the forms of the buildings and the landscapes surrounding them.... Year by year the house becomes more entwined in its natural landscape, because of the harmony of form and color.... This house ... is the most complete and satisfying work that I have done in architecture ... and I think it can be called modern and Mexican.[5]

The main portion of the house is built into a natural grotto, which forms the living room, enclosed largely by the natural rock formation, and around which the rest of the house is constructed (also of lava rock). A skylight has been inserted in the roof and there is a large ceiling mosaic with symbols from Aztec mythology. There are also many colored mosaics decorating the exterior walls, which are highly irregular in size and shape. These mosaics, says O'Gorman, "are reminiscent, chiefly, of the vegetation and the animal life of the Pedregal." On the upper terrace there is a

[5] As quoted in Clive Bramford Smith, *Builders in the Sun.* Architectural Book Publishing Co., 1967, p. 33. This book contains excellent photographs of O'Gorman's house.

large freestanding mosaic sculpture of a fanciful bird in yellow, red, and black that makes at least a passing bow to functionalism, since it serves as a windbreak. The landscaping with its lush vegetation, was done by Mrs. O'Gorman (the former Helen Fowler of Seattle, Washington), who is also a sculptress.

Mathias Goeritz (b. Danzig, 1915) is another artist who believes in ignoring categories in order to "achieve a unified totality in art." He has been active as painter, sculptor, architect, teacher, writer, and general gadfly of contemporary art in Mexico. He tells us of the deep impression made upon him by "the great works that united in themselves all the arts," and that he was never troubled by "the question of where there began or ended the elements of 'architecture,' 'sculpture,' 'painting,' or even 'poetry.' " The idea of creating an "emotional architecture" came to him when he was invited, in 1952, to build "whatever he pleased" on a lot in the center of Mexico City. He decided to construct an Experimental Museum in which the first experiment would be the building itself. As Goeritz describes it,

There were almost no right angles in the plan of the building. Some walls were thin on one side and thick on the opposite side. I always sought a strange and at times imperceptible asymmetry, like that found in the structure of any face, of any tree, of any living creature. There were no amiable curves, nor sharp vertices. The whole work was realized on the site itself, without exact plans. Plasterer, painter, sculptor, "architect"—all were practically one person.[6]

El Eco, as it was called, contained a large abstract sheetmetal sculpture by Goeritz, like an angular snake, that was used as the setting for modern ballet; murals embodying work by Goeritz, Henry Moore, Tamayo, and Mérida; and a "Plastic Poem" by Goeritz inscribed on a wall column and consisting of "a visual composition of abstract typography addressing itself solely to the sensitiveness of the spectator." The museum was eventually diverted from its original purpose and converted into a restaurant and then a nightclub. But it had aroused international attention and it had a decisive effect on Goeritz's future work. As he tells

[6] " ¿ Arquitectura Emocional?", in *Revista Arquitectura ENA* (May and June, 1960).

us, "I saw the problem of space with other eyes. I became interested in volumes of monumental size. I dreamed of constructing an immense cathedral, a pyramid of our century, a gigantic prayer."

The opportunity to realize something of this nature came to Goeritz in 1957, when the architect Luis Barragán commissioned him to design the main entrance for the Satellite City that was being planned near the capital under the general direction of Mario Pani.[7] "When I saw the deserted landscape," writes Goeritz, "I thought of some vertical columns, of the towers of San Gimigniano, of the skyscrapers of Manhattan." Actually, in 1955 Goeritz had made a painted wood sculpture titled *Here and There*, referring to the contrast between a typical Mexican village (horizontal group) and the skyline of Manhattan (vertical group). Taking as his basic concept the vertical elements of this sculpture, Goeritz designed the five triangular concrete pylons, ranging in height from 123 to 190 feet, that mark the main approach to the Satellite City (Plate 1, Frontispiece). Three of them are painted white, one yellow, and one orange. Goeritz had wanted them to be much higher—500 to 700 feet—but practical considerations prevented this. The effect is nevertheless both impressive and beautiful, both monumental and lyrical. Architects insist that *The Towers* are "nothing but a large sculpture." This does not bother Goeritz. He envisioned them as sculpture, painting, architecture, and music too: "I would have liked to place small flutes [with amplifiers?] in their corners so that the traveler passing along the highway would hear a strange song caused by the multiple songs of the wind." No wonder that Goeritz describes himself as "an absurd romantic in an age without faith." And he has stated the conviction that "Only when man receives genuine emotions from architecture can he once again regard it as an art."

In 1968, as artistic advisor to the Organizing Committee for the XIX Olympiad held in Mexico, Goeritz had an opportunity to design another group of concrete towers, consisting of seven columns fifty feet high—six painted yellow, one red—placed in front of of the new Sports Palace in Mexico City. This sculptural

[7] For a detailed description of this remarkable project, see *Arquitectura México*, 12, 60 (1957).

group is called *The Big Dipper*, because that is the design of its ground plan. It is one unit in a large plan conceived by Goeritz, that includes eighteen concrete sculptures designed by artists from many parts of the world, ranging in height from twenty to sixty feet, and placed at intervals along "The Route of Friendship," a peripheral route approximately eleven miles long and having the Olympic Village as its focal point. The three Mexican sculptors represented in this project, besides Goeritz, are Helen Escobedo, Jorge Dubón, and Angela Gurría. In addition, a bronze sculpture twenty-three feet high, by Germán Cueto of Mexico, was placed near the Olympic Stadium of the University City.

At a meeting of the artists involved in this project, Mathias Goeritz proposed the establishment of an International Council for artistic planning to counteract the chaos and ugliness of our urban environments: "An art integrated from the very inception of the urban plan is of fundamental importance in our age. This means that artistic work will leave its suroundings of art for art's sake and establish contact with the masses by means of total planning in order to raise these elements to the level of a spiritually necessary expression of contemporary society."

The architectural adviser for Goeritz's El Eco was Luis Barragán (b. 1902), who in spite of having no degree in architecture became one of the most successful and internationally famous Mexican architects, and who has done notable work in landscape gardening. His most spectacular accomplishment was the development of a formerly deserted area near Mexico City, on the edge of the volcanic lava field, known as Pedregal Gardens (*pedregal* means "a place full of stones"). The entrance area has a large stone sculpture by Goeritz, representing an indefinable beast, and a high jet fountain within a setting of monumental stone walls. Some of Mexico's finest houses and gardens are located in this development, which looks upon a sensational volcanic landscape. While Barragán is certainly not a romantic like Goeritz, nor an irrationalist like O'Gorman, he does use materials—preferably rough stone, mortar, and wood—primarily for their aesthetic effect, and he relies heavily on the use of vivid color for dramatic contrasts, enhanced by a skilfull deployment of natural light. All this adds up to his own type of "emotional architecture," and that is in fact the term that Barragán has used to describe his own house—"an emotional piece of architecture rather than a cold convenience for living."

Candela: Master of Shells

In 1936 a young Spanish architect named Félix Candela (b. 1910) won an award for a paper titled "The Influence of New Trends in Reinforced Concrete Techniques on Architectural Form." The award would have allowed him to travel and continue his training in Europe; instead, he found himself caught in the Spanish Civil War and ended up as a refugee in Mexico in 1939. He tried various ways of making his fortune (including motion picture production), but soon construction with reinforced concrete, especially folded slab or laminary structures, became his absorbing interest. He began to build concrete shells in 1949, starting with simple vaults in funicular or catenary form. From these he proceeded to more complex structures, particularly those based on the double curvature form of the hyperbolic paraboloid (called *hypar* for short), which permitted a wide variety of applications as well as extreme thinness of the shell.

Candela's first big opportunity came when he was invited to collaborate in building the Cosmic Rays Pavilion for the University City (1951). Although trained as an architect, Candela prefers to specialize in the design and construction of shells (for which he founded a factory in partnership with his brother) and to work with one or more architects for the general design of a building. In the case of the Cosmic Rays Pavilion, the architect was Jorge González Reyna. The basic plan was simple: a vestibule, two laboratories, and an air-conditioning unit. The structural problem arose from the functional requirement that the crowns of the shell have no more mass than about eight pounds per square foot, which meant that the thickness of the shell at that point had to be no more than seven-eighths of an inch. Candela designed and built a saddle-shaped vault, with a span of thirty-three feet, that fulfilled this requirement and that quickly became celebrated as "the thinnest shell in the world."

About the same time, Candela began to use the large sinusoidal (undulating) slabs that he was the first to apply as part of the interior structure of a private house in 1951. Used as an intermediate floor, the slab projects through the façade with a graceful and original effect—a fusion of structural and aesthetic elements that is characteristic of Candela's work. Commissioned (by the newspaper *Novedades*) to build five houses in the Pedregal Gardens with the architect Raúl Fernández, Candela again used the sinusoidal slab with stunning effect as a cantilevered carport for the "Novedades House No. 1." Candela strongly advocates the use of curvilinear forms in opposition to the rectangular, box-like structures favored by contemporary international architecture. He holds that imagination and inventiveness should have free play instead of being subservient to previously conceived mathematical schemes (he often does his own detailed mathematical calculations *after* the work is finished). Subservience to mathematical calculations, he affirms, is responsible for "avoidance of curvilinear and spatial structures whose mathematical analysis seems at first difficult to undertake." For Candela, functional structure is simply the means for the creation of new aesthetic dimensions.

Candela went on to build schools, factories, warehouses, laboratories, supermarkets, residences, clubs, restaurants, service stations, churches, and even monumental architectural sculptures—always seeking new and daring solutions for old problems, refusing to be bound by preconceived ideas, guided mainly by intuition and experience, and everywhere combining utility with beauty. In the words of Colin Faber, "some of his warehouses are as beautiful as his churches." This is well illustrated in Las Aduanas, the warehouses for the Mexican Customs in the Federal District (1953–54; architect, Carlos Recamier). There are three sheds of different lengths, each roofed by a central cylindrical vault (shell about an inch and a half thick), with two cantilevered vaults at either side. The structure is noteworthy for the simplicity and elegance of its design and the perfect proportion and articulation of the various elements.

Candela's architectural masterpiece—the only structure he

designed and built entirely by himself—is the Church of the Miraculous Virgin in Mexico City (1954–55). Here the idea of the Gothic church, with its multi-arched verticality and soaring vaults, acquires a new dimension—but no less lyrical and inspiring—through the use of predominantly triangular configurations, warped surfaces, prominent paraboloids, and what Colin Faber aptly calls "the insistent zizag of its edges through space." A tall, slender, asymmetrical, freestanding campanile complements the structure with another vertical accent. This is a truly neogothic (not pseudogothic!) church for the twentieth century.

Candela has constructed other remarkable churches: among them San Antonio de las Huertas in Tacuba (1956), Santa Teresa del Niño Jesús (1957–58) and San José Obrero in Monterrey (1959), St. Vincent de Paul Chapel in Coyoacán (1959–60), the Villahermosa Cathedral in Tabasco (1960). All these were done in collaboration with various architects. In regard to integration of the arts, special mention should be made of the Chapel of the Missionaries of the Holy Ghost in Coyoacán (1965), built by Candela with the architects Enrique de la Mora and Fernando López Carmona. It has a high V-shaped shell roof that rises to a peak above a massive rough-stone wall. The space between the wall and the roof, which forms two triangles, is filled with a stained glass designed by Kitzia Hofmann, *The Descent of the Holy Ghost*, done in a semiabstract manner. Intersecting metal bands, curved and rectangular, give a dynamic quality to the composition. On a high outside wall enclosing the atrium, punctuated by irregular rectangular apertures that in themselves form an interesting abstract pattern, the Stations of the Cross have been carved in concrete (low relief) by the sculptor Herbert Hofmann-Ysenbourg.

One cannot write about Candela without mentioning the extraordinarily successful design of the restaurant Los Manantiales in Xochimilco (1957–58), built in collaboration with the architect Joaquín Alvarez Ordóñez, which Candela himself is said to regard as his most significant work. Technically it consists of "an octagonal groined vault composed of four intersecting hypars." More poetically, it has the form of a lotus-flower, spreading over an area of 150 feet, with its high shell vaults forming hyperbolic arches in a circular pattern of gracefully undulating shapes. The result can only be described as enchanting.

In terms of wide acceptance and variety of application, Candela's most successful device has been the so-called "umbrellas," inverted concrete shells consisting of four sloping surfaces meeting at a common point and supported by a central pillar that also serves for drainage. Whatever the shape—rectangular, rhomboidal, polygonal—they are based on the same principle and have proved their versatility in practically every kind of structure, from factories to churches, warehouses to hotels, banks to residences. They are found all over Mexico, and according to Colin Faber in Mexico City alone Candela's firm has roofed more than three million square feet with umbrellas.

Among the most original of Candela's structures are the acoustic band shell at at Santa Fé (with Mario Pani) [Plate 11]; the open chapel near Cuernavaca, in the form of a single hypar shell (with Guillermo Rossell and Manuel de la Rosa); the monument in the Plaza de los Abanicos in Lomas de Cuernavaca (with the same architects), a free-standing fan-like ornamental monument; and the monument at the entrance to a resort development on Lake Tequesquitengo, Morelos (same architects), described by Max Cetto as a "double cantilever arm with hyperbolic–paraboloid wings, an amazing feat of construction." The two last-mentioned are clearly works of monumental art—among the most strikingly original to be found in Latin America.

CUBA AND CENTRAL AMERICA

Cuban architecture during the 1950's before Fidel Castro came into power, was progressive and had some distinguished achievements to its credit. One of these was the Office of the Comptroller in Havana (1952–54), designed by Aquiles Capablanca (b. 1907). It is a nine-story building which in general follows the formulas of Le Corbusier, including elevation on pillars and a honeycomb façade with rectangular sun-screens. Henry-Russell Hitchcock remarks that the building is especially effective for the "warm beige tone" and "rough texture of the limestone, with coarse

shell aggregate, with which the walls are sheathed."[8] Leopoldo
Casteda goes all out and calls it "one of the best realizations of
modern Spanish-American architecture," calling particular attention to the effectiveness—he calls it "the integrating tonic note"—
of the ceramic tile murals by Amelia Peláez.[9] These are indeed
among the best of their kind, in strong, dynamic, and skilfully
varied abstract designs that use both geometric and irregular forms.

One of the most important architects of Cuba, Max Borges Jr.
(b. 1918), who was trained in the United States, designed in 1952
the original and extremely attractive nightclub, Cabaret Tropicana,
on the outskirts of Havana. He used five thin-shell concrete vaults
for the main enclosed area, with arches ranging in span from
forty to ninety feet, placed eccentrically to one another and
decreasing in height as they approach the orchestra stage. The
entire front wall is of glass, with sliding doors. Borges said, "I
thought of the vault device because one cannot say where the
wall ends and the ceiling begins. Besides, it proved to be the
cheapest enclosure and provided an area uninterrupted by
columns." The principal artistic feature is the decorative stabile
over the orchestra stage, made of thin galvanized water pipes
bound in a frame of narrow steel plates. The total effect is—to
borrow Niemeyer's phrase—both very modern and very tropical.

Among the Central American countries, Guatemala has taken
the lead in the integration of architecture and the plastic arts.
Her leading artists, beginning with Carlos Mérida, have shown
keen interest in this type of work, and have received full encouragement and support from the government as well as from some
private sectors. Since about 1950 Mérida's absorbing concern
has been with architectural art. His first important architectural
project was executed for the President Juárez Housing Development in Mexico City (1952), for which he designed a series of
concrete reliefs carved on small panels that project from the
building façade. There are twelve panels on each façade, located
in symmetrical groups of six on each side. The designs are based

---

[8] *Latin American Architecture since 1945*, p. 73.
[9] "La Arquitectura Actual," paper presented to the Inter-American Sym-
posium on Intellectual Backgrounds of Latin American Art since
Independence (1966).

on highly stylized archaic Mexican motifs interpreting the legend of *Los Cuatro Soles*. Along the central wall of the exterior stairway Mérida designed a continuous low relief concrete mural depicting the origin of the world according to Aztec mythology, as recounted in the *Relación de Texcoco*. For this project he also executed semiabstract murals for several interior walls, and eight frieze reliefs depicting various Aztec deities.[10]

In Guatemala City's new civic center, Mérida executed his most important architectural projects for the City Hall or Municipal Building (1955–56) and the Social Security Institute (1958–59). For the former he designed a very large glass mosaic for an interior wall two storeys high (3,800 square feet), *The Mestizo Race of Guatemala*, which he treats in his usual later semiabstract manner, all the figurative elements geometrically stylized in complex and continuously interlocking patterns. The side walls of this building also have concrete relief murals by Dagoberto Vásquez and Guillermo Grajeda Mena, the latter strongly influenced by ancient Maya motifs.

For the Social Security Institute, Mérida executed a two-sided glass mosaic in the same style for a long freestanding wall near one side of the building. Another freestanding wall, further from the building, in front of the main steps, has a flat cut-stone relief in a more monumental style by Roberto González Goyri.

For another government building, the National Mortgage Credit, in 1964, González Goyri undertook a more ambitious project consisting of four concrete reliefs more than 40 feet high. Here indigenous and industrial themes of work and leisure are depicted in a highly stylized manner, intricate in form, with complex patterns, yet strong and clear in the overall design (Plate 14). More abstract and symbolic are the concrete reliefs for the Bank of Guatemala (1966), measuring forty meters in height and seven meters in width, on three projecting wall panels of the main façade. The powerful pictographic quality of these murals in their immense verticality, at once monumental and dynamic,

[10] Mathias Goeritz, "La integración plástica en el C. U. 'Presidente Juárez'," in Mario Pani, *Los Multifamiliares de Pensiones* (Mexico: Editorial Arquitectura, 1952), p. 101–8.

is one of the most impressive examples of architectural sculpture in Latin America.

Efraín Recinos, architect, sculptor, and painter, has also contributed some excellent concrete mural reliefs to the National Mortgage Credit (1963–64), consisting of three large vertical panels with stylized figurative Mayan motifs. Another artist, Dagoberto Vásquez Castañeda, in addition to his rather conventional concrete relief, *Chant to Guatemala,* for the City Hall, has done more distinguished work with his large wood sculptures mounted on the interior walls of the Banco Inmobilario in Guatemala City (1958), depicting Indians vigorously paddling one of their native canoes. For a frieze on the lower section of the Carranza Building, Vásquez executed a semifigurative concrete relief, *Man's Leisure.*

VENEZUELA

Venezuela zoomed into the modern industrial age when oil was found beneath Lake Maracaibo in 1917. Foreign exploitation of these resources went hand in hand with soaring national income; waves of immigration swept into the country; everyone was eager for progress and profit; and Caracas mushroomed into a sprawling metropolis. Shack dwellings—*ranchos*—huddled beside elegant apartment houses, and slum areas festered in the shadow of high-rise office buildings. Beginning around 1940, more careful city planning was undertaken, slum areas were cleared, and large housing developments were constructed. Many able architects contributed to building the new Caracas, among them Moisés F. Benacerraf, Guido Bermúdez, José Miguel Galia, Carlos C. Guinand, and Martín Vegas Pacheco. Many were trained in the United States (at Yale, Harvard, or elsewhere) and brought to their task the efficiency and sophistication of the prevailing international styles. But the architect whose personality has given its strongest individuality and its greatest international fame to contemporary Venezuelan architecture is Carlos Raúl Villanueva.

Carlos Raúl Villanueva

Son of a Venezuelan diplomat and a French mother, Villanueva was born in London on May 30, 1900. After obtaining his degree in architecture at the Ecole des Beaux Arts in Paris, he settled in Caracas and began his professional practice there in 1928. He was appointed Director of Buildings for the Ministry of Public Works and was an organizer of the National Council for Protection of Historic Monuments. His first important work was the Plaza de Toros (bull ring) in Maracay (1931), in which he combined traditional elements of design with modern construction methods, especially in the use of concrete. During this eclectic phase he also designed the Caracas Museum of Fine Arts (1935) in neoclassic style, and the Escuela Gran Colombia (1939), an elementary school along functional lines—significant as his "first attempt to find a design vocabulary free of historical embellishments."[11]

Villanueva's first big public project was the low-cost housing development known as El Silencio (1941), which involved clearing a midtown slum area and creating a modern neighborhood that would harmonize with the colonial pattern of old Caracas. The apartment units are located around or near an oblong Plaza into which a main thoroughfare debouches. This was monumentally adorned with a pair of fountains in the Renaissance tradition. The traditional Colonial colonnade—both ornamental and practical for providing shade—is reproduced in the buildings bordering the Plaza. Otherwise, all is modern and designed for health and comfort, including large balconies and loggias that can be used for sleeping in hot weather, ample cross ventilation, and protection from sun glare. This is said to be "the first such project undertaken with the support of any Latin American government."

In 1944 Villanueva undertook his most ambitious project and the one that brought him—and the city of Caracas—great international acclaim: the University City of the Central University of Caracas. At first, still under the influence of his Beaux Arts training, he had designed a conventional plan with buildings symmetrically arranged on either side of a monumental axis. But

[11] Sibyl Moholy-Nagy, *Carlos Raúl Villanueva and the Architecture of Venezuela*. Frederick A. Praeger, 1964, p. 20.

this was soon discarded in favor of a more open plan which provided for the long-range development of "activity zones" throughout the 500-acre campus, without a rigidly preconceived design. By 1947 ten such zones had taken shape, including dormitory and sports areas and a botanical garden in addition to the administrative, academic, and service buildings. In the first unit that Villanueva completed, the Technical Industrial School, the various buildings were made into a unified area by the novel use of covered walks—and this proved to be, in extended application, one of the most original and characteristic features of the University City.

Pedestrian circulation is mainly by means of a covered walk more than a mile long which goes through the heart of the campus in a wide curve. It gives a sense of containment and continuity to the University City and also furnishes protection from the tropical sun. Built with the assistance of the engineers Otahola and Benedetti, the covered walk is not uniform but offers a variety of structural features and a diversity of shapes in its concrete canopies. The simplest type of canopy consists of a cantilevered vault twenty-nine feet wide, supported by bent prestressed columns. The covered walk leads to the Covered Plaza, which is the sociocultural center of the campus. In this area are located the Library, Reading Rooms, Small Concert Hall, Great Hall (Aula Magna), Hall of Honor (Paraninfo), Rectorate, Administration, Court of Honor, and Museum. The Covered Plaza itself can be converted into an exhibition area by means of movable panels. Many of the artworks are also concentrated in this general area.

Villanueva's first major achievement in the University City was the Olympic Stadium (1950-52), to which were later added a baseball stadium and two swimming stadiums. As Sibyl Moholy-Nagy observes, "In the general context of Villanueva's development the stadiums signify the transition from the experimental use of reinforced concrete to full mastery over it." The basic plan of the Olympic Stadium is traditional, as such structures must necessarily be because their purpose has not changed for thousands of years. The striking originality occurs in the use of reinforced concrete for the huge yet graceful beams or ribs that form the cantilevered roof of the grandstand. The sustaining pillars that support the stand are slender and inconspicuous; but the immense ribs, soaring from the ground to the tip of the roof in a continuous movement, create a splendid effect of strength and elegance combined (Plate 12).

The Swimming Stadium, one of the largest and most complete in the world, conveys an impression of solidity and massiveness lightened by an eye-catching use of textures and colors: gray concrete juxtaposed with bright red walls and white trim, solid surfaces below with vertical louvered areas above, massive supporting ribs with the slender walls of ramps and galleries. The overall effect is extremely harmonious: even the diving towers and platforms combine functionalism with artistic design. The roof over the grandstand is a huge but gracefully modulated concrete slab.

The School of Dentistry, the School of Pharmacy, the School of Architecture and City Planning, the Central Library, the Small Concert Hall, and the Aula Magna are among the most notable buildings designed by Villanueva for the University City. What stands out in all these buildings is not merely their technical brilliance and efficiency but also the strong aesthetic component that lifts them above the standard style of contemporary international architecture. This is partly from the use of color, which Villanueva manipulates very much as an abstract painter might— for example, in the horizontal bands of bright red on one side of the façade of the School of Dentistry; on the other side the corresponding areas are left in pure white; the whole color pattern of this building is remarkably successful. One of his most distinguished buildings is the School of Architecture, with its solid rectangular *brise-soleil* panels and its exposed stair-tower enclosed in a frame of thin vertical slats that run unbrokenly from top to bottom of the tower. Here too, the use of color, particularly light and dark blue rectangular areas covering an entire wall, as well as various shades of gray and brown, is very effective. Actually, the School consists of eight units, including an auditorium and a Museum and Exhibition Hall.

The Aula Magna (1952) an assembly hall seating 2,600 persons, is one of the great achievements of University City (Plate 13).

The exterior is massively functional, wth none of the superficial embellishments commonly associated with such ceremonial edifices. The main building material is concrete, though a steel structure was used for the suspended ceiling. The roof is a planar slab of poured concrete, while the ceiling is of plaster. The whole structure is a triumph of engineering (done by the Danish firm of Cristiani and Nielsen). A large cantilevered concrete canopy leads to the main entrance. The foyer is spacious and imposingly grand, with curving ramps leading to the upper level. But it is in the auditorium itself that one appreciates the full extent of Villanueva's creative genius and the skill with which he has blended technical and artistic elements. Its most striking feature are the acoustical "clouds" (or "flying saucers," as they have been called) designed by Alexander Calder. Although technically they function as sound reflectors, their total effect, as they are suspended from the ceiling or mounted on the side walls, is that of animating the entire space with their colors, their varied shapes, their aspect of "floating clouds."

Integration of the arts is a major accomplishment of the University City. The works of art, chosen by Villanueva himself, reveal both his own cosmopolitan background and the absence of a nationalistic attitude in Venezuela. There are bronze sculptures by Henry Laurens (the monumental *Amphion*, sixteen feet tall), by Jean Arp (*Cloud Shepherd*), and by Antoine Pevsner (*Dynamism at 30 Degrees*). There are large glass mosaics by Fernand Léger and abstract ceramic tile murals by Victor Vasarely.

Venezuelan artists have by no means been overlooked. There are several ceramic tile murals by Mateo Manaure in abstract style, notably at the entrances to the Covered Plaza and to the Small Concert Hall. Manaure also designed the two acoustical wall-mounted units in the Small Concert Hall. All these are located in or near the Covered Plaza. Other art works may be found in various buildings throughout the campus: glass mosaics by Oswaldo Vigas in the Administration Building, the Communications Building, and the Museum; a mural by Armando Barrios on a façade of the Museum and one by Alirio Oramas in the Central Library; the sculpture *Maternity* by Balthasar Lobo. Other Venezuelan artists whose work is represented in the

University City are Carlos Bogen, Francisco Narváez, Alejandro Otero, Victor Valera, Jesús Soto, Héctor Poleo, Miguel Arroyo, Omar Carreño, Pedro León Castillo, and Braulio Salazar. Certainly national talent has not been neglected! But it has been placed in competition with some of the most famous contemporary artists of the Western World. Perhaps that is one reason why art in Venezuela today, whatever its limitations, is never provincial. It is not sheltered by the protection of nationalistic barriers.

COLOMBIA, CHILE, AND PERU

The architects Jorge Arango and Carlos Martínez, in their book *Arquitectura en Colombia* (1951), remark that "Colombian architecture leaped from the colonial to the contemporary." The main reason for this is that there was no prosperous nineteenth century in Colombia—as there was was, for instance, in Argentina and Peru—to replace the colonial dwellings "with the French or Italian styles then in vogue." The first school of architecture in Colombia was founded in 1936, just about the time that the country entered upon a period of rapid economic growth. This in turn coincided with the rise and potent influence of modern international styles in architecture under the leadership of such men as Le Corbusier, Gropius, and Mies van der Rohe, all of whom left their mark on the new generations of Columbian architects. Although by 1951 there were six schools of architecture in Colombia, most of the architects received at least some of their training abroad, chiefly in the United States. The absence of any strong trend toward aesthetic or cultural nationalism in Colombia encouraged the growth of "standard modern" construction, both for private housing and for office buildings.

In recent years there have been some notable examples of the integration of the arts in Colombian architecture. One of the most impressive is the Bank of Bogotá (1959), by the architects Pablo Lanzetta and Reinaldo Valencia, with an immense wall relief, covering 3,000 square feet, by Eduardo Ramírez. Two storeys in height, it consists of a high relief in wood covered with gold leaf, with abstract curvilinear forms that create a kind of visual counterpoint of strongly rhythmic character. The lavish use of gold (with which the background wall is also solidly covered) is consistent not only with the spirit of the bank but also with the ancient tradition of Colombia in pre-Hispanic times, when the Chibcha Indians excelled in ornamental gold work.

Eduardo Ramírez also executed the monumental bronze relief of the entrance to the Bank of the Republic in Cúcuta (1962). The relief is twenty feet high and in his usual abstract geometric style. As Paul Damaz observes, "The various flat planes of the relief, cut out in sharply defined geometrical shapes, create a graceful play of shadows which are a valuable complement to the architecture of the building." Unfortunately, it was impossible for local foundries to cast large sections of bronze for this work; hence it had to be made of 300 pieces bolted together, and the resulting joints detract somewhat from the overall effect, as may be seen by comparing it with the original model.

Two of the most important contemporary painters of Colombia, David Manzur and Alejandro Obregón, have executed murals for modern buildings in Bogotá. Manzur's mural in the lobby of the Arlequín Theater contains both abstract and figurative elements (the former predominating). Obregón's mural is in the Luis Angel Arango Library (1959), occupying the entire wall of the second floor stair hall. This is one of Obregón's most powerful paintings, in his usual semiabstract expressionist manner, with images and symbols completely integrated in the plastic concept. The library itself is one of the best modern buildings in Bogotá, designed by the architects Rafael Esguerra, Alvaro Sáenz, Rafael Urdaneta, and Daniel Suárez.

In Chile during the 1940's, the integration of art and architecture was attempted under the direct influence of the Mexican muralist movement, with murals executed at the public school in Chillán by Siqueiros (1940). The Social Club Aguirre Cerda in Santiago (1942), by the architects Jorge Aguirre Silva and Enrique Gebhard, has a large mural by Xavier Guerrero painted under the influence of Siqueiros, consisting of two monumental human figures. It covers most of the vaulted ceiling in a long and rather narrow room, which makes it impossible to view it in proper perspective.

The leading contemporary architect of Chile, Emilio Duhart H., achieved better results in his design for the Nilo Theater in Santiago (1958), which has a fine abstract mural, *Earthquake*, by the painter Nemesio Antúñez, as well as attractive ceramic tile murals. The most distinguished examples of artistic integration were created by Duhart in the Open Forum or Central Plaza of the University of Concepción (1962), to serve as the social, cultural, recreational, and ceremonial center for that campus. Different levels, with varied textures and colors, provide a harmonious setting for the principal works of art: a semiabstract monument to the university's founder by the sculptor Samuel Román, and a freestanding, double-faced wall, 120 feet long, covered with a mural in glazed brick designed by Mario Carreño (*Sun Wall*). The geometric design is completely abstract.

Mario Carreño collaborated with the architect Francisco Domínguez Errázuriz in designing a three-dimensional mural for a night club in the Casino of Viña del Mar (1961). This has been admirably described by Paul Damaz: "It is composed of three elements: large metal plates colored white, ochre and black and separated from the wall, metal rods assembled in an orthogonal arrangement, and red geometric forms painted on the wall. Indirect lights, concealed behind the plates, introduce a fourth element."[12] Another very successful mural by Carreño—also abstract and geometric—is one that he designed for an exterior wall of the Saint Ignatius Loyola School in Santiago (1960; architect, Alberto Piwonka).

Carreño and Duhart collaborated once again in the design (by competition) for the United Nations Regional Building in Santiago (1963–64). This is designed as a horizontal rectangular enclosure with sectioned patios and a central spirally-shaped building that provides a curvilinear contrast. A strong vertical accent is created by the *Tree of Nations*, designed by Carreño, which stands in a pool at the front of the building. It consists of twelve units cast in concrete, superimposed to a height of thirty-six feet, and with projecting rectangular panels in bright colors: red, yellow, orange. At the other side of the building is a freestanding wall

[12] *Art in Latin American Architecture*, p. 166.

with abstract-geometric mosaic designs by Carreño, also in bright colors.

Contemporary residential architecture in Chile is excellent in design and construction, though not particularly original. An example that combines functional logic with aesthetic appeal is the house built for himself by the architect Jorge Costabal in Santiago, with ferro-concrete construction (1954–55).

A somewhat similar situation prevails in Peru, where ex-President Fernando Belaúnde Terry happens to be an architect by profession, trained at the University of Texas (he was formerly Director of the School of Architecture). Until fairly recently there was much neocolonialism and historical eclecticism in Peruvian architecture, but since 1950 the modern international style has become increasingly conspicuous, with high-rise office buildings and apartments beginning to dominate the skyline of Lima. A new University City is under construction between the capital and its port of Callao. One of the earliest low-cost housing developments was the Unidad Vecinal Matute (1952), designed by Santiago Agurto Calvo, which includes both four-story apartments and units of one-story houses, all painted with gay colors. Luis Miró Quesada Garland, Max Linder, Mario Bianco, Enrique Seoane Ros, and Simón Ortiz are among the leading architects of Peru.

Luis Miró Quesada and Simón Ortiz were the architects for the Cemetery of the Angel in Lima (1958), which thus far represents the most notable examples of architectural art in Peru. This is an above-ground cemetery, where the coffins are sealed into compartments placed in long, high walls. The design for the entrance is simple yet extremely effective, consisting of a contemporary variant of the classic portico: seven rectangular columns faced with black granite and topped by an identical horizontal slab. Behind this is a graceful gate framed with metal strips in an open rectangular pattern, and to the left a long wall covered with glass and stone mosaics designed by Fernando de Szyszlo and with three-dimensional bronze sculptures by Joaquín Roca Rey on the theme of resurrection. The exceptionally harmonious collaboration between these two Peruvian artists, each a strong creative personality in his own field of painting or sculpture, has resulted in one of the best manifestations of artistic integration to be found in South America.

ARGENTINA

Of all Latin American cities, Buenos Aires is probably the one where the French Beaux Arts tradition had its strongest influence. Entire city blocks, both business and residential, look like transplanted sections of Paris. The lavish private mansion or *hotel privé*, in the French nineteenth century manner, became the ideal of the wealthy Argentines. A conservative or reactionary bureaucracy did nothing to promote or encourage the emergence of a modern architecture. At a time when other Latin American nations were leaping into the main currents of contemporary architecture, the dictatorial regime of Juan Perón set up mediocre conventional criteria for government-sponsored buildings and monuments and discouraged private or individual initiatives. After Perón's overthrow in 1955 the nation was disrupted by political and economic instability. While office buildings and apartment houses built during the last twenty years or so are often good examples of contemporary design and construction, Argentina has not as yet fully participated in the upsurge of modern architecture in Latin America.

Amancio Williams

It was in this unpropitious atmosphere that the most original and imaginative of Argentine architects, Amancio Williams (b. 1913), embarked upon his professional career. No wonder that he was beset by frustration from the beginning and that most of his projects have been realized only on the drawing board or in the workshop. Yet wherever modern architecture is studied, the designs and plans and writings of Amancio Williams are known, and his most important completed project, a residence at Mar del Plata, has received international acclaim. His designs for concrete shells of minimal thickness supported by a central column—to be used as "umbrellas" for roofing—were made as early as 1948 (in a plan for a hospital in the Province of Corrientes). In Mexico, Candela was able to make a big success out of the same idea (no question of priority is being raised here), while in Argentina little scope was found for such a practical innovation. The milieu made the difference.

Amancio Williams' aesthetic position was summed up by the Italian critic Gianni Rigoli:

> In the context of the modern movement in Argentina or more generally in South America, the work of Amancio Williams clearly belongs to the vein deriving from European rationalism, but finds its own independent expressive space through a precise and concrete technological base integrated with a few components of historical continuity and imaginative interpretation of the environment, without ever slipping into formalistic or stylistic involution.[13]

His work, adds Rigoli, is furthermore characterized by "the attention given to every detail, the careful analysis of functional components and of possibilities for new technological processes. . . ."

These qualities are evident in the house that Williams designed and built in a wooded section of Mar del Plata (1943–45), conceived essentially as "a form in space." The principal structural material is uncovered reinforced concrete, with large glass areas and plywood for the interior. The endeavor was to make "a really tridimensional structure, which works as a whole and not as a conjunction of separate elements." This unity is achieved largely through the use of two concrete slabs; one of these, curved like an arch and bridging a brook that flows under the house, acts as support for the horizontal slab that constitutes the main floor level. The curved slab is tied to the horizontal slab by two thin walls, and is "anchored" at either end by rectangular pier pillars that also contain the entrance and utility areas. The main slab is cantilevered at both ends. The roof is flat and provides an additional terrace area. A verandah-like peripheral area places the occupants face to face with the surrounding woods. Henry-Russell Hitchcock calls this house "a bold structural device" and praises "the

[13] *The Work of Amancio Williams* (Buenos Aires, 1966), p. 37. Reprinted from *Rivista Zodiac*, No. 16 (July, 1966).

continuity of interior space and the unbroken range of the windowband."

Amancio Williams' first project (1942) was for an apartment building designed on a continuous step-back principle, so that the roof of one unit formed the garden-terrace of the adjoining unit (later he developed this idea into a large housing project). In 1945 he designed an airport for Buenos Aires to be located in the River Plate (i.e. adjacent to the center of the city), with landing-strips supported by pillars standing in the shallow water (the bottom here is flat and uniformly resistant). The project, of course, has not been realized. Neither was the design of a Suspended Building for Offices (1948), based on the conjunction of two entirely different elements: (1) "the supporting structure of reinforced concrete composed of four huge pillars and two big beams"; and (2) "the building itself, a clear steel and glass construction hanging from the beams." According to the architect, the great advantage of such a suspended structure is that "the tension bars are much thinner than columns, leaving the surface of the floors practically free, with no problems of distribution, and also much lighter."

Those who say that Williams has his vision fixed on Utopia point to the rather fantastic design for the Hall for Plastic Spectacle and Sound in Space, upon which he worked for more than ten years (1943–53), including a great deal of time spent on acoustical research. As described by its designer,

> *Its principal form is somewhat like that of a large spinning-top or cabbage-head, within which the hall is enclosed; and this is, at the same time, the structure that sustains it. This form of a "spinning-top" . . . is the equivalent of the arch and the dome of antique architecture. Surrounding this principal structure is a ring somewhat like "Saturn's ring." This contains the public foyer, cloak-rooms, galleries, etc. The public passes from this ring into the hall by means of stairs that may be mechanized. The ring and the hall are located a good distance above the ground so that a park might be made underneath.*

Unusual though it may be, this design is by no means "Utopian." It is based on scientific principles, it is perfectly realizable, and it corresponds to the need for a new kind of audio-visual environment to meet the requirements of electronic music and the various intermedia that make up the "total theater" of today's space age.

Perhaps the future belongs to the scientific-humanistic thought that Amancio Williams represents. Upon being elected to the National Academy of Fine Arts in 1961, he said, "The paramount task of the new man, in order to achieve the welfare of humanity and even to assure its survival under acceptable conditions, is to apply scientific knowledge to life."

Teatro San Martín

By far the most notable example of the integration of arts and architecture in Argentina is to be found in the Teatro San Martín of Buenos Aires, built by the municipality and designed by the architects Mario Roberto Alvarez and Macedonio Oscar Ruiz (1961). The theater itself is located in a large, multipurpose high-rise building that also houses the Museum of Modern Art and various other cultural centers. There are actually two theaters, a larger one and a smaller one, both equipped with the most up-to-date technical facilities. Works of art by eleven Argentine artists are placed in various parts of the building—not always, it must be said, completely integrated with the architecture. The largest work is a mural one hundred feet long and thirty-five feet high by Luis Seoane, depicting *The Birth of the Argentine Theater*, in the lobby of the lower theater. It is figurative, with a background of geometric designs. A low relief in cast stone by the sculptor José Fioravanti covers the wall of the cantilevered projection booth of the upper theater, which juts out into the lobby. In this lobby there is also an abstract stainless steel sculpture by Enio Iommi. Extremely dramatic are the two large sculptures in cast stone by Pablo Curatela Manes, mounted high on the wall of the stage tower. A large semifigurative ceramic mural by Juan Battle Planas is in the exhibition hall, while a ceramic relief by Carlos de la Cárcova is in the lower lobby. Elsewhere in the building there are works by Libero Badii, Juan Ballester Peña, Antonio Fernández Muro, Sarah Grilo, and Miguel Ocampo.

URUGUAY

In Uruguay the integration of the arts received its chief impetus from the teaching and the example of Joaquín Torres García. His ideal of a "decorative monumental art" with humanistic significance is embodied in his *Cosmic Monument* for the Parque Rodó (1938). For the Hospital of the Colonia Saint-Bois in Montevideo, Torres García and members of his atelier painted twenty-seven murals in his constructivist style. A large universalist constructivist mural by Augusto Torres was painted for the dining room of the Medical Association of Montevideo in 1953 and 1954. The house of Horacio Torres, the great painter's son, has interior murals in a definitely archaic expression of this style, as well as wrought iron grilles of a more decorative character for the front door and windows. The residence of the architect Mario Payssé Reyes in Montevideo (1955), itself designed along the rectangular lines of universalist constructivism, has a number of well-integrated art works by followers of Torres García. These include a fresco mural in the covered patio by Julio Alpuy, titled *The Four Seasons*; a large semiabstract tapestry designed by Augusto Torres and executed by Elsa Andrada de Torres covering a living-room wall; and two sculptures outside: one in the form of a small decorated wall above the fountain in the patio, by Francisco Matto Vilaró, the other a sculpture-column made of brick with added ceramic elements designed by the architect and owner of the house, Payssé Reyes. Because the house and the art works in and around it are all drawn from the same aesthetic concept, the resulting integration is exceptionally fine and harmonious.

BRAZIL

By a fusion of outside influences and national genius, Brazilian architecture broke out of its academic and imitative shackles in the 1930's, with results that immediately placed it in the forefront of contemporary architecture. We have already mentioned the influence of the Russian-born Gregori Warchavchik, who worked

closely and effectively with Lúcio Costa when the latter was
appointed Director of the National School of Fine Arts in 1931.
Together they provided both inspiration and encouragement, as
well as sound training and an international outlook, for the
rising generation of Brazilian architects, among them Jorge
Machado Moreira, Carlos de Azevedo Leão, Oscar Niemeyer, and
Affonso Eduardo Reidy. From France came the stimulating
influence of Le Corbusier, whose writings in *L'Esprit Nouveau*
were known in Brazil even before his first visit there in 1929.
In 1936, when it was decided to build a new edifice for the Ministry
of Education and Public Health, Le Corbusier was invited to Rio
as consultant. During his stay he also gave six lectures, presented
a new city plan for Rio, and drew up plans for a University City.
In his book on city planning, *La Ville-Radieuse* (1935), Le
Corbusier had included plans for four South American cities:
Rio de Janeiro, São Paulo, Montevideo, and Buenos Aires. It was
in Brazil that his ideas found their most fruitful soil.

In Rio, Le Corbusier worked with Lúcio Costa and the group
of young architects already mentioned, drawing up plans for
the new Ministry of Education (1937–43). The building was
designed in two main sections: a two-story structure for serving
the public (lobby, auditorium, exhibition hall, and so forth); and
a fourteen-story block for offices, with a penthouse for recreational
and dining facilities. Its most striking features were the high
pilotis that raised the building some thirty-three feet off the
ground, and the northern façade (equivalent to southern exposure
in Rio), a honeycomb pattern formed of thin concrete ribs containing adjustable louvers (called *brise-soleil*) for protection
against sun glare. These were made of asbestos cement in metal
frames, painted light blue. According to Le Corbusier this was "the
first example of the use of *brise-soleil* in modern architecture."
He claimed that these horizontal panels should not have been
movable, for "It is the sun that does the moving."[14] Be this as
it may, the Ministry of Education building marks the coming of
age of contemporary Brazilian architecture and immediately
attracted world-wide attention.

[14] Le Corbusier: *Creation Is a Patient Search* (New York, 1960), p. 111.

This project was also notable for its ambitious effort to integrate the arts. The reception area has a large fresco by Portinari in his best neoexpressionist manner, and several ceramic tile murals (*azulejos*) by the same artist—purely and delightfully decorative. Roberto Burle-Marx designed one of his earliest gardens for the second-story terrace (seen from above he said, it looks like an abstract painting). Facing the building is a large sculpture in gray granite by Bruno Giorgi, representing a robust and healthy young couple (*Brazilian Youth*)—not inappropriate for a Ministry that included Public Health. The bronze sculpture *Prometheus* by Jacques Lipchitz perches somewhat uncomfortably on the exterior wall of the auditorium (it was reduced to one-third of the size planned by the artist). The Ministry of Education, at all events, established the precedent of collaboration between architect and artist that has since been followed in most public buildings in Brazil.[15]

Several of the architects involved in this project were to become the leaders of contemporary Brazilian architecture and to acquire international reputations. Jorge Moreira Machado was appointed chief architect for the University City of the University of Brazil in Rio. In this capacity he designed its first completed building, the Children's Clinic (1953), which has shell-vault roofing for recreational areas and makes effective use of tiles for both solid and screen-like surfaces. He also designed the National School of Architecture (1959) and the University Press (1963), both in the University City, as well as apartment houses (notably the Edificio Antonio Ceppas [1952]), office buildings, and residences.

Affonso Eduardo Reidy

Affonso Eduardo Reidy (1909–1963) was born in Paris of an English father and a Brazilian mother of Italian descent. He completed his training at the National School of Fine Arts in Rio, where he succeeded Warchavchik as professor of architecture. He was appointed Chief Architect for the former Federal District

[15] After the nation's capital was moved to Brasília, the former Ministry of Education building in Rio became the Palace of Culture.

of Rio de Janeiro and Director of the Department of City Planning—a field in which he did his most important and influential work. He also taught this subject at the National School of Architecture. He designed a large number of administrative buildings in Rio, as well as a Community Theater (1950–51), several large housing projects, and the Museum of Modern Art. Elsewhere, his most original and successful projects included an Aviation Training Center in São Paulo (1947) and an Experimental School in Asunción, Paraguay (1953). He also designed the Museum of Visual Arts in São Paulo (1954). Two of his most representative buildings will be briefly described here: a residential complex and an art museum.

The Pedregulho Residential Neighborhood was designed in 1947 as a low-cost housing project for municipal employees. The site covers about twelve acres and the main construction is on a hillside that rises to a height of 164 feet. The plan calls for four blocks of apartments, of which the largest is a long curvilinear structure (853 feet in length) that follows the contour of the hill (this also facilitates access from the rear at different levels). Each block is raised above the ground on pillars, providing shade and air circulation at ground level. The third floor of the largest building is mainly without partitions, providing space for a kindergarten, day nursery, and playground. Perforated ceramic screens are used whenever possible for protection against sunlight. The neighborhood includes an elementary school, shopping center, swimming pool, gymnasium, and health center. The gardens were designed by Roberto Burle-Marx. At the first Bienal of São Paulo in 1951, Reidy's design was awarded the prize for "the best plan for the organization of large areas." In 1952, he designed a similar but larger residential neighborhood (35 acres), on a still higher hillside that was formerly a densely populated slum area (Gávea Residential Project).

The Museum of Modern Art of Rio de Janeiro, located on the edge of Guanabara Bay and therefore close to the heart of the city, was begun in December 1954 and finished in 1962. (It was actually built on landfill recovered from the bay.) In keeping with modern concepts the museum was to be not merely an art gallery but also a cultural center including an art school, working studios, and a theater for lectures, plays, concerts, ballets, and films. The most radical departure from traditional design is the absence of large blind walls and permanent partitions. This is an "open" museum with large glass areas through which the visitor can look out over the bay as a refreshing change from gazing at pictures. There is a combination of natural and artificial lighting; some windows are provided with aluminum blinds to control the amount of outside light entering the rooms. The main exhibition gallery provides an unbroken floor space measuring 427 by 85 feet.

The principal structure is enclosed in a frame consisting of concrete ribs with a ground span of 85 feet, placed at intervals of thirty-three feet and projecting outwards to furnish further protection from excessive sunlight. These huge exposed concrete ribs, which also raise the building above the ground, are the most distinctive and impressive feature of the structure. Various ancillary installations are housed in a U-shaped building arranged around a garden courtyard. The varied and attractive garden and walks for the immediate surroundings were designed by Burle-Marx. The upper story of the administrative building has a glass-enclosed restaurant with a splendid view over the city and the bay, and a spacious terrace covered with a latticed sun-screen. Altogether a museum and cultural-recreational-educational center of which Rio de Janeiro may well be proud—and in which it may find some consolation for no longer being the nation's capital.

Oscar Niemeyer

Oscar Niemeyer Soares Filho was born in Rio de Janeiro on December 15, 1907. After graduation from the National School of Fine Arts in 1934 his first important assignment was as a member of the designing group for the Ministry of Education, which he directed after Costa withdrew from the project in 1939. His first independent work was a maternity clinic in Rio (1937). In 1939 he designed, together with Lúcio Costa, the Brazilian Pavilion for the New York World's Fair. After that he went from one important project to another—banks, office buildings, schools, hospitals, churches, apartments, private houses (including two of his own), often using his favorite curvilinear forms and always applying boldly imaginative solutions to each project. By 1956 he was not only Brazil's most celebrated architect but also one of the most famous in the world. Among his major accomplishments, besides those that have been mentioned, were the Boavista Bank Building in Rio (1946), with its vertical use of *brise-soleil*; the Montreal Office Building in São Paulo (1950), with its curving, horizontally banded façade; the headquarters for the Getúlio Vargas Foundation in Rio (1955), with its striking variation of the *brise-soleil* device in the form of vertical angled slabs reaching from the bottom to the top of the building; the Secondary School in Belo Horizonte (1954), with its elliptical, shell-enclosed auditorium; the Public Library in Belo Horizonte (1955), raised on pilotis, with its long curvilinear main reading room and its circular stack area; the Modern Art Museum in Caracas (1955), probably the most original of all his designs, projecting from a hillside in the form of an inverted pyramid with a large horizontal area at the top providing a maximum of daylight (sun glare is controlled by a horizontal sunbreak); the Residential Blocks in Petrópolis (1953), with their lavish use of "open" and curvilinear forms in Niemeyer's most "lyrical" manner; the Kubitschek Complex in Belo Horizonte (1951), where the supporting pillars of the main block, with their triangular and curvilinear shapes, anticipate the famous pillars of Brasília; the Air Training Center at San José dos Campos (1947), a varied complex of technical and housing facilities that demonstrated the architect's ability to combine functional and lyrical elements; and the Youth Center in Diamantina (1950), which demonstrated his masterly use of large arched forms in a very open kind of structure. By 1956 Oscar Niemeyer was ready for the greatest opportunity and challenge of his career: the building of Brasília. And once again he was brought into creative association with the man in whose office he had worked as a student: Lúcio Costa.

Brasília

The most important cities of Brazil, including its first capital, Salvador da Bahia, and its second capital, Rio de Janeiro, were established on or near the country's immense coastline. The idea of moving the capital to the interior, in order to encourage and facilitate the development of Brazil's vast hinterland, was first broached in the early nineteenth century and was never allowed to die. The Constitution of 1891 declared that a tract in the central highlands (State of Goiás) was the property of the federal government for the purpose of constructing a new capital there. The Constitution of 1946 made specific provisions for moving the capital, and in 1953 the Congress authorized the government to carry out studies for determining the exact site. The prime mover behind this enterprise was President Juscelino Kubitschek, who held that this westward expansion "expressed anew the pioneer spirit that has always characterized Brazilians." The site having been selected and approved, 585 miles to the north and west of Rio de Janeiro at an altitude of some 3,000 feet, the Congress authorized (August, 1956) the creation of an entity known as NOVACAP, with full responsibility for planning and constructing the new capital, which was to be named Brasília.

The first task of NOVACAP was to organize a competition (open to Brazilian architects only) for the overall plan of Brasília. From twenty-six entries, the International Jury chose the plan submitted by Lúcio Costa, remarkable for the simplicity and clarity of its design as well as for the boldness and originality of its conceptions. Basically the form might be described as that of an airplane, with the fuselage corresponding to the main monumental axis of the city. In the words of Lúcio Costa,

Brasília should not be envisaged merely as an organism capable of fulfilling adequately and effortlessly the vital function of any modern city, not merely as an "urbs," but as a "civitas," possessing the attributes inherent in a capital. And, for this to be possible, the planner must be imbued with a certain dignity and nobility of "intent," because that fundamental attitude will give birth to the sense of order, utility and proportion which alone can confer on the project as a whole the desirable monumental quality. Not, let it be clear, in the *sense of ostentation, but as the palpable and conscious expression, so to speak, of what is worthwhile and significant. The city should be planned for orderly and efficient work, but at the same time be both vital and pleasing, a suitable background for intellectual deliberation; it should be such a city as, with time, could become not only the seat of government, but also one of the more lucid and distinguished cultural centers in the country.*[16]

The skeletal design is that of two axes crossing at right angles. One of the axes was then curved "in order to contain it within the equilateral triangle which limits the urbanized area." The straight axis is the one that contains the official buildings of the federal government and is therefore known as the "Monumental Axis." As described by Lúcio Costa,

The most outstanding buildings are those which will house the governmental powers and, because these are autonomous and three in number, the equilateral triangle seemed the elementary form most appropriate to enclose them. . . . One of the buildings was placed at each angle of this Plaza—Plaza of the Three Powers as it might well be called—with the Executive Palace and the Supreme Court occupying the base of the triangle and the Congress the apex. The latter faces a broad esplanade set out on a second terrace, rectangular in shape and bordered along its entire length by a stone retaining wall. . . . Along this equivalent of the English mall—broad sweeping lawns to be used by pedestrians, processions and parades—the various ministries and autonomous agencies were placed. . . . The Cathedral, too, has been given a location on the esplanade but has a plaza of its own disposed laterally to it for three reasons: one of protocol, in that the Church is separate from the State; one of scale, in that the Cathedral's monumental qualities are thus enhanced; and finally, a question of architectonics—the perspective of the esplanade as a whole must run unimpeded beyond the intersection of the two main axes.[17]

With Lúcio Costa as the city planner, Oscar Niemeyer was appointed, in 1957, chief architect for NOVACAP. His first task was to design two buildings outside the general plan, which President Kubitschek considered immediately essential for the functioning of the new capital: the President's Palace (residential), Palácio da Alvorada, and the Brasília Palace Hotel (suitable lodging

[16] As quoted in Willy Stäubli, *Brasília.* Universe Books, 1965, p. 12.
[17] *Ibid.,* p. 14.

had to be provided for officials and visitors during the period of construction). These were both completed in 1958. In his design for the President's Palace, and particularly in his highly personal and lyrical solution for the modern equivalent of the classical exterior colonnade, Niemeyer set the distinctive tone for some of the most successful and characteristic official buildings of Brasília. His solution achieves (in his own words), "a continuous, undulating rhythm in constructing the columns as if they were laid on the earth lightly and with elegance." Because they are slightly arched at the bottom, these graceful curvilinear forms do actually appear to rest lightly upon the ground on their points. Meeting one another in wide curves at the base, they rise in tapering perpendiculars to sustain with their slenderness the widely projecting flat roof. The columns are faced with white marble. The building stands on the outskirts of the city, near the large artificial lake that surrounds Brasília on three sides. On the side toward the lake is the Presidential Chapel, remarkable both for its simplicity and for the harmony of its circular design.

The various arts are well represented in the Alvorada Palace. In a pool on the entrance side there is a bronze sculpture, by Alfredo Ceschiatti, of two seated women drying their hair. Facing the rear façade is a large abstract bronze sculpture by Maria Martins titled *Rhythm of Rhythm*. Another abstract bronze sculpture, by André Bloc, is in one of the interior hallways. There are also two tapestries by Di Cavalcanti and a mural by Firminio Saldanha.

Niemeyer's most important contributions to the architecture of Brasília within Lúcio Costa's master plan are the National Congress, the Supreme Court, the Planalto Palace (Executive Palace), the Ministry of Foreign Affairs, the Cathedral, and the National Theater. The first three are located in, and give a unique character to, the Plaza of the Three Powers, ceremonial terminus of Brasília's Monumental Axis.

The approach to the Plaza of the Three Powers is dominated by the twin towers of the National Congress building rising from a rectangular lagoon. Immediately adjacent is the low horizontal structure housing the assembly rooms of the Senate and the Chamber of Deputies, the most striking features of which are the two protruding cupolas, one in the form of a partial hemisphere (convex), the other in the form of a bowl (concave). As explained by Niemeyer, "Our aim was to emphasize their plastic appearance and therefore we transplanted them onto a huge esplanade where their forms sprout like a symbol of the legislative power." Once again Niemeyer found an original solution, both functional and aesthetic, for the conventional concept of the legislative cupola.

At the other end of the lagoon, and at a slightly lower level, is the Plaza itself, in the shape of an oblong rectangle (984 feet by 328 feet), which may also be regarded as the base of a symbolic triangle representing the Three Powers: Legislative, Executive, Judicial. At the end nearest the lake stands the Planalto Palace, housing the executive offices of the President. Using the same type of curvilinear column as in the Alvorada Palace to support the projecting flat roof, Niemeyer created a completely new concept of the classical peristyle, in keeping with his theory of free, lyrical forms. This can be seen also in the Supreme Court building, at the opposite end of the Plaza; but here again with a variant version of the columns that avoids monotonous repetition. Whereas in the Executive Office building the lower arch of the columns rises to the level of the first floor, here it rises only slightly, to the level of the ground floor periphery. The columns are on two sides of the building only, which emphasizes the impression of openness and dignified simplicity. The columns of both buildings are faced with white marble.

The relatively small Museum of Brasília stands between these two large buildings, on the side of the Plaza by the lagoon. On the other side of the Plaza a slim vertical accent is supplied by a tower-like dovecote, while nearer the Planalto Palace stands a heroic bronze sculpture by Bruno Giorgi, *Two Warriors*. In front of the Supreme Court is a stone sculpture by Ceschiatti—a rather conventional representation of Justice as a blindfolded female figure holding a sword in her lap. In the entrance hall of the National Congress building there is a mural designed by Athos Bulçáo, executed in black granite and white marble, which is more closely integrated with the architectural design than any other art work in Brasília.

The National Theater houses two theaters, one large, the other small, to be used for opera, ballet, and concerts as well as for plays. They are located tangentially, so as to make use of the same stage apparatus. The exterior of the building makes no attempt to be conventionally impressive. Described as "a blunt pyramid with a trapezoid base," its *raison d'être* is best stated by the architect himself:

> The functional problems of space and volume are not subordinated to external shape and thus there is no reduction in the areas indispensable for theatrical production. To this end, an architectural form has been devised which is different and contains the whole building like a shell, allowing the stage and annexes to be distributed without limitation of space or preoccupation with questions of finish, almost as though they were temporary structures—a treatment that enables them to be readily adapted and brought up to date.[18]

Here Niemeyer applies the formula that form follows function— but entirely in his own manner as usual.

The Ministry of Foreign Affairs was one of the earliest buildings designed by Niemeyer for Brasília (1958), but its actual construction was not begun until 1963 (completed in 1967). The Ministry as a whole consists of three main units, two of which are high-rise administrative office buildings. The offices of the Minister and his immediate staff, as well as the representational and ceremonial functions, are located in the three-story rectangular Palace of the Arches (Palácio dos Arcos), so-called because of the colonnade arches formed by a third variant of Niemeyer's columns. The architect said that he aspired to create an edifice that would be "both contemporary and tropical." In this he succeeded (Plate 10). Each floor is made of a different kind of Brazilian marble, in an ascending hierarchy of color and rarity: common gray, yellow marble from Bahia, pure white marble. Besides the usual gardens by Burle-Marx, there are tapestries designed by this multifaceted artist. Numerous art works were commissioned for the new Ministry, among them a nonobjective sculpture by Bruno Giorgi that stands near the reflecting pool.

On the whole Brasília, though still "a work in progress," thus

18 *Ibid.*, p. 105.

far lives up to the aspirations of its founders, planners, and builders in terms of Kubitschek's "grandeur and functional design," Costa's "fluency and unity of . . . layout" with "spaciousness on a noble scale," and Niemeyer's "richness of forms . . . surprising and breathtaking forms." The best buildings of Brasília already appear to have the rightness and permanence that we associate with the greatest architectural achievements of mankind.

Church Architecture

In Brazil, modern church architecture, integrated with art, owes its impetus to Niemeyer's daring originality. In 1942, he was commissioned by Juscelino Kubitschek, then mayor of Belo Horizonte, to design a series of buildings (including a casino, a yacht club, and a church) for the newly developed suburb of Pampulha. For the Church of St. Francis of Assisi at Pampulha (1943), facing an artificial lake, Niemeyer not only created a totally contemporary design but also achieved a remarkable integration of the arts with tile mosaics, paintings, and sculpture. The main structure, the nave, consists of a single parabolic concrete shell vault, with vertical louvers on the front façade letting in the light. A slightly smaller parabolic vault defines the area of the sanctuary, flanked by three considerably smaller vaults (two on one side, one on the other) of the same shape (for the sacristy and the vestry). The freestanding bell tower, tapering at the bottom instead of at the top, has projecting from it a large slab that serves as an entrance canopy for the church.

As one enters the church one first notices the fascia of the balcony and the exterior face of the baptistry screen (a freestanding wall), both decorated by Portinari with ceramic tile. The interior face of the baptistry screen is decorated with figurative low reliefs in bronze by Ceschiatti. Along the left wall of the nave are the Stations of the Cross painted by Portinari, who also executed the splendid fresco on the reredos wall, depicting Jesus Christ ministering to the poor and sick. The ceramic tile designs on the exterior of the pulpit are also by Portinari. On the outside of the church, the exterior nave vault has blue and white abstract mosaics by Paulo Werneck in freely undulating forms. But the great masterpiece of the exterior decoration is Portinari's mural in *azulejo* (blue and white tile), depicting scenes from the life of St. Francis and covering the entire area of the three rear vaults. Both in the overall effect seen from a distance, with the large curvilinear abstract patterns, and in detail, with the close-ups of the Saint and the various animals (a repeated pattern of birds and fishes appears as a kind of decorative background), the whole composition reveals the mastery achieved by Portinari in this typically Brazilian medium.

For the nation's new capital, Brasília, Niemeyer designed three churches: the Presidential Chapel (1958), the Chapel of our Lady of Fatima (1959), and the Cathedral (begun in 1959). The first of these, adjacent to the President's Palace (residential) and connected to it by a passageway, is designed on a very simple but effective circular plan, consisting of two crescent-shaped walls that face each other asymmetrically, the gap between them forming the main entrance. A lyrical effect is produced by the upward curvature of one wall, rising to a peak above the entrance. The Chapel of Our Lady of Fatima is entirely different in design, in the form of a canopy rising to a high peak at the front and supported by one of those curving columns to which Niemeyer is so partial. The most ambitious and original of these structures is of course the Cathedral, for which Joaquim Cardoso served as structural engineer. Under construction for ten years, its completion was delayed partly because of technical difficulties and partly because it was paid for by voluntary contributions from the people of Brazil. The general aspect of the Cathedral is described by Stäubli as "A huge bundle of hollow concrete ribs [that] towers into the sky like a cluster of sheaves." The result is a circular form, about 200 feet in diameter at the base, narrowing to about forty feet at the roof. The ends of the concrete ribs, which at this point curve outward, extend for some distance above the roof, forming a sort of crown. The walls (i.e., the area between the ribs) are of stained glass. Access to the Cathedral is by means of an inclined ramp because the floor is some ten feet below street level. Projected in the vicinity of the Cathedral are numerous annexes (Archbishop's Curia, Choir Residence,

Sisters' Residence, Salon, and Auditorium), most of them housed in a long rectangular L-shaped building. The Salon and Auditorium (including a cinema) will have a separate building.

On the whole, Latin American architects have produced some of the most imaginative and original architecture in the modern world. The University Cities of Mexico and Caracas are unique achievements, especially noteworthy for the integration of the plastic arts in the overall conception. Mexico and Brazil have taken the lead in developing new forms of church architecture, particularly through the work of Luis Barragán, Félix Candela, and Oscar Niemeyer. Great attention has been given to city planning and to large low-cost housing developments in which the aesthetic factor, far from being slighted, has been deliberately emphasized. Artists and architects have cooperated to achieve integrated and harmonious results on many projects, both private and public, commercial and industrial. The plastic arts have been well served by architecture in several notable museums, particularly the Museums of Modern Art in Mexico City, Rio de Janeiro, and Caracas. It may be a long time before another Brasília is built; but the modernization of older cities like Caracas, São Paulo, and Mexico City offers a different kind of challenge that Latin American architects have readily accepted and in which remarkable results have already been achieved.

Selected Bibliography

Art in Latin America Today. Washington, D.C.: Pan American Union, 1959—. A series of illustrated booklets by various authors, covering to date: Argentina, Brazil, Chile, Colombia, Guatemala, Haiti, Peru, and Venezuela.

Arango, Jorge, and Carlos Martínez. *Arquitectura en Colombia.* Bogotá: Ediciones Proa, 1951.

Bardi, P. M. *The Tropical Gardens of Burle-Marx.* New York: Reinhold, 1963.

Bienal Americana de Arte, Córdoba. Catalogs of the Biennials of 1962, 1964, 1966. Córdoba, Argentina.

Bienal de São Paulo. Catalogs of the Biennials of 1951–67. São Paulo, Brazil: Fundação Bienal de São Paulo.

Bonifaz Nuño, Rubén. *Ricardo Martínez.* Mexico: Universidad Nacional, 1965.

Born, Esther. *The New Architecture in Mexico.* Supplementary articles on contemporary painting and sculpture by Justino Fernández. New York: *The Architectural Record* and William Morrow and Co., 1937.

Cardoza y Aragón, Luis. *Mexican Art Today.* Mexico: Fondo de Cultura Económica, 1966.

———. *México: Pintura Activa.* Mexico: Ediciones Era, 1961.

———. *Orozco.* Mexico: Universidad Nacional, 1959.

Catlin, Stanton L., and Terence Grieder. *Art of Latin America Since Independence.* [Catalog]. New Haven: Yale University Press, 1966.

Cetto, Max L. *Modern Architecture in Mexico (Arquitectura moderna en México).* Bilingual edition. New York: Praeger, 1961.

Charlot, Jean. *The Mexican Mural Renaissance, 1920–1925.* New Haven: Yale University Press, 1963.

Chase, Gilbert. "The Artist." In *Continuity and Change in Latin America*, ed. John J. Johnson, pp. 101–35. Stanford, Calif.: Stanford University Press, 1964.

———. "Art in Mexico Today." In *The Caribbean: Mexico Today*, ed. A. Curtis Wilgus, pp. 169–75. Gainesville: University of Florida Press, 1964.

Cuevas, José Luis. *Cuevas por Cuevas: Notas Autobiográficas.* Prologue by Juan García Ponce. Bilingual edition. Mexico: Ediciones Era, 1965.

Damaz, Paul F. *Art in Latin American Architecture.* New York: Reinhold, 1963.

Faber, Colin. *Candela, The Shell Builder.* New York: Reinhold, 1963.

Fernández, Justino. *La pintura moderna mexicana.* Mexico: Editorial Pormaca, 1964.

———. *Orozco: Forme e idea.* Mexico: Ediciones Porrúa, 1956.

Franck, Klaus. *The Works of Affonso Eduardo Reidy.* New York: Praeger, 1960.

García Cisneros, Florencio. *Latin-American Painters in New York.* Privately printed, 1964.

Goldwater, Robert. *Rufino Tamayo.* New York: Quadrangle Press, 1947.

Gómez Sicre, José. *Four Artists of the Americas: Roberto Burle-Marx, Amelia Peláez, Alexander Calder, Rufino Tamayo.* Washington, D.C.: Pan American Union, 1957.

———. *Pintura cubana de hoy.* English version by Harold T. Riddle. Havana: M. L. Gómez Mena, 1944.

Goodwin, Philip L. *Brazil Builds: Architecture Old and New, 1652–1942.* New York: Museum of Modern Art, 1943.

Gual, Enrique F. *David Alfaro Siqueiros.* English version by Emma Gutiérrez Suárez. Mexico: Ediciones Galería de Arte Misrachi, 1965.

———. *Drawings by Tamayo.* Mexico: Ediciones Mexicanas, 1950.

Siqueiros. New York: Tudor Publishing, 1965. (Contains reproductions in color of 32 easel paintings.)

Heine, Ernesto. *Once pintores uruguayas*. Montevideo, 1964.

Helm, McKinley. *Modern Mexican Painters*. New York: Harper, 1941.

Hitchcock, Henry-Russell. *Latin American Architecture since 1945*. New York: Museum of Modern Art, 1955.

Jaguer, Edouard. *Gironella*. Mexico: Ediciones Era, 1964.

Lynch, James B., Jr. *Tamayo*. An Essay [with] A Commentary by the Artist. Phoenix, Arizona: Phoenix Art Musem and Friends of Mexican Art, 1968.

Merli, Joan. *Raquel Forner*. Buenos Aires: Editorial Poseidon, 1952.

Messer, Thomas M., and Cornell Capa. *The Emergent Decade: Latin American Painters and Painting in the 1960's*. Ithaca: Cornell University Press, 1966.

Moholy-Nagy, Sibyl. *Carlos Raúl Villanueva and the Architecture of Venezuela*. New York: Praeger, 1964.

Myers, Bernard S. *Mexican Painting in Our Time*. New York: Oxford University Press, 1956.

Myers, Irving E. *Mexico's Modern Architecture*. In cooperation with the National Institute of Fine Arts of Mexico. New York: Architectural Book Publishing, 1952.

Nelken, Margarita. *Carlos Mérida*. Mexico: Universidad Nacional, 1961.

Nessi, Angel Osvaldo. *Situación de la pintura argentina*. La Plata– Buenos Aires: Renacimiento, 1956.

Orozco, José Clemente. *An Autobiography*. Translated by Robert C. Stephenson. Austin: University of Texas Press, 1962.

Papadaki, Stamo. *The Work of Oscar Niemeyer*. New York: George Braziller, 1960.

Payró, Julio E. *Horacio Butler*. Buenos Aires: Emecé, 1954. (Spanish and English text.)

Paz, Octavio. *Tamayo*. Mexico: Universidad Nacional, 1958.

Plenn, Virginia, and Jaime Plenn. A *Guide to Modern Mexican Murals.* Mexico: Ediciones Tolteca, 1963.

Quem é Quem nas artes e nas letras do Brasil (Artistas e escritores contemporaneos ou falecidos depois de 1945). Rio de Janeiro: Ministério das Relações Exteriores, Departamento Cultural e de Informações, 1966.

Ramos, Samuel. *Diego Rivera.* Mexico: Universidad Nacional, 1958.

Reed, Alma. *José Clemente Orozco.* New York: Oxford University Press, 1956.

————. *The Mexican Muralists.* New York: Crown Publishers, 1960.

Rial, Antonio. *La pintura de Heiter.* Caracas: Carlos Maggiora, 1959.

Rivera, Diego. *My Art, My Life: An Autobiography.* In association with Gladys March. New York: Citadel Press, 1960.

————, **and Bertram D. Wolfe.** *Portrait of America.* New York: Covici, Friede, 1934.

————. *Portrait of Mexico.* New York: Covici, Friede, 1937.

Rodman, Selden. *The Insiders: Rejection and Rediscovery of Man in the Arts of Our Time.* Baton Rouge: Louisiana State University Press, 1960. Includes essays on Orozco and Cuevas.

————. *Renaissance in Haiti: Popular Painters in the Black Republic.* New York: Pellegrini & Cudahy, 1948.

Schmeckebier, Laurence E. *Modern Mexican Art.* Minneapolis: University of Minnesota Press, 1939.

Smith, Clive Bramford. *Builders in the Sun: Five Mexican Architects.* New York: Architectural Book Publishing, 1967.

Stäubli, Willy. *Brasília.* New York: Universe Books, 1965.

Stewart, Virginia. *Contemporary Mexican Artists.* Palo Alto, Calif.: Stanford University Press, 1951.

Torres García, Joaquín. *Historia de mi vida.* Montevideo: Talleres Gráficos "Sur," 1939.

————. *La recuperación del objeto* (*Lecciones sobre plástica*). Prólogo de Esther Caceres. 2 vols. Montevideo: Impresora Uruguaya, 1965. (Biblioteca Artigas, vols. 75–76.)

Traba, Marta. *La pintura nueva en Latinoamérica.* Bogotá: Ediciones Librería Central, 1961.

Westheim, Paul. *Tamayo.* Mexico: Artes de México, 1957.

Wolfe, Bertram D. *The Fabulous Life of Diego Rivera.* New York: Stein and Day, 1963.

Zúñiga, Olivia. *Mathias Goeritz.* (English text.) Mexico: Editorial Intercontinental, 1963.

Index

NOTE: Spanish-American names are indexed under the first surname, thus: González Goyri, Roberto; Portuguese-Brazilian names, under the last surname: Moreira, Jorge Machado. There are some exceptions (e.g., Siqueiros, David Alfaro).

Abela, Eduardo, 60, 67
Abramo, Lívio, 216-217, 220
Abstract expressionism, 48, 54, 58, 76, 88, 93-94, 112, 115, 117, 118, 123
  in Argentina, 142, 144, 148-152, 155
  in Bolivia, 117, 118
  in Brazil, 211-214
  in Chile, 123, 124
  in Peru, 107-108, 111
  in Uruguay, 178, 179
  in Venezuela, 76-77, 79-82
Abularach, Rodolfo, 48, 49-52
Acha, Juan, 100, 103
Action painting, 103, 151, 152
Aguirre Silva, Jorge, 254
Agurte Calvo, Santiago, 256
Aldave, Victor, 111
Alix, Gabriel, 71
Almeida, Guilherme de, 184
Alonso, José, 162
Alpuy, Julio, 261
Alva de la Canal, Ramón, 11
Alvarado, Antonio, 58
Alvarez, Mario Roberto, 260
Alvarez Ordóñez, Joaquín, 244
Amaral, Tarsila do, 183, 184, 185-187
Andrada de Torres, Elsa, 261
Andrade, Mário de, 181, 183-186 passim, 198, 199
Andrade, Oswaldo de, 183-188 passim

Angel, Abraham, 21
Angulo, Jorge, 37
Antúñez, Nemesio, 121, 124, 125, 255
Aparicio, Ernestina de, 48n.
Aquino, Flávio de, 190, 196
Arai, Alberto T., 233
Arango, Jorge, 253
Arche, Jorge, 67
Archipenko, Alexander, 119
Architecture, 227-279
  in Argentina, 257-260
  in Brazil, 212, 227, 231, 261-274
  in Chile, 254-256
  in churches, 243-244, 264, 272-274
  in Colombia, 253-254
  in Cuba, 245-246
  emotional, 258-262
  functional, 227-228, 229-232
  in Mexico, 228, 229-231, 232-245, 246-247
  in Venezuela, 248-256
Arece, Francisco, 229
Arévalo, Juan José, 45
Argentina, 20, 53, 125, 127-169, 206
  abstract expressionism, 148-151
  action painting, 151-152
  architecture, 257-260
  cubism, 136-148 passim
  figurative painters, 136-148
  geometrical abstraction, 157-160
  optical art, 158-159, 169

Argentina (*continued*)
  pop art, 154, 160-161
  sculpture, 161-168, 169, 260
Arias, Luis, 110
Arinos, Afonso, 216
Arosamena, Justo, 58
Aróstegui, Alejandro, 54-56
Arp, Hans, 119, 157, 158, 164, 252
Arroyo, Miguel, 253
Art Nouveau, 32, 151, 214, 228
Ashlander, Leslie Judd, 48. *See also*
  Portner
Asturias, Miguel Angel, 46
Atahualpa, Inca, 106
Atl, Dr., 2-6, 8, 14
Ayres, Lula Cardoso, 200-202

Badi, Aquiles, 139
Badii, Libero, 260
Ballester Peña, Juan, 260
Balmes, José, 124
Bandeira, Antonio, 210
Barnitz, Jacqueline, 86
Barragán, Luis, 240, 241-242, 274
Barreda, Ernesto, 125
Barrios, Armando, 75, 85, 252
Barrios, Gracia, 124
Basaldúa, Héctor, 138, 140-142
Batista, Fulgencio, 61
Battle Planas, Juan, 148, 260
Battman, Otto, 210
Behring, Edith, 219-220
Benoit, Bigaud, 71
Belaúnde Terry, Fernando, 256
Belkin, Arnold, 14n.
Benecerraf, Moisés F., 248
Bento, António, 215
Berdia, Norberto, 178
Bermúdez, Cundo, 64, 65-66
Bermúdez, Guido, 248
Bermúdez, Lia, 82
Bernabo, Hector. *See* Carybé
Berni, Antonio, 20, 53, 138, 146-147
Best-Maugard, Adolfo, 6-7
Bianco, Mario, 256
Bigatti, Alfredo, 138, 142, 161, 162, 163
Bigaud, Wilson, 71
Bill, Max, 212

Blake, William, 136
Blanchard, Sisson, 71
Blas, Camilo, 101
Bloc, André, 202, 269
Boaz, Franz, 7
Boccioni, Umberto, 129
Bogen, Carlos, 253
Bolivia, 115-120
Bonatti, Eduardo, 124
Bonevardi, Marcelo, 159-160
Bonnard, Pierre, 136, 170
Bonomi, Maria, 219, 220
Borda, Antonio, 115-116
Borges, Jacobo, 76-77
Borges, Jorge Luis, 133
Borges, Max, Jr., 246
Born, Esther, 228n.
Borno, Maurice, 71
Bosch, Hieronymus, 58, 217
Botelho, Adir, 221
Botero, Fernando, 87, 90-92
Bourdelle, Antoine, 162
Brancusi, Constantin, 29, 119, 132, 164
Brandt, Alberto, 82
Brandt, Mary, 82
Braque, Georges, 9, 24, 42, 130, 198
Brasília, 220, 222, 223, 225, 227, 232, 267-274
Bravo, Jorge, 233
Brazil, 181-226, 261-274
  architecture, 227-228, 231, 261-274
  art patronage in, 181-182
  graphic arts, 214-221, 226
  modern art, beginnings of, 182-187
  nationalism, 196-199, 225
  nonobjective art, 209-213
  primitive painters, 193-195
  regionalism, 199-208
    in Bahia, 204-208
  sculpture, 221-225, 263
    in Brasília, 269, 270, 271, 272
Brecheret, Victor, 183, 185, 221-222
Brennand, Francisco, 200n., 203
Breton, André, 32, 63, 103

Brito Moreno, Rodulfo, 36, 37
Brizzi, Ary, 157, 158
Bulção, Athos, 270
Bumba-meu-boi, 201
Burchard, Pablo, 120-121
Burle-Marx, Roberto, 188, 223, 263, 264, 265, 271
Butler, Horacio, 136, 138-140
Bryen, Camille, 210

Cabre, Manuel, 75
Cabrera, Geles, 37
Cabrera, Roberto, 49, 52-53
Cajahuaringa, Milner, 108
Calder, Alexander, 85, 252
Calderón, Constancia, 58
Camargo, Iberê, 180, 209, 220
Camigli, Massimo, 137
Camino Brent, Enrique, 101
Camões, Luís [Vaz] de, 222
Canaday, John, 21, 116
Cancela, Delia, 160-161
Candela, Félix, 235, 237, 242-245, 258, 274
Capa, Cornell, 85*n*., 88, 90, 105, 208
Capabianca, Aquiles, 245
Caracas, César, 55
Cardoso, Joaquim, 273
Cardoza y Aragón, Luis, 13, 14*n*., 18*n*., 42
Carrá, Carlo, 129
Carranza, Venustiano, 3, 19
Carrasco Núñez del Prado, Jorge, 117, 118
Carreño, Mario, 61, 64, 65, 255-256
Carreño, Omar, 85, 253
Carrillo, Lilia, 22*n*.
Carrington, Leonora, 32
Carvalho, Eleazar de, 189
Carvalho, Flávio Rezende de, 183, 188-189, 209
Carvalho, Genaro de, 206-207
Carybé, 206
Casanova, Teresa, 82
Cassou, Jean, 35, 178
Casteda, Leopoldo, 246
Castellanos, Julio, 21-22
Castillo, Carlos Aitor, 104, 107-108
Castillo, Marcos, 75

Castillo, Teófilo, 98
Castro, Fidel, 245
Castro, Juan José, 139
Castro, Pedro León, 75
Cavalcanti, Carlos, 194
Cédor, Dieudonné, 71
Cendrars, Blaise, 185
Central America, 39-57, 246-248
Ceramics, 37, 38, 61, 62-63, 72, 121, 124-125, 272-273
Cervantes, Pedro, 37
Ceschiatti, Alfredo, 223, 269, 272
Cetto, Max, 233, 239, 245
Cézanne, Paul, 9, 75, 103, 120
Chab, Victor, 151
Chabloz, Jean-Pierre, 195
Charlot, Jean, +*n*., 6, 11
Chateaubriand, Assis, 181
Chávez López, Gerardo, 110
Chávez Morado, José, 234, 235
Chávez Morado, Tomás, 235
Chicharro, Eduardo, 8
Chile, 20, 120-126, 254-256
Chili, Manuel ["Caspicara"], 113
Chire Barrientos, Moisés, 118
Clark, Lygia, 223-224
Cocteau, Jean, 185
Codesido, Julia, 101
Colina, Juan Manuel de la, 110
Colombia, 39, 87-95, 126, 253-254
Communism. *See* Marxism
Constructivism, 82-84, 119, 158, 160, 166, 168, 210, 214. *See also* Torres García
Consuegra, Hugo, 66
Corinth, Lovis, 183
Coronel, Pedro, 25, 28, 29-31, 37, 38
Coronel, Rafael, 31-32
Cortés, Hernán, 2
Corzas, Francisco, 14*n*., 32
Costa, Lúcio, 231, 262, 265, 266-268
Costabal, Jorge, 256
Cravo, Mário, 224, 225
Cruxent, José María, 79
Cruz Díez, Carlos, 85-86
Cuba, 39, 60-67, 245-246
Cubism, 5, 9, 77, 88, 98, 115, 117, 128, 130, 132, 137, 138,

Cubism (*continued*)
139, 172, 185, 198, 213
Cueto, Germán, 241
Cuevas, José L., 230
Cuevas, José Luis, 14n., 34-36, 38,
41, 59
Cuneo Perinetti, José, 178
Cunha, Luiz de Almeida, 187, 204,
205, 212, 213
Curatela Manes, Pablo, 128, 162,
260

Dacosta, Milton, 213
Dali, Salvador, 103, 113
Damaz, Paul, 83, 95, 174, 234, 254,
255
Da Silva, Alfredo, 118
Dávila, Alberto, 104, 107-108
Dávila, Jaime, 111
Dávila, José Antonio, 76
De Lamonica, Roberto, 219
De Staël, Nicolas, 80, 112, 124, 212
Deira, Ernesto, 152, 155
Demarco, Hugo R., 158, 159
Denis, Maurice, 170
Di Cavalcanti, Emiliano, 183, 184,
185, 188-191, 269
Di Chirico, Giorgio, 209
Di Prete, Danilo, 210-211
Diament de Sujo, Clara, 74, 79, 80,
84
Dias, Antonio, 221
Dias, Cícero, 200, 202-203
Diáz, Porfirio, 1, 2, 3, 12
Díaz Aldana, Luis Humberto, 53
Dickerson, Robert I., 16n.
Djanira, 193, 194
D'León, Omar, 55
Doesburg, Theo Van, 157, 172
Domínguez Errázuriz, Francisco,
255
Dorcely, Roland, 72
Dos Prazeres, Heitor, 193-194
Dreier, Katherine S., 173
Dubón, Jorge, 241
Dubuffet, Jean, 55
Duchamp, Marcel, 183
Dujour, Alfred, 72
Dufaut, Prefete, 71
Duhart H., Emilio, 255

Dutary, Alberto, 58

Echeverría, Enrique, 22n.
Ecuador, 112-115
Egas, Camilo, 112-113
El Salvador, 47, 51
Eluard, Paul, 103, 202
Enríquez, Carlos, 60, 67
Eppens, Francisco, 234
Ernst, Max, 63
Escobar, Marisol. See Marisol
Escobedo, Helen, 37, 241
Esguerra, Rafael, 254
Evers, Medgar, 150
Expressionism, 22, 76, 77, 89, 117,
126, 128, 138, 141, 178,
183, 187, 189, 190, 198,
205, 214, 216. See also Ab-
stract expressionism
Exter, Alexandra, 61
Exumé, René, 72

Faber, Colin, 243, 245
Fauvism, 9, 121, 138, 139
Felguérez, Manuel, 22n.
Fernández, Justino, 20, 21, 28, 30,
228
Fernández, Raúl, 243
Fernández Muro, José Antonio,
148, 149-150, 260
Ferraz, Geraldo, 207
Fierro, Pancho, 98, 102
Figari, Pedro, 138, 141, 169-170
Fioravanti, José, 161, 162, 260
Flores, Ricardo, 101
Folk art,
in Brazil, 194, 202, 207, 218, 225
in Guatemala, 41-42, 50, 52-53
in Mexico, 6, 7, 43
Forner, Raquel, 138, 142-145
Fowler, Helen, 239
Fresco painting; See Mural painting
Frey, Rosa, 111
Freyre, Gilberto, 181, 199-203
passim, 217
Friedeberg, Pedro, 32
Friedlaender, Johnny, 180, 214,
218, 219, 220
Friedman, Martin L., 204, 209, 211,
212, 219

Friesz, Othon, 103 138, 140, 146
Functionalism. *See* Architecture, functional
Futurism, 2, 98, 116, 128

Galdos-Rivas, Enrique, 108
Galia, José Miguel, 248
Gamarra, José, 179-180
Gambartes, Leónidas, 148
Gamio, Manuel, 1-2
García, Victor Manuel, 60, 67
García Ponce, Juan, 34
García Reino, Oscar, 178
Gaudí, Antonio, 171
Gauguin, Paul, 88
Gebhard, Enrique, 254
Generative painting, 157-158
Geometric abstraction, 85, 87, 126, 149, 152, 157-158, 160, 178-179, 210, 211, 213, 214, 223
Gerchman, Rubens, 211
Gerstein, Noemi, 162-164
Gheerbrant, Bernard, 218
Giacometti, Alberto, 55
Gindertael, Roger van, 165
Giorgi, Bruno, 222, 263, 270, 271
Giotto, 17, 142
Gironella, Alberto, 22n., 32-34, 38
Gleizes, Albert, 185
Goeldi, Oswaldo, 214-216, 217, 220
Goeritz, Mathias, 239-241, 247n.
Goitía, Francisco, 21
Goldwater, Robert, 25
Gómez Sicre, José, 53, 55, 58, 60, 61, 65
Góngora, Leonel, 14n.
González, Carmelo, 66
González, Daniel, 82
González Barahona, Jaime, 124
González Bogen, Carlos, 85
González Goyri, Roberto, 42, 43, 46-48, 50, 247-248
González Reyna, Jorge, 242
Goya, Francisco, 3, 33, 35, 57, 58, 59, 74, 217
Grajeda Mena, Guillermo, 247
Gramcko, Elsa, 81-82
Graphic arts, 58, 59, 60, 61, 65, 66, 67, 74, 100, 105, 113, 121

in Argentina, 128, 146-147, 148, 152
in Brazil, 213, 214-221, 225
in Guatemala, 41, 45, 46, 49-51, 52-53
in Mexico, 8, 14, 18, 22, 34-36
in Uruguay, 178-180
Grassmann, Marcelo, 217
Grau, Enrique, 92-93
Grau, Ricardo, 103-105
Greco, El, 91, 142
Grilo, Sarah, 148-149, 260
Gris, Juan, 9, 61, 130
Gropius, Walter, 228, 253
Groupe de Recherche d'Art Visuel, 84, 158-159
Guarani, Francisco Biquiba, 224
Guarnieri, Camargo, 188
Guatemala, 39-54, 246-248
Guayasamín, Oswaldo, 114
Guerrero, Xavier, 254
Guevara Moreno, Luis, 76
Guido, Angel, 162
Guignard, Alberto da Veiga, 191-192, 193, 209
Guillén, Arnaldo, 55
Guillén, Nicolás, 188
Guinand, Carlos C., 248
Günther, Rafael Yela, 46
Gurría, Angela, 241
Gutiérrez, Alberto, 93-94
Gutiérrez, Sérvulo, 102
Guttero, Alfredo, 142
Guzmán, Alberto, 112
Guzmán de Rojas, Cecilio, 116

Haiti, 39, 67-72
Happenings, in Buenos Aires, 160
in Rio de Janeiro, 221
Hayter, Stanley W., 121, 123, 124
Hector, George, 72
Heiter, Guillermo, 77-79
Helm, McKinley, 42
Heredia, Luis Alberto, 113
Hernández, Daniel, 98
Hernández, José, 130
Hernández Saavedra, Emilio, 111
Hidalgo, Miguel, 12
Hitchcock, Henry-Russell, 245, 258
Hoffman, Hans, 86

Hofmann, Kitzia, 244
Hofmann-Ysenbourg, Herbert, 244
Hudson, W. H., 139
Hunter, Sam, 154, 156
Hurtado, Angel, 80, 81
Hydraulic sculpture, 166-168
Hyppolite, Hector, 69-70

Ianelli, Arcangelo, 212
Imaná Garrón, Gil, 118
Impressionism, 5, 9, 41, 141, 205
Indigenism. *See* Nativism
Indoamerican art, aesthetics of, 173-174; *see also* Nativism
Informalism, 48, 66, 72, 111, 115, 148, 149, 150, 152, 181, 210, 211, 212, 214
  in Venezuela, 79-82. *See also* Abstract expressionism
Integration of the arts, in Argentina, 260
  in Brazil, 263, 269-273 passim
  in Chile, 254-256
  in Colombia, 253-254
  in Guatemala, 44, 246-248
  in Mexico, 232-234
  in Peru, 256-257
  in Uruguay, 261
  in Venezuela, 252-253
Iommi, Enio, 260
Irazabal, Fernando, 82
Iturburu, Córdova, 130, 134n.
Ivalfi, Humberto, 57
Izquierdo, César Antonio, 55
Izquierdo, María, 21

Jaimes Sánchez, Humberto, 80-81
Jasmin, Joseph, 70
Jespers, Oscar, 222
Jewell, Edward Alden, 65
Jiménez, Manuel, 108
Johns, Jasper, 80
Jolicoeur, George Hector, 72
Jolicoeur, Wilson, 72
Joseph, Antonio, 70, 71
Jouffroy, Alain, 109-110

Kahlo, Frida, 22
Katchaturian, Aram, 188

Kemble, Kenneth, 150-151
Kennedy, John F., 118
Kinetic art, 84-85, 129, 158, 179, 223
King, William, 86
Kingman Riofríos, Eduardo, 113-114
Kirstein, Lincoln, 113
Klee, Paul, 43, 136, 156, 218
Kleiser, Enrique, 105
Klimt, Gustav, 214
Kline, Franz, 115, 151
Knop, Naun, 168
Knopf, Alfred, 16
Kosice, Gyula, 158, 166-168
Koster, R. M., 59
Krajcberg, Frans, 211-212
Kramer, Hilton, 123
Kubin, Alfred, 215
Kubitschek, Juscelino, 191, 267, 272
Kubotta Carvajal, Arturo, 108

La Placa, Alfredo, 118
Lam, Wifredo, 39, 60, 61-64, 67, 70
Lanzetta, Pablo, 253
Laso, Francisco, 98
Laurens, Henry, 252
Lazo, Agustín, 22
Lazo, Carlos, 232
Le Corbusier, 122, 188, 228, 231, 245, 253, 262
Leal, Fernando, 11
Leão, Carlos de Azevedo, 262
Lee, Wesley Duke, 213-214, 221
Legarreta, Juan, 230
Léger, Fernand, 103, 185, 186, 223
Lenin, Vladimir, 12
León, Angel Acosta, 67
León Castillo, Pedro, 253
Le Parc, Julio, 158-159, 169
Letycia (Quadros), Anna, 219, 221
Levoyer, Jorge, 113
Lhote, André, 61, 103, 137, 138, 140, 146, 150, 185, 206, 209
Liautaud, George, 70
Lichtenstein, Roy, 161
Lima, Grauben Monte, 195
Linder, Max, 256
Lipchitz, Jacques, 271
Lira, Pedro, 121

Llanque, Antonio, 118
Llinás, Julio, 151
Llorens, Antonio, 179
Lobato, Monteiro, 183
Lobo, Balthasar, 252
Long, Richard A., 72n.
López Carmona, Fernando, 244
Louys, Pierre, 146
Lucas, Désiré, 136
Lugo, Genaro, 55
Luque, Angel, 76

Mabe, Manabu, 211
Macció, Rómulo, 152-153
Mac-Entyre, Eduardo, 157, 158
Machado, Gerardo, 60, 61
Madí Group, 166, 168, 179
Magalhães, Aloísio, 203-204, 209
Magalhães, Roberto, 221
Magritte, René, 103
Maillol, Aristide, 222
Maldonado, Tomás, 212
Malevitch, Kasimir, 85
Malfatti, Anita, 183, 184, 185
Manaure, Mateo, 85, 252
Manolo, 63
Manzur, David, 93, 254
Marca-Relli, Conrad, 86
Marceau, Marcel, 79
March, Gladys, 8n.
Mariaca Arguedas, Antonio, 118
Mariátegui, José, 96, 97, 98, 108, 113
Marín, Lupe, 29
Marinetti, Filippo Tommaso, 128
Marisol (Escobar), 86-87
Martín Fierro Group, 130-131, 134
Martín, Vicente, 178
Martínez, Balthazar, 36
Martínez, Carlos, 253
Martínez, Ricardo, 26-28, 31, 38
Martínez de Velasco, Juan, 232
Martins, Aldemir, 217-218
Martins, Luis, 189, 190
Martins, Maria, 222-223, 269
Marx, Karl, 12
Marxism, 9-10, 12, 97, 98
Massaccio, 17
Masson, André, 63
Matisse, Henri, 63, 66, 192

Matta Echauren, Roberto, 121-125 passim
Matto Vilaró, Francisco, 261
Méndez Dávila, Leonel, 52
Mérida, Carlos, 22-23, 39-40, 41-44, 49, 53, 239, 246-247
Mesejeán, Pablo, 161
Messer, Thomas M., 76, 88, 107, 108, 214
Mestrovic, Ivan, 221, 225
Mexican muralists, influence of, 98, 99, 102, 112, 113, 114, 117, 119, 178
Mexican Revolution, 1-5, 6, 9, 11, 19, 38
Mexico, 1-38, 227, 228-231, 232-245
  architecture, 227, 228-231, 232-245
  artistic trends, variety of, 21-22, 32
  easel painting, 19, 22, 24-34
  graphic arts, 8, 14, 18, 22, 34-36
  Indian culture, 1-2, 11-12, 17, 23
  mural painting, 3, 6-21, 22, 24, 39, 234, 236, 239
  Museum of Modern Art, 28, 29, 33, 36, 236-237
  National Museum of Anthropology, 2, 234-236, 237
  sculpture, 26, 36-38, 239, 240-241, 243
Meza, Guillermo, 32
Mies van der Rohe, Ludwig, 228, 253
Mijares, Rafael, 235, 236, 237
Milián, Raúl, 66, 67
Millet, Sergio, 185
Minujin, Marta, 161
Miranda, Silvio, 55
Miró, Joan, 43
Miró Quesada Garland, Luis, 256
Mishaan, Roberto, 48-49
Modigliani, Amadeo, 49
Moholyi, Yolanda, 213, 220
Moholy-Nagy, Sibyl, 249n., 250
Molina, Benjamín, 32
Monasterios, Rafael, 73
Mondrian, Piet, 85, 158
Monsanto, Edmundo, 75
Montani, Andrés R., 178

Montecino, Sergio, 121
Monteiro, Vicente do Rego, 184-185
Montenegro, Roberto, 6, 7
Montparnasse Group (Chile), 120-121
Moore, Henry, 111, 163, 222, 239
Mora, Enrique de la, 230, 244
Moral, Enrique del, 229, 232, 234, 237
Morales, Armando, 56-57
Morandi, Giorgio, 141
Moreira, Jorge Machado, 262, 263
Morelos, José María, 12
Morera, Gabriel, 82
Mori, Camilo, 120, 121
Morrow, Dwight, 11
Mota e Silva. *See* Djanira
Mujica Lainez, Manuel, 137, 141, 148
Munch, Edvard, 215
Muñoz, José, 19n.
Mural painting, 44, 51, 75, 79, 102-103, 114, 151, 171, 254, 260
 in Brazil, 196-198, 201-202, 218
 in Chile, 254-255
 in Mexico, 3, 6-21, 22, 24, 39, 234, 236, 239
 in Uruguay, 178, 180
Murillo, Gerardo. *See* Atl.
Myers, Bernard S., 18, 20
Myers, Irving E., 231n.

Narváez, Francisco, 253
Nationalism, in architecture, 228, 231
 in Brazil, 196-199
 in Mexico, 2, 35, 127
 in Peru, 98-100, 106-108
Nativism, 103, 106, 116, 117, 125, 155, 186
 in Bolivia, 116-120
 in Ecuador, 113, 114
 in Peru, 97-102, 103, 104, 106-107, 108
Navarro, Pascual, 85
Negret, Edgar, 88, 94-95, 126
Neofiguratism, 46, 49, 52, 53, 55, 58, 66, 74-75, 110, 118-119, 121, 123, 126, 140, 214
 in Argentina, 141, 144, 145, 147,
 151, 152-157
 in Colombia, 87-90, 94
 in Uruguay, 165, 178, 179
 in Venezuela, 75-76, 77
Neoprimitivism, 64, 156, 157, 165, 185
Neorealism, 92, 124-125, 145-146, 210
Neruda, Pablo, 146, 188
Neyra, Varela, 111
Nicaragua, 54-57
Niemeyer, Oscar, 223, 225, 246, 262, 265, 268-274
Nishasahua, Luis, 22n.
Noé, Luis Felipe, 152, 153-154
Nueva Presencia, La, 14n.
Núñez del Prado. *See* Carrasco
Núñez del Prado, Marina, 119-120
Nuño, Rubén Bonifacio, 27

Obin, Antoine, 69
Obin, Philomé, 69
Obin, Séneque, 69
Obregón, Alejandro, 87, 88-90, 92, 93, 126, 254
Obregón, Alvaro, 6
Ocampo, Miguel, 150, 260
O'Gorman, Juan, 228, 229-231, 232, 233, 238-239, 241-245
Oliva, Tomás, 66
Oliveira, Raimundo de, 207-208
Ong, Walter J., 177
Op art, 85, 86, 152, 157, 158-159, 169, 212
Opazo, Rodolfo, 124
Oramos, Alirio, 252
Orlando, Felipe, 64, 66
Orozco, José Clemente, 3, 5, 7, 11, 13-18, 20, 22, 36, 38, 41, 114
Orozco Romero, Carlos, 22, 31, 38
Ortega Flores, Salvador, 234, 237
Ortega y Gasset, José, 10, 54
Ortiz, Emilio, 14n.
Ortiz, Simón, 256
Ortiz de Zarate, Manuel, 120
Ossaye, Roberto, 40, 44-46, 49, 50
Ostrower, Fayga, 219, 220
Otero, Alejandro, 35, 82-83, 87, 253
Ozenfant, Amédée, 61

Pacheco, María Luisa, 117
Páez, Jorge, 178
Páez Vilaró, Carlos, 180
Palma, Ricardo, 96, 98
Panama, 39, 57-60
Pancetti, José Gianini, 204-206
Pani, Mario, 232, 234, 237, 240, 245, 247*n*.
Pantosa, Oscar, 118
Parada, Domingo, 119
Pardo, Mercedes, 79
Paredes, Diógenes, 113
Paris, School of, 5, 60, 61, 112, 186, 210, 212
Parpagnoli, Hugo, 146
Paparella, Aldo, 168
Paternosto, César, 160
Pavlova, Anna, 7
Payró, Julio, 132
Paz, Octavio, 29
Pedraza, Carlos, 121
Pedrosa, Mário, 209, 224
Peláez (del Casal), Amelia, 39, 60-63, 65, 67, 246
Pellegrini, Aldo, 133, 134, 135
Peluffo, Martha, 151-152
Peñalba, Alicia, 162, 164-166, 169
Peñalba, Rodrigo, 54
Pereira Pacheco, Armando, 117
Pereyra, Rafael, 49
Pérez Martínez, Alberto, 124
Pérez Palacios, Augusto, 233
Perón, Juan Domingo, 257
Perotti, José, 120, 121
Peru, 96-112
  abstract expressionism, 105-108
  architecture, 256-257
  modernism, 102-105
  nativism, 97-102, 103-108 passim
  sculpture, 111-112
Peters, Dewitt, 68, 69, 70
Pettoruti, Emilio, 102, 128-133, 134
Pevsner, Antoine, 252
Phases Group, 151
Picasso, Pablo, 9, 24, 35, 41, 42, 45, 61, 63, 77, 92, 102, 114, 132, 170, 189-190, 198, 202
Pierola della Francesca, 142
Pierre, Fernand, 71
Pinchinat, Max, 72

Piqueiras, Jorge, 108, 109-110
Pirovano, Ignacio, 157
Piwonka, Alberto, 255
Piza, Arthur Luiz, 218-219
Pogolotti, Marcelo, 67
Pons, Isabel, 219-220
Poisson, Louverture, 71
Poleo, Héctor, 75-76, 253
Polesello, Rogelio, 151, 152
Ponce de León, Fidelio, 60, 67
Pop art, 53, 74, 80, 110, 111, 152, 154, 160-161, 178, 212, 214
Portinari, Cândido, 102, 114, 187, 190, 196-199, 213, 220, 225, 263, 272-273
Portner, Leslie Judd, 35, 48
Portocarrero, René, 64-65, 67
Posada, José Guadalupe, 8, 14
Prat de la Riba, 171
Presas, Leopoldo, 148
Presno, Lincoln, 178-179
Prete, Juan del, 140, 141-142
Price, Lucien, 71-72
Primitive painters, in Brazil, 193-195
  in Haiti, 67-71
Pucciarelli, Mario, 150, 151
Puvis de Chavannes, 171

Quintana Castillo, Manuel, 82
Quinquela Martín, Benito, 136
Quiroa, Marco Augusto, 53
Quiroga, Facundo, 153

Ragon, Michel, 147
Ramírez, Pablo, 120, 126
Ramírez Plancarte, F., 4*n*.
Ramírez Vázquez, Pedro, 235, 236, 237
Ramírez Villamizar, Eduardo, 87, 253-254
Ramos, Nelson, 178
Rauschenberg, Robert, 86, 161
Recamier, Carlos, 243
Recinos, Efraín, 51, 53, 248
Realism. *See* Neorealism; Social realism
Rego, José Lins do, 189
Reidy, Affonso Eduardo, 262, 263-265

Renard, Emile, 186
Rendón, Manuel, 112
Renoir, Auguste, 146
Reverón, Armando, 73-75, 77
Reza, Jorge de la, 116
Richier, Germaine, 223
Richter, Louisa, 76, 79
Rigoli, Gianni, 258
Reinoso Vinatea, Jorge, 101-102
Ríos, Juan, 101, 104
Riva Agüero, José de la, 97
Rivera, Diego, 7-13, 14, 15, 17, 22, 29, 31, 36, 38, 50, 99, 100, 102, 117, 128, 198, 230, 233, 234
Roa, Israel, 121
Roca Rey, Joaquín, 111-112, 256
Rockefeller, John D., Jr., 13
Rodman, Selden, 69-70
Rodríguez, Ida, 37
Rodríguez, Mariano, 67
Rodríguez-Larraín, Emilio, 108-109
Rodríguez Lozano, Manuel, 21
Rodríguez Saavedra, Carlos, 108
Rohe. *See* Mies van der Rohe
Rojo, Vicente, 22n.
Rolando, Maruja, 79
Romera, Antonio R., 120-124 passim
Romero Brest, Jorge, 153, 169
Rosa, Manuel de la, 245
Rossell, Guillermo, 245
Rouault, Georges, 77
Rousseau, Henri (Douanier), 67, 172
Ruiz, Macedonio Oscar, 260

Saavedra, Gustavo, 232
Sabelli, Eduardo, 168
Sabartés, Jaime, 40-41
Sabat, Hermenegildo, 178
Sabogal, José, 98-101, 103, 108, 113, 116
Sáenz, Alvaro, 254
Sáenz, Leoncio, 55
Salazar, Braulio, 253
Saldanha, Firminio, 269
Salinas, Raúl, 233
Sánchez, Félix, 237
Santelices, Raúl, 212

Santos, Agnaldo Manoel dos, 224
Sarmiento, Domingo Faustino, 153
Sartoris, Alberto, 133
Satie, Erik, 185
Savain, Pétion, 67-68
Schiele, Egon, 214
Schmeckebier, Laurence E., 12, 16, 17
Schulz Solari, Oscar Agustín. *See* Solar, Xul
Scott, William, 67
Sculpture, 51-52, 56, 70, 72, 121, 126, 180
   in Argentina, 128, 158, 161-168
   in Bolivia, 199-220
   in Brazil, 187, 221-225
   in Colombia, 88, 94-95
   in Guatemala, 46-48
   in Mexico, 36-38
   in Peru, 111-112
   in Venezuela, 85, 86-87
Seeley, Jason, 70
Segall, Lasar, 183, 187-188, 216
Segui, Antonio, 152, 155-156
Semana de Arte Moderna. *See* Week of Modern Art
Seoane, Luis, 148, 260
Seoane Ros, Enrique, 256
Sepúlveda, Artemio, 14n.
Serpa, Ivan, 195, 212, 213
Seuphor, Michel, 166, 167, 172, 223
Seurat, Georges, 9
Severino, Gino, 120
Shinki Huaman, Venancio, 108
Signac, Paul, 17
Silva, Carlos, 157, 158
Silva, Carmen, 124
Silva, Francisco Domingos da, 195
Silva, José Antonio da, 195
Sinclair, Alfredo, 57-58
Siqueiros, David Alfaro, 3, 7, 11, 19-21, 22, 34, 36, 38, 45, 101, 102, 234, 254
Sjölander, Waldemar, 22n.
Smith, Clive Bramford, 238n.
Smith, Robert C., 197
Sobalvarro, Hernando, 55
Sobrino, Francisco Matarazzo, 181
Social realism, 22, 44, 66, 99, 114, 128, 187, 193, 198, 202

Solar, Xul, 129, 133-136
Solari, Lis, 178
Soldi, Raúl, 145-146
Somavilla, Godofredo, 169
Soriano, Juan, 25, 26, 28-29, 37, 38
Soto, Jesús, 82, 83-85, 87, 253
Soulages, Pierre, 81
Spilimbergo, Lino Eneas, 20, 136, 137-138
Springett, Sabino, 104, 107
Staempfli, George, 109
Stalin, Josef, 44
Stäubli, Willy, 273
Stéphane, Micius, 71
Strocen, Stefan, 156-157
Suárez, Daniel, 254
Suro, Dario, 172
Surrealism, 21, 22, 49, 52, 53, 63-64, 103, 104, 109, 112, 116, 122, 123, 124, 144, 148, 198, 214, 223
Svanascini, Osvaldo, 164
Szennes, Arpad, 223
Szyszlo, Fernando de, 35, 105-107, 117, 125, 256

Tabouis, Geneviève, 119
Tachisme, 49, 103, 110
Tamayo, Rufino, 22, 23-26, 30, 38, 45, 46, 49, 50, 51, 89, 239
Tapies, Antonio, 211
Testa, Clorindo, 150
Texada, Leonardo, 113
Thoby-Marcelin, Philippe, 68, 69
Tomasello, Luis, 159
Torre, Macedonio de la, 103
Torres, Augusto, 261
Torres, Horacio, 261
Torres García, Joaquín, 45, 136, 169, 170-178, 179, 261
Toulouse-Lautrec, Henri, 170, 190, 214
Traba, Marta, 90, 94, 114
Trujillo, Guillermo, 58-60
Turner, Luce, 71, 72
Tyler, Parker, 35

Ubico, Jorge, 45
Ugarte Eléspuru, Juan Manuel, 102-103, 104

University City, of Caracas, 227, 232, 249-253, 274
of Mexico, 20, 227, 232-234, 237, 242, 274
Urbino, Luis, 55
Urdaneta, Rafael, 254
Urteaga, Mario, 102
Uruguay, 125, 169-180

Vaca, Lorgio, 118
Valcárcel, Luis, 96
Valencia, Reinaldo, 253
Valenti, Carlos, 40-41, 53
Valera, Victor, 253
Valladares, Clarival, 188, 192, 194, 195, 224
Vallejo, César, 108
Van Gogh, Vincent, 77, 205, 215
Vanegas, Leonel, 55
Vantongerloo, Georges, 172
Varela, Victor, 80, 85
Vargas Rosas, Luis, 120
Varos, Remedios, 32
Vasarely, Victor, 151, 158, 252
Vasconcelos, José, 6, 7, 23
Vásquez Castañeda, Dagoberto, 247, 248
Vásquez Ceballos, Gregorio, 92
Vázquez Díaz, Daniel, 117
Vega, Fernando, 108
Vega, Jorge de la, 152, 154-155
Vega Pacheco, Martín, 248
Velázquez, Diego, 33, 52, 57
Venezuela, 39, 73-87
abstract expressionism and informalism, 79-82
architecture, 248-256
geometric abstraction, 82-86
sculpture, 86-87
semiabstract and neofigurative painters, 75-79
Ventayol, Juan, 179
Vergara, Carlos, 229
Vestrini, Renzo, 82
Victorica, Miguel Carlos, 136-137
Vidal, Miguel Angel, 157, 158
Vigas, Oswaldo, 80, 81, 252
Villa, Pancho, 3
Villacres, Atahualpa, 113
Villagrán García, José, 228, 229-230

Villa-Lobos, Heitor, 184, 185
Villanueva, Carlos Raúl, 83, 85, 248-252
Vital, Pauleus, 71
Vlady, 22n.
Volpi, Alfredo, 191, 192-193, 209
Vuillard, Edouard, 136, 170

Warchavchik, Gregori, 227, 231, 261, 263
Week of Modern Art, São Paulo, 182, 183-185, 187, 189, 229
Wells, Alberto, 168
Werneck, Paulo, 273
Westheim, Paul, 44
Williams, Amancio, 257-260
Winternitz, Adolfo, 105
Wols, 210

Wright, Frank Lloyd, 228

Xirau, Ramón, 37
Xylography, 66, 147, 215, 216-217

Yáñez, Enrique, 230, 231n., 237
Yaya Arias, Daniel, 108
Yrarrázaval, Ricardo, 124-125
Yrurtia, Rogelio, 161

Zadkine, Ossip, 163, 164
Zañartu, Enrique, 121, 123, 124, 126
Zanini, Walter, 190
Zapata, Emiliano, 3
Zilveti Calderón, Luis, 118-119
Zuloaga, Ignacio, 99